NO NEED TO DIE

AMERICAN FLYERS IN RAF BOMBER COMMAND

GORDON THORBURN

HAYNES PUBLISHING

First published in 2009

A catalogue record for this book is available from the British Library.

ISBN 978 1 84425 652 5

Library of Congress control no. 2009923198

Published by Haynes Publishing, Sparkford, Yeovil, Somerset BA22 7JJ, UK
Tel: 01963 442030 Fax: 01963 440001
Int. tel: +44 1963 442030 Int. fax: +44 1963 440001
E-mail: sales@haynes.co.uk
Website: www.haynes.co.uk

Haynes North America Inc.
861 Lawrence Drive, Newbury Park,
California 91320, USA

Printed and bound in the UK

CONTENTS

By the same author

Bombers, first and last
Cassius. The true story of a courageous police dog
Animal Spy
Men and Sheds
The Appleby Rai

FOREWORD

No Turning Back
by Hubert Clarence 'Nick' Knilans

It's a long time ago but I can remember clearly the concern we felt in our family about the way that the war in Europe was punishing the innocent. I heard on the radio and read in the American papers about the dreadful loss of life in London and other English cities, and at sea too, from the untargeted attacks of German bombers and U-boats.

I turned the concern into action and joined the Royal Canadian Air Force, which trained me to be a pilot, and a bomber pilot. I never did put the USA shoulder patch on my uniform, I don't quite know why, but that meant that everyone on the station in England, except the Canadians, thought I was a Canadian.

Being a bomber pilot is a world away from being in fighters. You have a big, big plane to fly, with four engines and, in a Lancaster, a crew of six guys who expect you to get them through. You fly for hours and hours, usually at night, over enemy territory where everybody tries to kill you. I had no fear of being shot down. I was so confident that I thought, if I'm attacked, I'll deal with it.

My plane was shot up seven times, and I had an engine knocked out seven different times. One of my crew was killed and others were injured by enemy action but I never turned back to base because of damage to men or aircraft. Others did, and they were entitled to do so, but I didn't, and I took a lot of criticism over it.

In particular, gunners from other crews would have a go at me for not doing my duty towards my crew. I always believed that my main duty was to get to the target and bomb it, and so I put that first, and my own crew knew that and were ready to fly with me knowing it.

It was a very different kind of war then. We had no guided precision weapons. Accuracy was something achieved by people's skill and determination under fire, not by technology, and it was not something you took for granted. I have to admit that, eventually, bombing cities full of civilians did get to me. There was no question that I wanted to keep fighting the war, and that I would have done whatever was asked of me, but I was glad to have the chance of volunteering for special duties, some of them very experimental indeed by the standards of those days.

I very much hope you enjoy this book and I commend it to you. There's a lot about me in it, but then, I came through. So many didn't. So many had much shorter careers, going down in flames or exploding in the night sky, and I saw it happen scores of times. If you can get a sense of what that was like from these stories of Americans in RAF Bomber Command, then the author will have done his job.

Nick Knilans
Wisconsin, USA
March 2009

ACKNOWLEDGEMENTS

9 Squadron Association; 97 Squadron Association; Fred Aldworth; Robert Bard; Jonathan Bashein – Nixon Peabody LLP; Roger Beckwith; Donald A.L. Bell; Bernice – volunteer, Madison County Historical Society; Maggie Land Blanck; Jim Brookbank; Dan Buechler; Clarissa Chavira – Texana/Genealogy Department, San Antonio Public Library; Jessica Day; Jim Earl – registrar, San Antonio Genealogical & Historical Society; George Ellison, Kati Baumann – Glendale Public Library, California; Wally Fydenchuk; Ron Goebel; Harold Gough – Herne Bay Historical Records Society; John W. Grimstone; Gretchen Grozier – Jamaica Plain Historical Society; Wendy Hall – Carnegie Library, Boulder, Colorado; David Hayes – Nixon Peabody LLP; Tracy Herold – Whitefish Bay Public Library; Linda Hocking – Litchfield Historical Society; Hans Houterman; Glenda Insua – Bentley Historical Library, Ann Arbor, Michigan; Dick James; Daniel L. Kentowski – librarian, Milwaukee Public Library; Hubert Clarence Knilans; Terry Lintin; Barbara McGrath; Jason Mann; James B. Richard – Wilkinsburg Historical Society; Jackie Saturley – librarian/archivist, Roseville Public Library, Michigan; S. Parkman Shaw; Jim Shortland; James Storey; Sandee Storey – *Jamaica Plain Gazette*; Robin Joseph Tate; Robert McG. Thomas, Jnr – *New York Times*; Barbara Wilson – Oxford University Boat Club; Tom Wingham; Geoffrey H. Womersley.

Photograph Credits

Images courtesy of 9 Squadron Archive, Jessica Day, Wendy Hall, David Hayes, Harold Gough, Terry Lintin, Mark Postlethwaite, S. Parkman Shaw and Jim Shortland.

PROLOGUE

American airmen flew – and died – with RAF Bomber Command from the earliest days of the Second World War, mostly enlisting before Pearl Harbor, before their own country was at war. Throughout and always, it was very, very dangerous taking the war to Germany, and there was nothing compelling those Americans to go apart from their own wishes and beliefs.

Our story is of a particular group of men, more than 20 of them, who joined 2 elite Royal Air Force bomber squadrons, Numbers 9 and 617 (the dam busters). As far as it is possible to trace at this distance, these are all of the Americans who served with those squadrons. For most of them, four out of every five, their brief encounter with life at the very edge was cut short by a death which, though sudden, generally allowed for terror and pain before.

These men knew the odds were against them, so why were they doing it? Some sought the ultimate test of themselves, as young warriors will. Some thought it the proper thing to do. Nick Knilans, for example, a country boy from Wisconsin, was moved to action by a Nazi atrocity, when a U-boat sank an ocean liner carrying children from the UK to safety in Canada.

Ray Ramey, an unscholarly, ordinary fellow from Milwaukee, learned to fly and joined via the Royal Canadian Air Force, saying that he thought all red-blooded young men should do the same. Another, Andy Storey, son of a fine old Massachusetts family, horrified his folks by failing Harvard and joining the RCAF instead. Maurice Buechler's parents, Harry and Minnie, were Hungarian Jews living in Newark, New Jersey. What did they feel when Maurice left the University of Tennessee to fight for the Brits against the Nazis? Ray Baroni, from Glendale, California, went as a gunner like Maurice, on the shortest training course for the worst job.

Jonah Reeves, known as Jonie, was a member of the Student Council, Oneida High School, State of New York. He was Treasurer of and actor in the Dramatic Club, Vice President of the Modern Problems Club, voted 'Wittiest Boy' in the popularity contest, played in the orchestra and, most poignantly, was President of the Science and Engineering Club, the aim of which was to 'prepare students who are interested in the sciences for a useful and interesting life'.

Nick would last out the war. Jonah, the two Rays, Andy and Maurice would be killed.

Chapter 1

THIS IS WHAT WE CAME FOR

Coming up to half past ten at night, 14 June 1943, and 13 4-engined Lancaster bombers were forming an orderly queue towards the head of a tarmac runway in rural Lincolnshire. Steering these enormous, black, terrifying aircraft around the perimeter track, from their segregated parking places (called dispersals) to their take-off position, was too slow a business to use the rudder, so the pilots manoeuvred on engines and brakes. The few people watching put hands over ears while Rolls-Royce Merlins roared, brakes squawked and screamed, hydraulic undercarts groaned, and this little group of the world's best bringer of destruction made ready for yet another enterprise of war over Germany.

At the front of the queue, facing down the runway, Flying Officer Robert Owen Van Note, of Boulder, Colorado, bomber pilot, kept his brakes hard on while all four engines bellowed with impatience. Bob Van Note, a good-looking, round-faced, dark-haired chap, of no more than average height and always well turned out, had been a mechanical engineering student at the University of Colorado in 1940. Now he was captain of Lancaster ED493 WS/A-Apple, of 9 Squadron, 5 Group, RAF Bomber Command.

He shared the impatience somewhat, for tonight was special. The night before last he had bombed Bochum, and the night before that Düsseldorf, night off before that, and so on and so on, going back to January and his first trip. That had been Düsseldorf too. Tonight was Oberhausen but that wasn't why it was special. No, tonight was Bob Van Note's thirtieth operation, of a tour of duty of 30. After tonight, he'd have done his bit. He'd be heading for a desk job. He'd be transferred probably, to the USAAF; Captain Van Note he'd be, maybe major one day, and he'd marry his English girlfriend, Marjory. Always provided, of course, that he came home from this one.

He knew of another American pilot with 9 Squadron who'd gone down on his thirtieth op, all crew killed. Over Berlin, that was. That

1

had been the news greeting him when he'd turned up, keen and raw, at the ramshackle collection of huts and hangars they called RAF Bardney and found his way to the officers' mess. Oh, American are you? Just lost one of yours, nice fellow, very tall. Flight Sergeant Storey. Dashed bad luck. On his thirtieth. Yesterday, wasn't it? Or the day before. Anyway, what are you having?

In the officers' mess they wouldn't have noticed that yet another American pilot, not an officer but a flight sergeant like Andy Storey, had started flying ops 16 January 1943, the day before Storey was killed. In the officers' mess, they never would have had time to notice Frank Nelson from Wilkinsburg, Pennsylvania, killed the second time he took his crew to Germany. Van Note might have remembered him as a fellow Yank but that was all, and it was months ago now. A week was a long time in Bomber Command, never mind months.

The Aldis lamp that served for Lancaster traffic control still showed red. Nothing was said in A-Apple but there was certainly a feeling. It wasn't only the skipper who would score 30 tonight. They all would. Van Note and his six crew had flown together all that time. The odd missed trip here and there had been made up flying as spare bod with another skipper. A Lancaster crew was a team, a fighting unit. If they were going to die, they would die together. If they were going to finish their tour, same thing.

At 22:29 hours Double British Summer Time (DBST), the man in the striped caravan with the Aldis lamp turned it to green. Van Note pushed the four throttles forward until the engines shrieked and the aircraft shuddered enough almost to shake herself apart. Brakes off. Huge surge of power. Ground speed up to 60mph in the twinkle of an eye. The pilot gave the joystick a touch forward to raise the tail and felt the rudder bar at his feet go stiff. Both hands on the stick now as Sgt Harry Hounsome, flight engineer, took over the throttles. Speed up to 100, 105, 110. Stick back. Airborne, with a load of over 11,000lb of high-explosive and incendiary bombs. Oberhausen, here we come.

Bob Van Note had had a quite remarkable career. He'd seen all the worst of the Battle of the Ruhr in the first half of 1943, a time when there were big losses on virtually every raid. On his last 3 ops, he'd come home unruffled while 45 other Lancasters, each with 7 souls aboard, had fallen to earth. He'd never had anything bad enough to be noted at interrogation (debrief) apart from flak damage, holes in the aircraft that they all had all the time, but otherwise, well, piece of cake really. The crews called the pilots 'Drivers, airframe' and often made remarks about a secure job with a bus company after the war.

Since Van Note started flying ops, his own squadron had lost 22 Lancasters with the great majority of crew killed. Of these, two had had American pilots. In just 20 weeks, 22 Lancasters down, or 'failed to return' as they called it, was a turnover of a squadron and a half. If No. 9 was going to lose a Lanc a week right through 1943,* that was the equivalent of three or four complete squadrons gone and replaced. If you started counting also the number of aircrew wounded, the number of Lancs staggering home in that time on two or three engines and/or with large parts of aircraft shot away, you would have to wonder what kind of protection, divine or otherwise, kept Flg Off Van Note and his boys in such good condition.

The arithmetical benchmark for heavy bomber losses was 5 per cent per night's raiding. Less than that was good, more than that bad. Crews in the mess didn't know the figures across all the squadrons. They saw empty chairs where men used to be, and spaces at dispersal where Lancasters used to be. That 5 per cent meant that an aircraft, and therefore a crew, should expect – on average – to come home from no more than 19 ops. In fact, it was worse than that. Average life expectancy taken over the whole war was 13 ops.

Some crews were lost on their first, second or third trips, therefore, some would have the luck to survive to 28, 29 or, praise the Lord, 30. That was reassuring to those who felt themselves to be very lucky. Another way of looking at it was to say that the lost Lancasters were replaced so, each time you went, you were one of many again, 95 per cent unlikely to be the one that had a prang, bought a packet, bought the farm, went for a Burton, got the chop.

New boys, sprog crews, were more likely to be lost than old hands, that was observably true, but the powers that be counteracted that by giving the worst jobs to the old hands. And, there was that little matter of actually becoming an old hand.

But for now, as he put A-Apple into a steady climb and headed for the rendezvous, none of this was on Van Note's mind. He checked

---

* 9 Squadron losses in 1943, 55 Lancasters.

around the crew on the intercom. The two gunners, endlessly searching the night sky from the tail-end turret and the dorsal turret called mid-upper, the wireless operator, the navigator, the bomb aimer (bombardier) below him in the nose, and Harry beside him watching his instruments, yes, they were all fine, thank you. All about them, 197 Lancs were gathering before setting off in their long, thin, formation in the dark, the bomber stream, for Oberhausen.

With the 197 were 6 de Havilland Mosquitos equipped with a new, high-tech navigation aid, Oboe, that used radar transmissions to and from ground stations back home. The Mosquitos, superfast, agile twin-engined aircraft, were going to mark the target for the heavy bombers. In the dense cloud that was forecast, they would have to drop flares according to their Oboe readings. The flares would cascade towards the given point, red and green stars for the bombers to aim at.

First there was the flak to pass through, from the Dutch coast onwards. There were two sorts of flak (*fliegerabwehrkanonen*: flyer defence guns). Light flak was tracer, a continuous stream of small calibre shells; heavy flak was a series of bigger shells, precisely fired, which exploded at a height set by the flak gunners. In your bomber, you saw the light flak zipping up and, hopefully, past. You didn't see the heavy kind until it went off below you, above you or beside you, in neat black and red thunderclouds.

The other great peril at this time of the war was the nightfighters. Tonight, 17 of the 197 Lancasters would be shot down, 8.63 per cent, mostly by nightfighters, some on the way there, some on the way back. Maj Günter Radusch and Hauptmann (Captain) Hans-Dieter Frank, both of *1 Gruppe, Nachtjagdgeschwader 1*, would get two Lancasters each. Of the 119 bomber aircrew thus dismissed from the war, nine would be taken to prison camp while the rest were for the cemetery. The Germans were very good at that, burying the dead. Meticulous, they were.

A-Apple reached the target without interruption from Hauptmann Frank or anybody else. There, the crew found the usual maelstrom of flak and searchlights. When they'd first witnessed it, they'd believed it impossible to go through once, let alone 30 times, and since then they'd seen plenty of strong evidence for that belief. A common sight for bomber aircrew, a regular fact of life you might say, was of somebody else being hit by flak and going down. It was one of the few occasions on which they saw another bomber, in the dark. They knew what it was, this loosening assembly of flame diving through the clouds, slowly spinning perhaps, exploding maybe, another aircraft exactly like theirs becoming a glowing puffball of smithereens, a victory for the enemy in orange and yellow against a black background.

They might also see nightfighter action, represented by the exchange of tracer between invisible opponents. There'd be cannon and machine-gun fire from a Messerschmitt or a Heinkel or a Junkers with guns fixed in its wings, and machine-gun bullets from the bomber's movable turrets. You might even be able to tell which one won.

The Germans also had an upward firing gun, amusingly called Jazz (*Schrägemusik*, literally sloping/angular/off-key music). The fighter pilot would put himself underneath his target, his Tommy, in the blind spot, and fire his jazzy cannon shells up into the bomb bay. Another crew watching this would see only a great flash as bombs, aircraft and crew were atomised in a fiery instant. This flash, RAF Intelligence told the bomber boys, was a harmless German bogeyman trick called Scarecrow, a petrol-fuelled flare designed to frighten you off.

Oh, really? So, if the fighter pilot fired from further away for his own safety, or missed altogether, what were those weird looping strings of tracer appearing from nowhere, coloured fairy lights making croquet hoops in the sky? What were they?

Such were the forces intent on preventing the bombers from doing their job, and the job tonight was Oberhausen. Van Note and his men were among the early ones to the target. At 01:26 hours DBST from 21,500ft, it was bombs gone and homewards as fast as could be. They'd been the squadron's first up and away. They were going to be first home too. It was a kind of tradition. Crews on their last op felt it absolutely necessary to be first home. As they left they could see the fires beginning to spread. Take a good look, chaps. You won't be seeing that again for a while.

Oberhausen, a town of the industrial revolution, population 190,000, iron and steel, coal, chemicals and the centre of a spider's web of railways, had 267 buildings destroyed in this raid and 584 seriously damaged, 85 people killed and 258 injured. Van Note and co. didn't know about that. They'd hit the target through the cloud if the flares had been accurate. Now they had around an hour and three-quarters of their operational tour remaining.

SECRET No. 9 Squadron Combat Report
Date: 14/15 June 1943. Pos: Oberhausen. Lancaster: 'A'. Captain: Flg Off
Van Note.

Our aircraft was intercepted by a T/E E/A* on the return journey from
the target at 01:54 hours in bright moonlight at Soesterburg,
23,000 feet, rectified airspeed 165mph. The Boozer** had shown
Yellow and the pilot had been doing a moderate weave for about ten
minutes when the rear gunner (Sgt Dale) reported E/A 500 yards
astern flying the same course. On instruction from the rear gunner
the pilot made a diving turn to port and the E/A followed the bomber
down. At 400 yards both the rear and mid-upper gunners fired bursts
which appeared to enter the fuselage of the E/A. The pilot then
started a barrel corkscrew*** and the E/A broke away starboard
quarter from which direction it made another attack firing short
bursts with cannon and machine guns, the tracer of which was
observed to pass well above the bomber. Rear and mid-upper gunners
fired long bursts and the tracer was seen to enter the E/A which broke
away in a dive and was not seen again. No damage was sustained by
the bomber. The E/A is claimed as damaged. No ground co-operation
of any kind was observed and no unusual phenomena.
Mid-upper turret 250 rounds, no stoppages.
Rear turret 1200 rounds, no stoppages.

'On instruction from the rear gunner the pilot made a diving turn to
port' – well, how else would one put it? And this is how the squadron's
Operations Record Book noted the achievement of Bob Van Note and
his crew, a tour of 30 ops when the average was 13: *DOWN 0309*.

So, Bob could marry his girl from Lincoln. He was statistically
unusual but, for 9 Squadron that night, the statistics were otherwise
accurate. Sergeant John Evans, pilot, aged 20, and his crew in
Q-Queenie didn't come back, FTR, and he'd flown 13.

*Twin-engined enemy aircraft.
** An unreliable enemy-radar detector.
***Escape manoeuvre of rapid half rolls, dives and climbs.

Chapter 2

THE EARLIEST BIRDS

In England in the late 1930s, working at the offices of an advertising agency, was Sedgwick Whiteley Webster, known as Bill, of Litchfield County, Connecticut, born in South Africa of American parents in 1904, the year the *General Slocum* caught fire in New York harbour.

At his age, he needed have no truck with wars and fighting, though he surely felt a deep concern at the rise of German power and a gallant wish to defend the England he was so fond of. In any case, there could hardly be a possibility of the forces taking him on. The army certainly wouldn't have him, or the navy.

Up in Burnley, Lancashire, a boy called John Edward Stowell was working for an engineering company. He was born 21 November 1921, in Royal Oak, Michigan, an old farming village recently grown to city status with a population increased to 6,000 on the back of the burgeoning automobile industry in nearby Detroit. His English parents had returned home in 1932 when the boy, known as Ed, was 11. As soon as he was old enough, he would take his engineering abilities to the air force as a mechanic. He wanted to be a pilot, too; his education, particularly his maths, was not of a high enough standard but the lad was a hard worker and very, very keen. He'd be all right. When the war ended in 1945 he would go back to the USA, his homeland, as one of this earth's rarest creatures, rarer than unicorns, a serving American bomber captain in the RAF who could say he'd joined up in 1939 and lived right through it.

In the USA in 1938, not everyone felt concern for what the wily, sabre-rattling old Europeans might be up to. The President saw himself on the Allies' side in the looming confrontation but could not envisage all of the people agreeing, even for some of the time. Columnist Boake Carter was syndicated in 83 newspapers with a combined circulation of over 7 million:

Where does the Roosevelt Administration derive the idea that Americans want to go gallivanting forth to play Sir Galahad again? The question that Americans should remember is: Do we or do we not want to help one gang of thieves against another gang of thieves? We saved the first crop of thieves twenty years ago – and made the world a safe place for a new set of thieves.

David Lawrence, syndicated in 196 newspapers, with a circulation of 7½ million wrote: 'While nobody condones for a moment the Nazi measures, it would be misrepresenting the state of opinion in Washington to say that our officials regard the Allied policies of the last twenty years as truly contributory to a permanent peace.'

Westbrook Pegler, 117 newspapers, over 6 million circulation: 'Perhaps the American people, if consulted, would say that if Britain and France must fight a war that is just their hard luck and, after all, only another war in the long series of wars between jostling European countries.'

The doyen of them all, Walter Winchell, 150 newspapers, 8½ million circulation, went to the heart of it: 'The future of American youth is on top of American soil, not underneath European dirt.'

Smaller voices sided with the British. Mark Sullivan, 46 newspapers, approaching 3 million circulation: 'Free government has its principal home in America and Great Britain. If it is destroyed in England by a foreign foe, then it will be more difficult to defend it here. England is our shield.'

'Hear, hear!' said England but, while these scribes were writing and Ed Stowell was bashing metal in Burnley and Bill Webster was lunching with clients, the problem was the state of the shield. If it became necessary to fight Nazi Germany and defeat it, how was this to be done? Could the Royal Navy do it? Sinking warships and U-boats and shelling coastal towns would not bring victory by itself, so perhaps the French and the British armies would hold the Germans at the Maginot Line and eventually turn them back. Perhaps.

More likely an answer was air power. It was the view of soon-to-be Prime Minister Churchill that he who held the skies had the ways and means to military success. Current Prime Minister Neville Chamberlain didn't seem to have a view. But how air-powerful were the British?

In America, the prototype 300mph Boeing B-17, the four-engined Flying Fortress, had flown in 1935 and was about to come into service with the USAAF. The first British four-engined bomber, the inadequate Short Stirling, was being developed but would not fly in anger until February 1941, the Handley Page Halifax shortly after, while the Avro Lancaster hadn't been thought of yet. In fact, while Walter Winchell and colleagues were burning typewriter ribbon, all the types of aircraft in service with RAF Bomber Command were unsuitable for contemporary warfare. The senior squadron, No. 9, still had the Handley Page Heyford biplane, more of a flying monument than a fortress. It could carry 3,500lb of bombs but certainly not as far as Berlin, particularly if it was to try and get back. It might make such a journey carrying a couple of 500-pounders but it would take a very long time, assuming the Germans didn't interfere on the way.

In the 20 years since the end of the First World War, very little had happened to improve the effectiveness of British bomber squadrons. Those biplanes were flying 40mph faster but they still had large fixed undercarriages, open cockpits and only a couple of Lewis guns for protection. If Chamberlain had not been granted his war postponement in 1938, the Germans' Messerschmitt 109 fighters would have eliminated RAF Bomber Command in no time at all.

Winchell may have had a wry smile on his face as he watched the newsreel pictures of Prime Minister Chamberlain landing back from his meeting with Hitler, waving his bit of paper and waffling about peace in our time. What Winchell didn't know was that No. 9 Squadron and others had been briefed for operations should Chamberlain fail. They were to get in their Heyfords and take full loads of bombs to targets in the Ruhr. On the return journey, as they ran out of petrol over Holland, they were to put on their parachutes and jump for it.

The first step in modernisation was the Armstrong Whitworth Whitley, also known as 'the flying barn door'. It was a twin-engined monoplane with enclosed, movable gun turrets front and rear and a retractable undercarriage, but it was so slow and feebly powered that it was already obsolete before it went on its first raid. There was also the Handley Page Hampden – 'the flying suitcase' – entering service in late 1938, another medium bomber with two engines. Both these aircraft would be sent to bomb Germany in the war about to start but, thankfully, would be overtaken by better types.

With the accepted policy being strategic, long-range bombing, for some reason the Air Ministry wanted more twin-engined, medium bombers and in the mid-1930s had requested submissions from some of the many rival aircraft manufacturers. Vickers and their key engineer Barnes Wallis came up with the Wellington. It doubled the Heyford's performance, taking 4,500lb of bombs 1,500 miles at 240mph, and it could reach up to 18,000ft, although its ceiling in practical terms was much lower.

One arrived at 9 Squadron, 31 January 1939: *Squadron took possession of its first Wellington aircraft.*

By 24 April 1939, No. 9 Squadron was fully equipped with the new bomber, entirely replacing their Heyfords. The Wellington was equivalent as a bomb-carrier to the B-17 Fortress but, with much less defensive armament, two engines fewer and a fuselage made of a rigid metal net covered in fabric, it was a great deal cheaper to build. It had a smaller crew, too: pilot, second pilot, observer, two wireless operator/air gunners and one extra gunner as required, initially for the 'dustbin turret', the retractable belly turret soon discontinued.

Whitleys and Hampdens were obviously better than the old biplanes but, Wellingtons apart, the RAF was still ill-fitted for strategic bombing, and this from the country that had been the leading prophet and proponent of bombing as a means to victory in wars. The world watched while others proved the principle. An American eye witness described a Japanese air attack on the Chinese city of Hankow:

At the Kiang An station Japanese planes with incendiary bombs finger for gasoline tanks on a siding. One car explodes in a flaming gust that dissolves the hundred coolies who are trying to push it to safety. A group of houses nearby is incinerated, their trapped inhabitants screaming as they are cooked to death. Beside the depot a row of eating stalls and a small hospital become, in one quivering moment, a churned mass of wood, tin, brick dust, human fragments.

Not only didn't Britain have the aircraft to make such attacks on Germany, she didn't have the crews, or the system for training them in the numbers that would surely be needed. And neither did she have any navigation aids to help find the target in bad weather or at night, nor effective devices for marking the target or for aiming the bombs at it if anybody got there, and she did not expect to attack largely unopposed as the Japanese were in Hankow.

By September 1939, the start of the war, only seven active-service RAF squadrons were equipped with the Wellington, or Wimpy as it was universally known, called after the character in the Popeye cartoons J. Wellington Wimpy. Those seven squadrons would be able to put about ten Wimpys each into the air; with a hundred or so Whitleys and Hampdens, they represented The Shield, that segment of Britannia's hope and glory able to take the fight to Germany and get home again. This was the sum total of bombers capable of carrying a worthwhile amount of bombs on a round trip to the enemy.

This was the RAF Bomber Command which, in early November 1939, recruited an apprentice groundcrew mechanic with a very strange accent, a mixture of Michigan and Lancashire, Ed Stowell. His reason for enlisting was plain; he wanted to fly and this was his way in.

A couple of months later a man of 36, twice Ed's age, from Connecticut, applied to join up for reasons known only to himself. Perhaps the RAF was old-fashioned enough to be able to find a place for an American gentleman who simply wanted to help. Despite Walter Winchell, in training from March 1940 was Plt Off Sedgwick Whiteley 'Bill' Webster, and he was a very singular bird indeed.

If being a US citizen in RAF Bomber Command was not enough to make him unique at that moment, his other qualifications certainly were. He was new aircrew yet positively ancient. He was not some young daredevil pilot wanting to climb into a fighter to test himself in combat. They made him an air gunner, probably to give him something to do since he'd so kindly volunteered to fight and it was a short training course. They made him an officer, only Plt Off, the lowest rank, the equivalent of army lieutenant, but an officer nevertheless.

At that time air gunning was not really considered a separate skilled trade in the RAF. At the start of the war, air gunners were wireless operators – WOp/AGs – who manned the guns when they needed to. Or they could be pretty well anybody who would fill in. The first Distinguished Flying Medal (DFM) of the war was won by a 9 Squadron groundcrew fitter/rigger, Aircraftman (AC) Charles Driver, aged 18, who was pressed into flying as a temporary air gunner, 18 December 1939.

Webster thus was one of the first designated gunner-only aircrew, not wireless trained, and one of the first, if not the first, wartime volunteer of officer rank in that job. Most WOp/AGs were aircraftman grades (aircraftmen, 'erks', equivalent to privates and corporals); some of the longer serving regulars had reached as high as sergeant. Bill

Webster was all this, and an American, and he was destined to become more unusual still.

Since March, he had had some basic training with No. 214 Squadron, not at that time flying operations but stationed at Stradishall, Suffolk, where crews were assembled ready for active service. The Germans began their *Blitzkrieg* on 10 May so, ready or not, Webster was posted down the road to Honington, to No. 9 Squadron, on 12 May with his pilot pal Bertram 'Jimmy' James (all those with the surname James were likely to be nicknamed Jimmy, after a much-loved comedian of the time). They crewed up with B Flight Commander, Squadron Leader (Sqn Ldr) George Peacock DFC, an officer with long service in Empire policing and an acknowledged brilliant pilot. James was second pilot; Webster took the rear turret.

Jimmy James recalled: 'Bill was ten years and more older than the rest of us so he was the old man of the crew, a nice, friendly fellow whom we held in great respect.'

Just eight days after the Germans launched their invasion of Holland, Belgium and France, 9 Squadron was ordered to take the war into Germany, to Cologne and, in Peacock's case, to Duisburg, on 18 May 1940. While the *fliegerabwehrkanonen* of the advancing German Army were very effective, defence of Germany itself against air attack was not yet properly organised. Hitler had promised his people that no British bomb would ever fall on the Fatherland, and so flak there had been considered unnecessary, unpatriotic almost. Over the previous three nights, Hitler had seen his promise broken with the first air raids on German targets beyond the Rhine. Bomb damage to several cities, although light, had caused a sensation throughout the country.

Clearly, a vicious and thoroughgoing response to such Allied airborne arrogance had to be expected soon but, in bright moonlight, Peacock and crew in their Wellington searched nervously but unhindered for their target in Duisburg. Like every other RAF bomber in 1940 they had no navigational tools beyond map, clock, compass and possibly sextant if the observer had one. If they were indeed at Duisburg, their aiming point had to be seen to be believed.

They circled the area undisturbed for 15 minutes at 10,000ft, clearly visible and audible from the ground. Flak or no, the tension inside the aircraft was near tangible. Some of the crew might have wondered if having a pre-war, old-school, press-on type of senior officer for your captain was such a good idea after all. Maybe it would be better to have someone who gave up more easily.

Never a shot was fired but suddenly moonlight was drowned by a much brighter, much more sinister light, a searing, blinding ignition that filled the eyes and painted the inside of the aircraft a brilliant white. As George Peacock threw the Wimpy into a fierce diving turn, Bill Webster fired his machine-guns down the searchlight beam. Amazingly, it went out. Nice shooting, Bill. Yes, sure, thank you. With that little local difficulty solved, they went on to bomb what they believed to be the target and came home after 6 hours in the air.

Two nights later, 9 Squadron was over the battle area in northern France: Le Cateau, Arras, Cambrai. The squadron at full strength, 12 Wimpys, took off in 3 sets of 4, around 20:30, 21:30 and 22:30. They were bombing and machine-gunning roads and railways, in effect armed reconnaissance at low level, and once again Peacock and his crew were away the longest on another 6-hour trip.

Several more such raids followed, looking for targets of opportunity which were generally either a SEMO or a MOPA: Self Evident Military Objective or Military Objective Previously Attacked. An exception was the raid on the bridge over the River Maas at Namur, Belgium, 22 May, furiously defended by the all-conquering Wehrmacht. George Peacock settled his Wellington P9232 WS/M-Mother at 2,000ft to begin his bombing run in a shallow dive. The observer (navigator), Sgt Ronnie Hargrave, lay in the aircraft nose, staring into his bombsight. As with gunner, bomb-aimer was not yet considered sufficiently demanding to be a specialised trade. The observer or sometimes the second pilot did it, with a bombsight based on a First World War design.

As Peacock went into his dive, hell broke loose. Volley after volley after volley of anti-aircraft shells, light flak, streamed towards them in a tangle of colours, as if a thousand deadly gardeners were aiming a thousand fiery hoses up into the air. It seemed a certainty that the bomber would be hit. While the rest of the crew saw uncountable death sentences rushing towards them, Bill Webster in his rear turret could only watch the shells whizz past and fade away as he prayed that the great man George Peacock DFC would get them through.

At 500ft it was bombs gone; Peacock pulled his shaking aircraft up into a climb. Now Bill could see the flak hurtling up, and he could see their bombs exploding and, seconds later, feel their aircraft kicked another few hundred feet upwards by the force. Home, George, and don't spare the horses.

Two nights later they were hunting in a hazy moon for SEMOs. The intention, according to their orders, was *to interfere with enemy movements and prevent both rest and activity of troops*, but they couldn't stop the Wehrmacht and so to Dunkirk, 3 June, trying to keep German heads down while the British Army made for the boats. After the desperate evacuation was over, the ghastly truth was evident for all to see – Roosevelt, Churchill, Walter Winchell, Plt Off Webster and the man in the moon. With remarkable ease, the Germans had taken as much of mainland Europe as they seemed to want for the moment: neighbour Poland, Denmark, Norway, Holland, Belgium and France. Britain surely had to be next and the only way to hit the Germans back was by air. For attacking, for prosecuting the war, RAF Bomber Command was it. There wasn't anything else.

On the night of 5/6 June, a dozen of 9 Squadron were on ops, some to northern France, to the Somme, and some back to Duisburg, including Peacock, Webster and crew. A city target by night must have seemed almost a relief after all that diving into German Army flak. Civil defences were still not up to the job, nor the nightfighters. Once they were through the Wehrmacht gun positions at the newly conquered Dutch coast, they could feel themselves free-ish agents of the darkness.

The squadron CO was a New Zealander, Wing Commander (Wg Cdr) McKee, who one day would be Air Marshal Sir Andrew McKee KCB, DSO, DFC, AFC but was ever known as 'Square' because he was about 5ft up and 5ft across. Square McKee always went to the control tower to say a last word to the boys flying on operations. He would wait until the bomber had taken off and then speak on the radio telephone. His message was always economical and always the same: 'Good luck.' Pilots, especially the superstitious ones, which was almost all of them, generally had a stock reply. Peacock always said 'So long, sir.' Tonight, he said something different. He said 'Goodbye.' Square McKee was taken aback. 'Come off it, George,' he said. 'We never say goodbye.' There was no response from Peacock.

An hour later, they were across the sea and approaching enemy territory. As they reached it, where the rivers Rhine and Maas join, south-west of Rotterdam, searchlights probed the sky but this time there was no putting them out. They were caught, and held long enough for a heavy flak shell to find them. No one was wounded but the port engine was on fire and the flames were growing and licking back. Soon theirs would be an aircraft with only one wing.

Bill Webster: 'The pilot gave the order to put on parachutes. I called him up on the intercom but as I got no reply I bailed out.' It wasn't quite as simple as that, was it, Bill? For a start, parachute training in Bomber Command consisted of being shown how to put the pack on and which was the thing you pulled to open it. Well, there's a first time for everything, Webster might have thought as he swung his rear turret open. Those turrets swung around to starboard. His way out therefore was on the port side, where all the flames were. Hesitating, hanging half out of the turret, uncertain if his parachute would catch fire, Bill got his leg caught in his guns. Uncertainties became academic as the flames spread and the aircraft went into a steep dive with Webster trapped. As the dive increased in speed and angle, his chest-mounted parachute pack whipped up past his head in the wind. The chute opened with a crack and the sudden force of it hauled Webster clear, leaving only a little skin, blood and RAF cloth behind when he might have left a whole limb.

As he floated down he saw his Wellington blow up and go in. The skipper had had no chance to get out himself; it was a matter of unbreakable honour that the captain held his machine steady while the others jumped. One had jumped in vain. His parachute was touched by the fire and that was that, a brief candle falling to earth with no possibility of survival.

The white-painted village church of Simonshaven has only a small graveyard. In the south-eastern corner of it were placed the bodies of Sqn Ldr George Ernest Peacock DFC, age 26, of the Durham town of Spennymoor, and Sgt Ronald Charles Hargrave DFM, age 25, of the Warwickshire borough of Sutton Coldfield.

Bill Webster, Jimmy James and Sgts Murton and Griffiths survived. The nice, friendly fellow who was very probably the first American bomber aircrew in the RAF thus became the first American to be shot down with Bomber Command. Soon he became the first American airman taken prisoner in Europe:

I landed in a field about 15km south of Rotterdam. I hid my parachute, harness and Mae West, then walked to a house and asked for help. This was refused and I made my way to a railway track intending to follow it. Unaware of my exact location I walked across country to a road and I was captured by a German patrol about an hour after bailing out.

After interrogation in Amsterdam, Webster was displayed in Berlin with the other officer, Jimmy James. The locals, who had seen countless foreigners before the war, now found them as curious as Martians. On they went via three short-term imprisonments to Stalag Luft I, their home, they must have expected, for the duration.

Jimmy James:

It was about a year after our capture and we were in Stalag Luft I, Barth, and Bill Webster was in the top bunk above me. One night, everybody in the hut was woken by a noise, and somebody got up and put the light on. There was Bill, lying on the floor groaning but not too badly hurt, and he said 'I was dreaming. I thought I'd bailed out of a Wimpy.'

They would both end up in Stalag Luft III where, in 1942–43, Webster would work on three tunnel digs in the east compound, none of them successful, and James would take part in – and survive – the Great Escape of March 1944. By the time Bill was liberated in 1945, he was a flight lieutenant with a lot of back pay due.

Webster's family would have known, very soon after he was posted missing, that he had been taken prisoner. The American mother of Charles Douglas Fox, pilot, Mrs Elizabeth Lippitt Fox of Berryville, Virginia, would have had longer to agonise. Flying Officer Fox might well have known Bill Webster from his time at Stradishall but he missed him at No. 9, where he arrived on 25 July and heard about the first air raid on London, night of 24/25 August.

In fact, it wasn't an air raid. It was a navigational blunder, like the earlier one on 10 May when some Luftwaffe Heinkel He111s lost their way to a French target and bombed one of their own cities – Freiburg – in error, killing about 60 civilians. Hitler claimed it was the inhuman British who had done it and so, at a stroke, legitimised the bombing of non-military targets.

The August case was of equal import. Hitler had forbidden bombing London, purely for political reasons, part of his strategy to keep the USA out of the war. Although capital-city bombing would have come anyway, this was different because it developed into a major change of policy and a missed opportunity for Germany. Most of the Luftwaffe believed that they had won the Battle of Britain, that Fighter Command was weakened almost to the point of no return. All it needed was another few weeks of attacking RAF bases and the Germans would have air supremacy. They could invade.

The Short Brothers aircraft factory at Rochester, where the Short Stirling four-engined bomber was being developed, was attacked on 15 August with great success and a follow-up was ordered, unnecessarily as it happened because production had been put back a year by the first raid. A few of these follow-up bombs destined for Rochester somehow were dropped near Croydon, just inside the London boundary. Churchill ordered an immediate riposte and, after several more deliberate Bomber Command raids on German cities, Hitler and Göring ordered the Luftwaffe from then on to stop going for air bases and concentrate on London. 'Since they attack our cities, we shall wipe out theirs,' said Hitler. The bomber war had begun in earnest and the Germans had made their first big bombing mistake.

Charles Fox was sent on his first operation as skipper on 26 August, to Germany. It was small beer, very small, compared to what was to come but here were the beginnings of organised, co-ordinated mass efforts against military/industrial targets in cities. The cities themselves were not yet the targets, as London now was for the Luftwaffe, and Hannover, Leipzig, Leuna and Nordhausen were not unduly disturbed by the 99 bombers sent against them.

Over the next four weeks, Fox and his crew added five more trips to Germany, one to Italy and two to the Channel ports where shipping was waiting for the signal to invade Britain. On the first of the new month, they took off in their Wellington at 18:30 aiming for the Air Ministry building in Berlin. They didn't find it; nobody did, nor would anyone until 1944. Whether they found Berlin at all is doubtful but they certainly got lost on their way home. *Aircraft R3282 (Flt Lt C.D. Fox and crew) failed to return. This aircraft made contact with Cullercoates at 0246 when it reported it was coming down into the sea off Lowestoft owing to shortage of petrol. No further communication was received.* No bodies were found either, despite searches by nine Wellingtons of the squadron from half past six in the morning to half five in the evening. Elizabeth Lippitt Fox of Berryville, Virginia, had lost her son. His name and those of his crew would be carved in stone at Runnymede, and that was all she had of him.

Chapter 3

FLYING IN FROM CANADA

On the day war broke out, Royal Canadian Air Force (RCAF) Air Vice-Marshal William Avery Bishop, veteran of the First World War of course, had foreseen the need for American airmen in this new war and the likelihood that many of the more adventurous types would be clamouring for the opportunity.

There were quite a few dilemmas and clashing priorities here. One, the most pressing requirement was for a large-scale training operation; they were desperately short of qualified pilots and American flyers could be a huge help. Two, it was likely that the flyers in question mostly would want to get into the fighting, not be school teachers. Three, there had to be some sort of organisation in the USA, recruitment offices, to select and screen and do the paperwork. Four, it was against US law to recruit American citizens to fight for another country. Five, the law was drafted before the Wright Brothers flew and so didn't mention airmen; in any case, the most senior people in the US government and air force were happy so long as the recruitment didn't affect the USAAF.

That there would probably be no such adverse effect was ruefully prophesied by USAAF General Arnold: 'According to the rules I'm working under, if a flying cadet gets fractious, goes in for low stunt flying, gets drunk one time, or we discover he's married, we must oust him. If I was fighting a war, they'd be the kind I wanted to keep, but I can't.' These 'frustrated washouts' as he called them, would doubtless be joining the RCAF, and good luck to all concerned.

In addition to General Arnold's personality test, the more orthodox selection criteria for qualified pilots were not as strict as those of the USAAF, which, for example, wanted a college degree. The RCAF wanted a high-school certificate, a birth certificate, 300 hours' flying time, a US Civil Aviation Authority private pilot's licence and experience with two-seaters. It would have been down to the individual interviewer how he balanced the urgent need for experienced pilots with a judgement on potential for low stunt flying and other venial sins.

Training schools were opened across Canada to try and cope with the flood of Canadian volunteers. Opinion in that country was largely behind the war, although not entirely. Many remembered how they'd been dragged into the First World War without any consultation by the Imperial Power; French Canadians in particular were reluctant until Hitler drove into Paris. Such hindrances were nothing to the RCAF. Queues of people were forming to sign up and the mother country was in dire straits.

By the time Bill Webster was shot down, the first US citizens with pilot's licences were installed and at work, taking an oath to obey orders rather than the Oath of Allegiance to King George. By the time Charles Fox was killed, the RCAF had received enquiries from 6,000 Americans who wanted to serve. On the strength in round numbers were 100 staff pilots at bombing and gunnery schools, 40 instructors and another 40 ferry pilots on the Atlantic route. They were well treated, well paid and were a big hit with the girls, but there was something missing for a lot of them, something to do with point two listed above. As one put it, 'I didn't come up here to be a damned elevator operator.' Eventually there was a quiet revolution, featuring petitions and mild strike action. By mid-1941, overseas postings seemed to happen more easily.

Among the earliest of the RCAF Americans to make the Atlantic crossing to the war was Warren Thompson Ramey of Whitefish Bay, near Milwaukee, Wisconsin. Warren Ramey, known to everyone as Ray, only son of Josephine and First World War veteran Eric, telegraph operator, was raised on the shores of Lake Michigan, 100 miles or so north of Chicago. At the age of 17 he left the local high school, where he'd been keener on sport and the drama group than his books, and learned to fly in his spare time at the Lawrence J. Timmerman airfield, Milwaukee. He found himself a girl, got married and listened to the radio as the war in Europe exploded. With his own country not involved, he enlisted in the RCAF in October 1940, trained for eight months and, before sailing for England, visited home in June 1941 to see his folks and his wife Dolores, shortly due to give birth to their first child. In an interview with the local evening paper, the *Milwaukee Journal*, he was quoted as saying, 'I believe that every young man with courage and a desire to end this bloody war should enlist in the Royal Canadian Air Force.'

Completing his training in England, Sgt Ramey was posted to a grass field in Suffolk by the village of Honington, home of No. 9 Squadron, at the end of October 1941 as captain of a Wellington bomber. Earlier in the war he would have come in as a second pilot like Jimmy James, ready to serve as helpmate to an experienced skipper for a while, before he was judged capable of being made up to skipper himself. Under pressure to get more crews in the air, this captain-apprenticeship period could not be afforded. Crews were arriving ready assembled with pilot captains but there was still a reluctance to send freshmen on ops on their own for their first time.

The way around this was to send new skipper and crew on a couple of work-experience trips to allegedly less-dangerous – that is, non-German – targets with an old hand doing the driving. This was all very well but there were still two pilots in a standard Wellington crew, and the loss of two trained pilots with every aircraft going down was exercising minds in Bomber Command.

Soon it would be decided to do away with second pilots as standard, although the practice of work experience for pilots only would remain. These were universally known as 'second dicky' flights. The novice pilot going as learner/passenger was second to Dicky, the captain-pilot, and it would be the custom until late in the war. The last second dicky on 9 Squadron would fly in July 1944.

Ramey's guide to war was Sgt Bosher, who had been there for all of two months which made him a veteran. He took Ramey and crew to Ostend and Boulogne, then Ramey was the man, flying his boys to two French targets and to Germany, to Emden, in ten-tenths cloud. No unseemly incidents were experienced. If this was war, it didn't seem very dangerous so far.

Also looking for excitement was another son of Wisconsin, Hubert Clarence Knilans, known as Nick. The family farm was near Delavan, Walworth County, a busy manufacturing town roughly halfway between Milwaukee and Chicago. He'd left Delavan High School in 1935 and worked on the farm in the summer months, milking the 40 cows, looking after the 10 horses that pulled the plough and seed drill and reaping machine. Come the winter and he was off to the Windy City to find a job in a factory, hospital or restaurant. One winter he was taken on by a detective agency.

He had a deferment from the Wisconsin draft board, which had issued his call-up papers in April 1941. It ran out in the October, after harvest, coming up to Nick's twenty-fourth birthday, but he could probably have got it extended indefinitely as he was the only son on the farm. He didn't want that, nor did he want to be a GI in the US Army but he did want something. His decision had been made some time before when he heard the news of the sinking of the *City of Benares*, a passenger ship of the Ellerman Line built for the India run. She'd set sail from Liverpool on Friday 13 September 1940, her passengers including 90 children being evacuated to Canada.

After four days' Atlantic sailing in a convoy of 19 vessels she was 600 miles out and into the periscope of *unterseeboot* U-48, through which instrument the submariners had already watched the departure of the convoy's warship escort. The weather was rough, very rough, and while the U-boat captain could not have known there were so many children aboard, that the *City of Benares* was a passenger ship was obvious, likewise the minimal chances of survivors.

The crew of *City of Benares* noted misses by two torpedos at 23:45 hours on 17 September. At a minute after midnight, the third hit her in the stern. 'Abandon ship' was ordered after 15 minutes and she sank after another 15.

Of the 406 passengers and crew, 259 were drowned as lifeboats capsized in the wind and waves. Among them was the convoy commodore Rear Admiral Mackinnon DSO, who had not followed the standing order to disperse the convoy once the escort had gone.

A Royal Navy destroyer, HMS *Hurricane*, arrived on the scene some 16 hours later and picked up survivors. At first it was thought that only 7 of the 90 children had lived through this ordeal, but the lifeboats had been miscounted and HMS *Hurricane* had left a boat behind. A week later, on the same day that the captain of U-48, Kapitänleutnant Heinrich Bleichrodt, was awarded the Iron Cross First Class, this last lifeboat was spotted from the air and rescued by another destroyer, HMS *Anthony*. Among the souls thought to have been lost were six evacuee boys. Mr Cordell Hull, the American Secretary of State, described the sinking as 'A most dastardly act.'

Bleichrodt would finish the war with 25 sunk ships to his name, including one warship, and the Knight's Cross with Oak Leaves. Nick Knilans had no idea if he would finish the war or not, but the *City of Benares* made sure he would start it.

The RCAF now had the resources to be able to recruit all sorts of trainees, not just ready-made pilots. Nick the farmer wanted to become a pilot, so he told his folks that he was taking a short trip to Chicago to see some friends, which was true as far as it went. A fine weekend was had with his pals and some girls from Mundelein College, a Roman Catholic establishment run by nuns. As every young man used to know, such schools of great strictness and devout study can produce a strain of rebellion and devil-may-care in some of their students, and days and nights of dancing, beer and merriment were just the thing for girls like this and boys who were off to the war.

Two of Knilans's friends were already in the US Army. They went back to barracks while Nick, $5 left in his pocket, bought a ticket for $4.50 on the Detroit bus, and a sandwich for 40 cents, leaving him a dime for the short bus ride across the border to Windsor, Ontario. Nick Knilans showed the Canadian immigration officer his Wisconsin driver's licence:

'I suppose you've come to join the air force,' he said. I said I hoped so. He gave me directions to the recruiting office and off I trudged under the afternoon sun, to find a RCAF sergeant with questions to ask. Did I by any remote chance have my birth certificate and my high school diploma with me? This was clearly an inquiry expecting the answer no, and the sergeant sighed when I gave him the anticipated response. Obviously, Americans were not intelligent enough to bring with them the essential qualifications for joining His Majesty's flying Canadians.

Nick would have to have these papers sent up, and the air force would arrange for him to be billeted in a private home:

The sergeant then said 'I don't suppose you have any money either', not so much a question as a statement. 'We'll give you three dollars a day. Collect it at ten o'clock every morning.' He passed me three dollar bills and a piece of paper with an address written on it. I asked if I would pass a post office on the way. The nod told me yes, in that direction.

With an airmail sent to his parents, explaining his change of vacation plans and requesting his certificates, Nick presented himself to his new family, a local reporter, wife and very attractive daughter, and was with them a week including a Sunday picnic. Such civilised sabbath events would soon became a dim memory and the first stop was the national showground at Toronto, where Aircraftman Knilans and colleagues were led into a large building with a sign over the door saying 'Sheep'. How true, they thought, as they headed off for rifle practice, parade-ground drills, inoculations, kitchen duty and all the other enticing elements of armed forces basic training.

Posting to Ground School came next, to Belleville, Ontario, quartered in a former school for the deaf:

> We had formal classes in mathematics, navigation, Morse code and military regulations. Here were the first sortings out as more intensive medical examinations showed that some would be unable to cope with aircrew duties. One fellow American claimed he heard voices in the central-heating pipes; he was sent home, although the pipes were indeed complaining as they struggled to cope with the onset of the Canadian winter.

Thus began the long and bumpy road to war-pilothood for Nick Knilans, in November 1941. On the evening of 27 November, a man who had already made the journey took off in his Wellington, one of nine of No. 9 Squadron, for Düsseldorf. Warren Ramey was first up at 17:13; last man was away at 17:37. Nine bombers, a grass airfield, almost half an hour to get going; this was how it was at the time. Bomber men flew in individual fighting units with a great deal of discretion. Crews were told what the target was for the night, the weather forecast and the opposition they were likely to meet. Earlier in the war they'd had lists of targets, maybe eight or ten, and they used to decide for themselves pretty well what time they would go. By now they were given one target in one town to visit, a general take-off time and a point at which to cross the English coast. Otherwise everything was still their decision. The navigator would plan his route and the captain might or might not take an interest. When they found what they believed was the target, the skip would decide how and when to attack.

The expression 'blind faith' comes to mind when considering the modus operandi of 1941 Bomber Command. Looking back, it is obvious that a navigator with a map and a compass was not going to find this engineering works or that oil refinery on a cloudy night in blacked-out Germany, having had to fly a long way to get there in crosswinds they couldn't forecast or measure accurately. Yet, the crews were given such specific targets and, since they often thought they'd found their targets and hit them, or were bullied into saying so, the blind senior officers at home continued to lead their blind aircrews in the same direction.

This night of 27 November was fairly typical, except that losses were light. There were 86 bomber crews altogether that set off for the railway yards of Düsseldorf; 52 later claimed to have hit the target and started good fires. In fact, only 1 or possibly 2 bombers dropped on Düsseldorf, setting a water-purification plant on fire with no casualties, while over 100 houses were damaged in nearby Cologne with 4 killed and 15 injured.

One returning Hampden missed its base in Lincolnshire, flew on a further 100 miles, ran out of fuel and crashed in a Worcestershire field. Another Hampden flew into a 'stuffed cloud' – one with a hill inside it – in Gloucestershire, similarly way past its own airfield. There were no casualties in either incident but a third Hampden was last heard of 300 miles out into the Atlantic.

Sgt Ramey and his crew bombed what they believed to be Düsseldorf. Even steered by a navigator with an Oxford degree, it was almost certainly Cologne. They saw the bursts and were dismayed to hear their starboard engine cut out. At only 7,000ft on one engine, home seemed a lifetime away but they did have some good fortune. While two other 9 Squadron aircraft were attacked by fighters and escaped, the Luftwaffe did not find half-power Ramey – and, he got that engine going again and climbed to 12,000ft. With confidence restored, they could all think again about breakfast in Suffolk, and things were looking good until they reached the sea.

Flames appeared from that same engine as they left Holland behind. With one motor still healthy, plenty of height and nothing but a short stretch of oggin to fly over, they might still have felt reasonably happy about making it, and they could have done, perhaps, had it not been for a navigational error that put them off track well to the south. Second pilot Armstrong was at the controls when they crossed the English coast, not somewhere near Lowestoft as expected, but on the southern edge of the Thames Estuary, 135 miles away, above Herne Bay in Kent.

They'd had quite an exciting time at Herne Bay lately. Only four days before, the RAF had dropped HE (high-explosive) bombs and incendiaries by mistake on some local woodland, killing three horses. On the same day, a lifeboat stolen from a German ship had landed with a crew of ten Dutch refugees. Now something even more spectacular was about to happen.

Notwithstanding the darkness of blackout, Ramey and his men knew that the shoreline they could see wasn't the right shoreline. Recognition of that fact came only seconds before their petrol tanks exploded. Gerry Armstrong pulled the aircraft around, thinking that ditching in the sea was preferable to a flaming crash in a town, and Ramey gave the order to jump. Sgt Rutherford, the Scots front gunner went first, followed by Londoner Sgt Stevens, the wireless operator. Ramey and the navigator, Sgt Amphlett, were the last to go, they believed, by which time they were down to about 600ft. Ramey suffered burns as he went but luckily not to his parachute.

Rutherford came to earth about 2 miles inland, at Bullockstone, a rural hamlet on the edge of old Herne. Stevens also found a happy landing on Poplar Drive, now part of the Greenhill estate but then rather more rural. Amphlett and Ramey dropped into the sea, while their aircraft ditched or rather crash-landed, the water there being so shallow, 100yd east of Herne Bay pier, still burning. This was a few minutes before 20:00 hours.

A story still current in Herne Bay says that an airman climbed up the structure of the pier and, in the dark, fell back into the sea when he failed to notice the gap cut in it to hamper the Wehrmacht should they have tried to invade Kent that way. If the story is true, it must have been Ramey as he was the nearest one to the shore after the drop. In any case, by 20:05, one policeman had waded and swum out to try and find the airmen whose cries could clearly be heard, and boats had been launched for the same purpose.

Two men in a motor boat found Ramey at 20:20, thus guaranteeing themselves a rich supply of stories to tell their grandchildren about how they plucked a Yankee flyer from certain death in the cold, cold, sea on a bleak November night. Sgt Amphlett had to bob around in his Mae West life-jacket for rather longer, until 20:45 when a man and a boy in a rowing boat found him.

Rutherford was unhurt but Ramey and the rest had shock and minor injuries, so they would be kept in for a few days at the Queen Victoria Memorial Hospital. All of them were quite certain that Gerry Armstrong had jumped, although they couldn't say about Peter Bilsborough because he'd been in the rear turret. The police searched but couldn't find them.

By two o'clock in the morning, the aircraft was no longer burning and the tide had gone out. Inside the machine, still in flying jacket and parachute harness, was the body of Gerald Gordon Armstrong, 23, of Macoun, Saskatchewan. At the next tide they were able to get inside the rear turret and pull out the body of Peter William Bilsborough, 21, of Shipley, Yorkshire, in leather flying suit and burned Mae West.

Bomber Command took little account of psychological wounds. There was a war on. When the physical hurt was mended, a man was fit again. After all, a spell in hospital was a bit of a holiday, wasn't it? Bombers and crews were being lost at a phenomenal rate – very nearly 200 in November/December – so convalescence did not figure in the calculations.

Pearl Harbor: 7 December 1941. There were now some 6,000 Americans in the RCAF, including about 4,000 aircrew at some point in their training and 800 operational aircrew in the UK with Fighter, Bomber and Coastal Commands. After the Japanese attack and the American declaration of war, many of the US/RCAF boys naturally wanted to transfer to their own air force. Such transfers would be administratively and practically difficult and so could take a while. President Roosevelt's advice was to stay put. He said that those involved 'can best serve the interests of their country through continuing to contribute loyal and effective service in the units in which they are now enlisted'.

Some of Knilans's comrades requested permission to transfer to the USAAF: 'I asked our flight commander if I could transfer from pilot training [which meant another year in Canada] to Gunnery School, a six week course. He said my results made me well qualified for pilot training and the need for pilots was far greater than that for gunners.' So, Knilans did what his flight commander and his President said.

It was an especially merry Christmas when Sgt Ramey could write home to America, land of plenty of everything, and tell the folks back in Whitefish Bay about the warm, watery English beer that the pubs

27

kept running out of, and about the extra rations the government had allowed, of 4oz of sugar and 2oz of tea per person.

With the festivities over, there was neither excuse given nor favour asked by Warren Ramey and his fellow parachutists when they saw themselves slated on 28 December for Germany. Ramey, with a new second pilot and rear gunner to replace his ghosts but the rest of the crew as before, attacked the docks at Emden and made two cloud-ruined attempts on the warships *Gneisenau, Scharnhorst* and *Prinz Eugen* at Brest. These ops were followed by top-secret trials and exercises with a new radio navigation aid initially called TR but later known as Gee.

The system worked by using phase differences in radio signals sent from a triangle of ground stations, far away from each other in the UK. A magic box in the aircraft received these signals, analysed them and deduced where the aircraft had to be. In the early 21st century it is still easy to find places where a cell phone will not work. In 1941 it was very easy indeed to find places where Gee wouldn't work, assuming the box itself was fully functional. Even so, the senior commanders and the boffins were ultra-enthusiastic. Gee was not merely there to guide bombers to navigational pinpoints. It was a system for blind bombing. When aircrews were flying over the Ruhr, where thousands of factories closely resembled each other, where cities and towns in a featureless sprawl overlapped and blended beneath a thick screen of smoke and smog, with the difficulties quadrupled by flying at night with every light 12,000ft below them turned off, the technological miracle of Gee would lift their cares away.

The aircraft used in the secret trials generally had crews quite different from the norm, with several navigators and an instructor working with the Gee box, one pilot, a wireless operator and a rear gunner. One such aircraft, on 19 January, had a piece of starboard wing break off. Among the seven men killed as they fell at Folly Farm, near Thetford, Norfolk, was Ramey's observer and fellow swimmer, Sgt John Amphlett BA (Oxon), aged 24, of Clent in Worcestershire.

Sergeant Ramey couldn't mention such a hush-hush matter as the Gee box in his letter to an old school pal back at the Bay, nor did he say that he was expecting to be transferred to the war in the Pacific. Expectations were one thing in the forces; reality was another. The friend showed the letter to the editor of the *Milwaukee Journal*, who printed it in full. Other news in the papers that day, 25 February 1942, was of anti-aircraft guns firing at an unidentified flying object over Los Angeles, air-war successes in the Far East for the USAAF and the RAF, and two months' supply of thiamin chloride (vitamin B1) flown to the daughter-in-law of Dr Sun Yat-sen, founder of the Chinese republic.

Ramey's letter, as reproduced in the *Milwaukee Journal*:

> I can tell you I'm with one of the best bomber squadrons in England. It is one of the [censored] and has a shining reputation of marvellous deeds. If there is any special task to be done, we get it! Can't tell you the type of plane, but I can tell you it is as big as a house, goes like the very Devil himself is after it, carries tons and tons of bombs, has guns covering every available angle of attack and is as powerful as a fleet of trucks.

In case any old Flying Fortress, Liberator, Halifax or Lancaster aircrew are reading this, it must be confirmed that it is the Vickers Wellington he's talking about.

> They are really swell to fly. I'm glad I decided to be a bomber pilot instead of sticking to the single engine ships. I'm kinda proud of myself for being able to fly these big ships. They run about a mile down the field before taking off. You can fly around for [censored] hours without landing if you wish. I'm getting all sorts of flying in – day, mist, fog, night, beam flying, low flying and just plain flying. My hours are piling up daily.
>
> I've been all over Germany, France, Holland, Belgium and England by air. Have visited all the important places in this country and met people from every country in the world. New Zealand, Newfoundland, Iceland, France, Czecho-Slovakia, Russia, Poland, Belgium, Holland, Italy, Spain, South Africa, Australia, Rhodesia and plenty of others. I've bombed every city in the countries I've been over that has anything of value in it. I've been shot at by every anti-aircraft gun in Germany, been hit by a couple, flown a burning plane across the Channel and bailed out by parachute just half an hour's swim from the shore (England's shore).

Ramey's description of Gee training is as near as he could get it: mist, fog, night, plain flying. Even given a certain poetic as well as pilot's licence, the rest of his account fits well into the RAF tradition of 'shooting the line', or making one's stories slightly taller. At the point he wrote the letter he'd been on Gee exercises for most of January and February. Before that he'd been to Brest twice, Emden twice, Boulogne twice, Ostend, Dunkirk, and Cologne instead of Düsseldorf. Still, you can't blame the lad for wanting to impress an old friend back home.

Perhaps you would like to go with me on a raid to, say, Hamburg? Okay, here we go. In the morning you go over your plane, from nose to tail, from aerial mast to tires, everything must be perfect. You don't get a second chance in this game. Then you air test it, which consists of flying it around to see that everything is in order. If not, you tell the groundcrew when you land and they fix it immediately. The gunners check, double check and triple check their guns, turrets and sights. Guns must be in perfect harmonization and working order. Wireless operator checks all his equipment. He has a radio station of no small power to look after. His equipment may be the difference between arriving safely home through heavy fog, or not.

With the arrival of Gee, wireless operator became a separate trade once and for all. No longer was the w/op expected also to be up and around the aircraft as a gunner. His equipment now included the Gee box, which would run into problems over the Ruhr but really was brilliant at helping the crews find their way home. If they'd had Gee, that ditching in Herne Bay would never have happened.

The morning is gone – dinner – then to the briefing to learn the target for tonight and each aircraft's duty. Can't tell you much about that or what follows but – we are on the line ready to take off – we get the signal and away we go down the runway, [censored] horsepower roaring out their challenge to the cold night air. Finally you are in the air – wheels up, everything set, you set course for your target.

It may take three and one half hours to get there or only one or two. Your crew are at their posts doing their special tasks. Gunners swinging turrets around looking for enemy aircraft, observer checking the course by star sights or ground fixes, wireless operator listening for signals of various natures, second pilot back in the fuselage checking oxygen delivery, oil consumption, petrol consumption and just generally keeping busy – pilot at the controls of [censored] tons of aircraft with its big load of bombs, keeping on

30

the course given by the observer navigator, climbing, ever climbing into the cold night skies.

The temperature steadily drops, 10, 15, 20, 25, 30 below zero [Fahrenheit]. Now you are over enemy territory, searchlights probe the skies for the plane. Huge cones are formed and must be avoided, the flak begins to burst in the sky about you, you 'jink' away, diving a bit when the shells are on your level, turning left or right or climbing, but always on toward your target. Finally you near it – Hamburg – way down there [censored] below, sirens are sounding, people are rushing to their shelters, gun and searchlight crews are rushing to their posts. Puzzling dummies are lit to mislead you, searchlights spring into brilliancy from all over. Flak begins to blot the sky with fiery patches of flame. You see your target – let's say, a railway yard.

The observer is at his bomb aimer's position, his bombsight set, his finger on the bomb release – you are getting near the target – the ground defenses realize you are there, they multiply the shells by tens, the sky is filled with flying steel, stench of burned cordite and multicolored flashes. 'Left, left, left,' says the bomb aimer. 'Bomb doors open,' you say.

In the spacious belly of your plane is cradled a load of high explosive bombs, the doors swing open, the target passes across the sight. 'Bombs gone,' says the observer and the plane leaps into renewed vitality as thousands of pounds of its weight screams downwards toward the target. A few seconds later the whole world seems lit up by the blast as your bombs hit the earth – what happens on the ground we don't see – we close the doors and head for home.

The gunners below won't give up and the shells scream through the air all about you, causing you to do things with the huge plane that people who have never been over wouldn't believe can be done. Then the long trek home – gradually descending – the sea – then the English coast and silently everyone breathes a sigh of relief – back to the field and down on good old terra firma. Gee, how good it is to be back.

There. You now have one operation under your belt. We have hundreds – really it isn't so bad – the shells lose their terror and the dodging becomes natural after a few trips. Don't know how much of that the censor will let through but can't see what I've given away so I figure all will get through. Hope so at least.

I reckon that's about enough for one letter. I'm well and fairly happy – I'll be happier when all this is over.

Still with no idea of what or when he would be flying, and certainly not thinking about all this being over, Nick Knilans was on Canadian guard duty:

> Winter storms had held up the pilot training of those ahead of us on the scheme, so we were sent to mark time at a storage depot 30 miles south of Montreal, to guard some crated-up Airspeed Oxfords waiting to be delivered to training bases. Our CO was a young pilot who had been grounded for unauthorised low flying, and he didn't want to be there any more than we did.
>
> At first, we thought enemy saboteurs were all about us and we marched up and down enthusiastically in our heavy overcoats and many layers of long underwear, but we soon realised that the snow and boredom were much greater threats. Some squads used to hide in a warm hanger until shortly before they were to be relieved. My friend Willie and I threw open the hangar door and shouted 'Sergeant! Get all their names and I'll have them on a charge in the morning', and watched them jump out of the windows.
>
> One member of our flight had been writing home to New York, telling his family that he was flying impossible bombing raids to Germany across the Atlantic. When he came back from leave one time, he found the barracks festooned with celebratory toilet paper, a 'Welcome Hero' sign over his bunk, and his photograph hanging inside a toilet seat.

This same loo-paper hero would retire one day as a colonel in the USAAF.

As with any group of lively, go-for-it fellows, beer and girls were important components of a satisfactory existence, and Nick Knilans was no exception:

> I'd been spending a pleasant evening at a dance and I was sitting at a table with an attractive girl who asked me back to her apartment. I was busy accepting her proposal when a sergeant came up and told me I was wanted on the telephone. When we got out into the hallway, he told me the girl I was with had syphilis, that she delighted in passing it on to airmen, and that I would be discharged if I got it. 'Oh yeah?' I said. 'And when I give her the heave-ho, you'll pile in where I left off.' Luckily for me, the sergeant didn't take offence. He told me to look between her fingers. I went back in, she

was lighting a cigarette, and I could see little sores and cracks in her skin. I told her I was recalled for guard duty and went out to thank the sergeant. 'That's okay, son,' he said. 'I don't want the King wasting his training money on Yanks with VD.'

With the Gee box tested and proved as Bomber Command's first real navaid, it would still be months before every aircraft could be fitted with it so select squadrons like No. 9, Gee-equipped, would have to lead the rest. Ray Ramey, on leave, missed the first Gee ops but he was there for the famous attack on Lübeck, a moderately important Baltic harbour and trading town, less well defended than the major industrial cities of the Ruhr and selected by the new chief of Bomber Command, Arthur Harris, to test a novel plan, 28 March 1942.

The first wave of bombers would go in and mark the target with incendiaries; the second and third waves, instead of looking for their own targets, would aim at the incendiaries and smash the place to pieces. The raid would feature over 230 aircraft and they all had to bomb in 2 hours. Such numbers, restrictions and discipline had never been known in a force that had been used to bombing as a loose collection of solo efforts. In the Gee-equipped incendiary wave on that Palm Sunday, 9 Squadron found the town already alight. Sgt Ramey dropped his load *in centre of island but no bursts seen owing to fires which appeared to be solid.* Lübeck, with an old town centre of narrow streets, was ideal for burning. When thousand upon thousand of incendiary bombs fell in back alleys and city lanes, fires started straight away, spreading widely and wildly, beyond any control. Germany had never seen anything like it. Small scale though it was, those officials sent to inspect afterwards – not having seen Coventry after the Luftwaffe raid of 14 November 1940 – were shocked to their souls. Something like 3,500 buildings were destroyed or badly damaged.

For Ramey and the squadron it was back to the Ruhr, 'Happy Valley' as they called it, to Essen, whence Ramey and everyone else bar one had to return early, with engine trouble or because of impossible flying conditions with ice and electrical storms.

A big show was planned for 5/6 April, a maximum effort on Cologne, and the squadron planned to send 11 Wellingtons to be part of the record-size force of 263. Plt Off Taylor, who'd been around a while and no longer had a settled crew, was short of a second pilot. Ray Ramey said he'd go. Out of the 11, 1 FTR so 10 crews reported *dropped incendiaries in centre of town*, and saw *Power Station and huge transformers illuminated by fire*. Taylor and Ramey saw *seven good fires dispersed over Cologne*.

Their target had been the Humboldt engineering works. Good results were reported by more than 200 crews, yet the only hit in the right area was a small mill; otherwise the nearest bomb to the target fell 5 miles away. At least the losses were light; only four Wellingtons and a Hampden altogether. According to a German report, the most incendiary incident of the night occurred while a crowd in the Cologne area was watching a crashed Wellington burn. It was a 9 Squadron aircraft, X3415, or it could have been X3489 of 75 Squadron. Either way, it had six dead men inside. It exploded, killing 16 spectators and injuring another 30.

Ray Ramey took his own boys to Dortmund, 15 April, where they bombed on a Gee fix through thick cloud, and Hamburg two nights later. The rear turret went u/s (unserviceable) so he had to come home; he never would get to Hamburg, in his imagination or in awful reality.

The top brass were planning a Lübeck-style operation to Rostock for 23 April but Sgt Ramey and his crew were detailed on 22 April for another raid to Cologne, a much smaller, experimental one testing the Gee box again as a blind-bombing tool in cloud. There were 69 bombers, all using Gee, and 1 in 5 at the most dropped on the city. For results so poor, the price for 9 Squadron was extortionate. Of the eight 9 Squadron Wellingtons that went, one fell at the target and another was brought down by flak over Holland. A third, Ramey's, was very badly damaged. Outstanding pilot that he was, Ray Ramey struggled back to within sight of the home flarepath. With less than a mile to go and his emergency landing lined up, the aircraft gave up on her crew and they went in near Sapiston with only the rear gunner surviving. They found him next day, still in his turret, in the back of a hedge. Ramey and the rest, including two Canadians, were buried in the churchyard at All Saints, Honington.

Warren Ramey's wife, Dolores, received the dreaded telegram from the RCAF Chief of Air Staff only an hour after the postman had brought her a new photograph of her husband, with a cheerful note hoping that she and Steven, the son he never saw, were well. A week later, the 700 pupils of Whitefish Bay High School held a memorial service and sang 'The Star Spangled Banner'.

At about the time they were singing, Ray Ramey's wireless operator at Herne Bay, Ken Stevens, 21, married to Irene, was killed at Kiel. Just two months later, front gunner James Rutherford, having survived another crash that wrote off a new Wellington, disappeared into the sea somewhere after a mining trip and still only 20 years old. So that was all of them.

Nick Knilans had never heard of Ray Ramey but he was very keen to replace him. Flying school was at St Eugene, a small Ontario village, where the instructors were mostly American civilians. They found this status a disadvantage in bars and dance halls and so had created their own non-specific uniform from air force and navy bits and pieces, without rank or other insignia but sufficient unto their need to be treated as they felt they should be, by girls and bartenders.

Learner drivers had to solo within 12 hours of lessons in a single-engined biplane, a Tiger Moth, 125hp. Nick was away in 10 but, coming in to land, on the tarmac runway they had there to make things harder than they would have been on grass, he was a little miffed to see his instructor sliding off into a hangar so he wouldn't have to watch. Flying along in a forgiving, well-tried biplane is easy enough. It's the taking off and the landing that find you out. When his undercart collapsed, Nick went skidding and spinning down the runway like a fallen figure skater. Another time, when he was wrongly cleared to land in a strong crosswind, 'I did a ground loop, rose up on one wing and crashed over upside down. I released my seat belt and promptly fell on my head on the runway. An alert mechanic ran out and climbed under the aircraft to shut off the petrol and the ignition.'

The French-Canadian girls were friendly, the Molson's and Labatt's went down a treat, and an African-French-Canadian chef in the airmen's mess produced the best steaks and could be relied upon for midnight feasts after an energetic evening at the village hall. Knilans kept up his record of average passes in flying and ground studies and so could expect to graduate to the next stage, the much more powerful, low-wing monoplane trainer, the North American AT6 Harvard at Advanced Flying School.

Chapter 4

THE ARISTOCRAT AND THE ORDINARY JOE

Charles Moorfield Storey was a partner in the law firm Peabody, Brown, Rowley & Storey (forerunner of today's international firm Nixon Peabody LLP), a prominent civic figure and national secretary of the Society of Cincinnati. A few months before his government posting to Europe to work on the First World War settlement, his wife Susan Jameson Sweetser had a second son, born 1 August 1917. They called him Anderson after her maternal grandfather, Samuel J. Anderson, one-time Mayor of Portland, Maine.

Back from Paris, Geneva and Budapest, Charles bought 229 Perkins Street, Jamaica Plain, a most desirable address overlooking Jamaica Pond and a rambling 19th-century mansion suitable to modern eyes for a Hitchcock movie. Charles Storey was well known in the neighbourhood anyway but he added to his reputation one winter by falling through Jamaica Pond ice while demonstrating its safety for skating.

There had been Storeys in the Boston, Massachusetts area since the 1700s. Storeys were pillars of the community, Harvard graduates and respected members of the bar.

Such a well-set family could send their highly intelligent son to one of the best boarding schools, and across the Atlantic for a summer with his sister. Anderson and Susan bicycled 2,200 miles through England, Scotland and Wales and absolutely loved it.

By the time war broke out in Europe, Anderson Storey had been sent down from Harvard, the family alma mater, for the appalling grades he got in his freshman year, classified as 'extremely poor', much to the anguish of his mother and father. The parents must have been equally disconcerted when their son proposed filling in time with a year working around their home town. He was a good auto-mechanic and took a job in a garage, then he said he was going to fight the Nazis.

The Harvard rustication had been a severe blow. He could make amends, and prove his worth to his parents, by doing something he believed was eminently worthwhile:

> I felt America should be taking part in the war, that it was essential, but at that time we were still neutral, so the only course for me was to cross the border and join up. I suppose I had everything at home but when I heard what was happening in England, the bombing and the destruction, I couldn't bear the thought of it.

He asked his old headmaster at Deerfield Academy (founded 1767) to write him a reference for the Royal Canadian Air Force, 3 October 1940, to help him go to war. The headmaster, Frank L. Boyden, obliged. 'Anderson Storey is from one of our oldest and best New England families, a young man of high character, fine personality and good scholastic ability. He is very sincere in his desire to be of service at this critical time.'

Andy Storey was certainly a high character, around 6ft 4in, but away from school he was rather shambolic, the kind of young man who would automatically cause ulcers in the vital organs of sergeant-majors and adjutants. He was also a bit of a comedian and liable to fool around. These aspects of his character would prove faults rather than assets, initially at any rate.

The universal elementary trainer, the Tiger Moth, had a Canadian cousin, the Fleet Finch, a simple, learner-friendly, two-seater biplane cruising at a gentle 85mph, initially with open cockpits but, in its second winter, now fitted with a Perspex canopy. This was Aircraftman Storey's first chariot, 23 February 1941, at No. 10 ETFS, Mount Hope, Ontario. By the end of April he'd flown solo and transferred to the two-engined Avro Anson, in which he practised until 21 July when he was judged ready for graduation to warplanes. He went home for a spot of leave then across the sea to the Wellington bomber, 23 October, and more training until, only a year and three months after his first student ride in a Finch, his posting to B Flight, 9 Squadron, late in May 1942. At 24 years of age, with his prematurely thinning fair hair, he would have seemed one of the older novitiates. Some of the new pilots coming in were hardly out of their teens, while one of the new wireless operators, an American called Howard Burton, from West Virginia, was almost of pensionable age at 31. He'd volunteered and found himself at No. 4 Bombing and Gunnery School, Fingal, Ontario, back in September 1941. He arrived on squadron a few days before Storey.

After two French ops, Burton's crew was sent with 1,046 other bombers to Cologne on the first of the famous 'Thousand Plan' raids. When Air Marshal Harris became Bomber Command C-in-C he had taken over the same objective as his predecessors: 'The progressive destruction and dislocation of the German military, industrial and economic system and the undermining of the morale of the German people to a point where their capacity for armed resistance was fatally weakened'. The difference with Harris was that he had a notion about how the objective might be achieved.

He'd tried his ideas at Lübeck and Rostock. Now he proposed the biggest air raid yet seen, one that would have massive propaganda value as well as inflict unsustainable damage on the enemy, using twice as many aircraft as the Germans had ever sent to the UK. It was also more than twice as many as the RAF currently had on operations.

The raid was set for the last day of May, a Sunday, in the moon. Winston Churchill personally approved the plan and Harris's deputy, Air Vice-Marshal Saundby, began the urgent job of collecting 1,000 bombers. By including 369 from the training units with crews that were mixtures of instructors, many of them tour-completed veterans, and pupils, the symbolic number began to look possible. Soon after noon, Saturday 30 May, the order went out. The preferred target had been Hamburg but bad weather forced the decision to Cologne, Germany's third city.

Gee-equipped Wellingtons of 9 Squadron, 14 of them plus others of 3 Group, were to be raid leaders, dropping flares and incendiaries for the rest to aim at. The pressure was on, to field as many aircraft as possible. One of the most experienced 9 Squadron pilots, a regular from before the war, didn't help matters by making a mess of a new Wellington, Z-Zola, landing after an air test, but someone had scrounged two of the old Wellington Mk IC from somewhere, a type of aircraft the squadron hadn't used since the previous October. The IC had the less powerful Pegasus engines, the Mk III the much better Hercules.

Sqn Ldr Turner, who had pranged Z-Zola, was given another new Mk III to fly. Burton's men were allocated one of the Gee-less Mk ICs and the other went to a similarly inexperienced crew. Elsewhere, records claim that 14 went to Cologne, because that was the plan, but the two elderly ICs made it 16 from No. 9.

The weather was poor on the way but cleared over the target as forecast. This was the first use on a major scale of the 'bomber stream' tactic with all the bombers flying the same route, at heights and times specified, so as to overwhelm with sheer numbers the nightfighter pilots and their controllers who were used to the haphazard arrangements of the past. Some of the RAF top brass predicted confusion and collisions with this method, but they were wrong and Harris was right.

Most of the bombers, just under 900, found the target and dropped almost 1,500 tons of bombs in 90 minutes. In round figures, 3,300 buildings were destroyed and 9,500 damaged, including 2,500 industrial and commercial properties; 500 people were killed, 5,000 injured and 45,000 bombed out of their homes. Something like 150,000 people left the city after the raid. The damage done in this one raid was almost equal to the total of all such damage inflicted by Bomber Command so far in the war. Air Marshal Harris felt vindicated:

[it] proved that in a successful operation the damage increased out of proportion to the numbers involved. It also showed that the destruction of German industrial centres by bombing was a realisable aim if sufficient resources were devoted to achieving it. From this time onwards one target, against which practically all available forces [could be] used was selected for each night's operation. Co-ordinated plans for each attack and common routes were laid down at Command HQ, in consultation with the Groups, and the planned concentration of bombing [was set at] ten aircraft per minute.

Bomber losses were a record too, but proportionately not so bad as might have been expected. Excluding 5 write-offs that were not to do with enemy action, 48 bombers were lost, of which 21 were from training units, almost all of them Wellington ICs. The two lost by No. 9 Squadron were Mk IIIs.

Apart from three minor operations, Bomber Command had a night off before the next 'Thousand Plan', to Essen, home of the vast Krupps works and the manufacturing core of the German war machine. They didn't quite make the number this time, sending 956 including 13 of 9 Squadron leading with the Gee box, loaded with more flares and fewer incendiaries than at Cologne, plus an old Wellington IC, DV672, taking off with the rest, as before with Howard Burton on the wireless set.

The weathermen had prophesied reasonable conditions but it turned into a hazy night with low cloud. The Gee-box scouts missed their mark. Losses were relatively light, damage in Essen was very light indeed, and heavy bombing was reported in Oberhausen, Duisburg and Mülheim.

Storey's initiation was as second dicky with Canadian Plt Off George Cooper, who was only 21 but, as he'd been flying with 9 Squadron since last December, was well qualified by this time, 3 June. Burton was there too, back in a Mk III. It was a bit of a mixed start for Storey, with 3 of the 12 aircraft failing to take off *for various reasons* and one coming home early with an engine u/s but, on a trip of slightly over 4 hours, Cooper and Storey saw the target and bombs were dropped across the aiming point. The Focke-Wulf and U-boat factories escaped while the harbour suffered serious damage and many houses were flattened too. By contemporary standards, it was a very successful raid, although 11 bombers went down out of 170, 6.5 per cent.

Next up was Emden, 6 June. Sitting there with Cooper again, waiting to take off, Storey may have felt that he had found the right air force, the one to match his own well-meaning but slightly chaotic nature. Two other Americans were also watching, station guests Majs Chilvers and Douglas of the USAAF, as the first two aircraft collided on the way from dispersals, another burst a tyre and Burton and co. had to give up with only one engine firing.

As a result, seven of them got away including Storey's, thus missing the final act of the drama when the eighth Wellington in the air lost all power at 100ft and crashed. Although the aircraft was soon a ball of flame, all the crew got out with only a few cuts and bruises. Storey would hear about this next morning, and about another of the squadron's Wellingtons coming home apparently out of petrol having been less than halfway to Emden, and another crashing while landing at a different airfield. Still, the student skipper Storey again saw the target, saw his bombs dropped near it and came home without further incident. Crews' reports of good results were confirmed by photoreconnaissance. Out of 233, 9 aircraft had been lost, less than 4 per cent, which made it a good night, overall, although the USAAF majors may have carried away a different impression.

Now Storey was ready to take his own crew, 8 June, to a French target as was usual for first-timers, attacking shipping and docks at Dieppe. Squadron Operations Record Book (ORB): *Sgt Storey reached mid-channel when hydraulic failure forced his return.* Storey flew to the Rouen area, 16 June, to drop leaflets and the next night was briefed for gardening, as mine laying at sea was called, around Borkum Island. As well as the mines, referred to as vegetables, they generally took two 500lb bombs to drop in case they came across enemy shipping. Generally, they brought these home with them *as no suitable target was found.* This was so for Howard Burton, although they laid their mines in the right place, but *Sgt Storey in aircraft 'T' did not take off.*

So far, not so good for Andy Storey. The one successful start out of three had been a French leaflet drop. He did much better on 19 June, one of four to go to Emden. The others bombed on Gee fix while Andy Storey said he'd identified the north-western districts of Emden though a gap in the cloud: *The weather was not very kind and Sgt Storey was the only one claiming to have seen the target. This crew also had minor encounters with two FW190s after bombing but returned without damage and did not claim a victory.*

The encounters were minor in the sense that the Wellington, carrying 540 4lb incendiaries and 3 500lb bombs, beat off the first attack. Storey's report: *Horizontal visibility was good owing to Northern Lights. Rear gunner fired three short bursts as our A/C prepared to make a diving turn into the attack. The E/A . . . broke away without firing and was not seen again.* After bombing was the second half of the minor encounter, as another Focke-Wulf 190 came in at high speed from 100yd, misjudged the approach under fire from the Wellington, could not get in a shot and was not seen again.

Life for some and death for others were the consequences of an odd incident a few days later, presaged in eerie fashion by a few words that same rear gunner, Plt Off Brian Moorhead, let slip in the mess. 'It's not fighters or flak I'm scared of,' he said, 'when I'm flying with that crew.' This remark was deemed sufficiently amusing to be written down in the officers' mess Line Book, the unofficial record of witty gems and other notable sayings.

The odd incident was the crew going for an air test with Andy Storey at 11:15 in Wellington WS/T, 22 June, and another in the same aircraft at 16:50 with Flt Lt Stubbs DFM. In between the two air tests, the crew had changed skippers. Storey's early flying career had not gone well. His crew had lost confidence in him and, likeable good company that he was as a person, they could not see themselves getting it back. They went to the CO and said that, for the sake of their own preservation, they would like a new skipper. Stubbs was new on squadron but beginning his second tour of operations. A first tour, initially defined as 200 operational flying hours, later was redefined as 30 ops; a second tour was 20 ops. Stubbs, very experienced, extremely competent, a highly professional stickler, was everything Storey was not. Storey went back to school for some revision and his crew boarded their Wimpy that night for Emden with Stubbs.

Howard Burton had his first experience that night of being coned, of being trapped by many searchlights at once. When this happened, the flak gunners turned all their attention to such a brightly illuminated target and the pilot had only a few seconds to twist and wriggle his way out of it, if he could. Burton, in his small corner of the aircraft with his wireless set and his Gee box, could not have seen what it looked like outside. He would only have known that he was suddenly sitting in a permanent flash of lightning, and that no white-knuckle ride on any fairground could equal the sensation of being in an aircraft that his captain was trying to turn inside out.

This fearsome experience was reported later, at around four in the morning, to the intelligence officer at the interrogation: *Bombs dropped on aiming point but no results seen owing to avoiding action being taken.*

They were off mining near St-Nazaire the next night, then to Bremen, where they found such thick cloud that they could only bomb on Howard Burton's Gee fix and hope for the best, which, as one of the leading aircraft on the third of the 'Thousand Bomber' raids, was quite a responsibility. Including Coastal Command's contribution, 1,067 aircraft went, of all available types, and most had no Gee and so bombed on the flares and the fires started by the incendiaries of crews like Burton's.

This was the largest raid of the war so far, the most variegated ever in terms of aircraft types, and with the most losses suffered so far. Bomber Command lost 52 and Coastal Command another 5. These ghastly figures included a grossly disproportionate 33 aircraft from the 200 or so supplied by training units, mostly Mk IC Wellingtons and Whitleys, old and obsolete bombers that should never have been carrying trainee crews on the long journey to Bremen. Trained and now experienced crews like Burton's, in their Mk III Wellingtons, fared rather better against the flak, and against the nightfighters which had become much more of a menace.

Results at Bremen were better than at Essen but still no compensation for all those losses, and they had to go back twice more in the same week to inflict serious damage on the main targets, including the Focke-Wulf aircraft works, the Korrf refinery and the A.G. Weser U-boat factory. After a mining trip to the Friesian Islands, which made 13 ops in 5 weeks, Howard Burton and the crew were given leave.

A Jewish family called Buechler emigrated from Hungary in 1889 to the USA with an 8-year-old son called Harry. He grew up, trained as a dentist and married a much younger girl, only 15, Minnie. They had three daughters, Janet, Corrine and Beatrice, and settled at 566 High Street, Newark, New Jersey. On 15 April 1920, their son Maurice Emanuel was born. He went to the B'nai Abraham Hebrew School and to West Side High School, Newark, on to Franklin and Marshal College, Lancaster PA and to the University of Tennessee. In September 1941, three months before Pearl Harbor, he upped and joined the RCAF, trained as a gunner in Canada and shipped over to the UK in January 1942 for his final, operational phase of training.

There was an accident on 15 July. Maurice wrote home about it:

It was about 03:15 in the morning when we hit the hillside, and before that one of our motors had cut out. Thanks to our pilot who worked miracles with the craft, we got back to within 15 miles of our base when the old kite wouldn't go any farther. We would have bailed out long before this but weather and visibility were practically nil and we didn't jump for fear of hitting the top of the mountains before the parachutes fully opened. When we finally could see, we were falling too fast to allow us all to jump, and only one man got out above 1,000 feet. His chute had just fully opened before he hit the trees, and he climbed down without a scratch. The only reason that we're alive is that we weren't expecting to hit when we did and we were completely relaxed.

Burton came back from leave, and Storey was back too, promoted to flight sergeant, refreshed and, it was hoped, fully prepared, as he went twice to Duisburg as second pilot with Plt Off Mullins, another young Canadian old hand. On Storey's second Duisburg with Mullins, 23 July 1942, there were 14 pilots of 9 Squadron, of whom 13 would not survive the war. One was killed that night and three more only five days later, including Storey's two 21-year-old Canadian mentors. James Mullins had George Cooper with him as a second pilot at a time when the squadron was usually flying with crews of five and just one pilot. They were shot down by flak on 28 July over Hamburg with no survivors.

Foul weather in England had meant that the greater part of the planned force couldn't get off the ground. Of the 256 that did, many were recalled as the weather worsened, and more turned back. Around 70 got through, inflicting no significant destruction. The damage was felt by the raiders: 7 Stirlings from training units, 3 more Stirlings from operational squadrons, 4 Wellington Mk ICs and a Whitley from training units, and 17 Wellington Mk IIIs from the squadrons including 3 from No. 9.

This trip was the first for Burton's crew in one of the squadron's four BJ Wellingtons, those specially adapted to carry the 4,000lb 'cookie', the light-case blast bomb known as the blockbuster. About 90 minutes into the flight the rear turret went u/s so they jettisoned all their bombs in the sea and came home. Lucky them, possibly, but an abbreviated trip like that was classified DNCO – Duty Not Carried Out. Despite 3 hours in the air in the worst of flying weather, half of it with the main means of defence not working, Burton and the rest could not tick off one more op on their target of 30.

The Avro Lancaster was coming to 9 Squadron and their last act in Wellingtons was to send 12 to Düsseldorf. Burton's was among the ten crews who returned. It was another of those raids where demands were made on the training units to bump up the struggling numbers and out of the 630 total they sent 105, of which 11 went down including 4 Hampdens from No. 14 Operational Training Unit (OTU). An American called Joe McCarthy, from Long Island, was on this one representing 14 OTU, but he and his Hampden came back, as he would always come back, from busting dams and everywhere else.

No. 9 Squadron was to move to a new home, from the grass of Honington in Suffolk to the tarmac of Waddington in Lincolnshire; to a new Bomber Command Group, from No. 3 to No. 5; and convert to the new aircraft. After almost 2,500 sorties in the much-loved Wimpy by 9 Squadron, away the machines went to various parts of the RAF. As August began, Plt Off Howard Burton had 16 operations counted in his log book, and Flt Sgt Anderson Storey 7.

Storey was made captain of a Lancaster with an entirely novitiate crew. There were seven of them: pilot/captain, flight engineer, navigator, bomb aimer, wireless operator, mid-upper gunner, rear gunner. Over that August, without any formal instruction, the pilots learned to fly a much bigger aircraft with four engines and everyone else got on with learning whatever they had to. The armourers, mechanics and other groundcrew had about four weeks to become used to these new monsters. Some aircrew from the Wellington days had to retrain to a new trade, gunner to bomb aimer for example. It was a frantic time.

Ex-Wellington pilot Plt Off Leslie Musselwhite had American Maurice Buechler as his rear gunner. Later in the war there would be a system called 'crewing up', where new heavy bomber crews would assemble themselves around a captain, with every man having a say in whether he joined this skipper or that. Now, in the late summer of 1942 with everyone working flat out around the clock, there were no systems and no choices. You, Flt Sgt Buechler, you're with Plt Off Musselwhite. Yes, sir.

In fact, Musselwhite was something of a minor hero. As second pilot, back in April at Rostock, his Wimpy had been badly shot up by a fighter, with the tail gunner killed and a furious fire in the rear section. In putting the fire out and trying to rescue the gunner, Musselwhite had been badly burned. His skipper was awarded the DFC for getting them home; Leslie Musselwhite was awarded a spell in hospital.

The Lancaster, able to fly higher, further and faster with more bombs than any other aircraft of the time, was also expected to last longer. Its superior performance would mean relatively fewer losses, it was said, and 9 Squadron's first ventures with Lancasters seemed to reinforce that belief. Storey's old crew flew with Stubbs and three other Lancs to Düsseldorf, with five others to Bremen and four to Wilhelmshaven. No casualties were suffered and no damage worse than a few flak holes and one undercarriage collapsing on landing.

The night of 16 September was different. This was to be a major raid and, exactly five weeks since the first Lancaster had arrived, the squadron was clearly ready to join it in style. After a massive effort by the mechanics, sparks and armourers, 13 crews could be briefed for Essen. One couldn't take off and two came back early with mechanical trouble. The ten flying on included W4186 WS/S-Sugar, captain Plt Off Musselwhite and rear gunner Flt Sgt Buechler who, like the aircraft and everyone in it except the skipper, was going to Germany for the first time.

Essen was the target of targets. Naturally, it was exceptionally well defended and, in the smog and darkness, very difficult to identify among all the other industrial hotspots sprawling across the Ruhr Valley. Despite many efforts by Bomber Command, Krupp and the rest of Essen had yet to suffer any really serious damage, of the sort that halted production for any length of time.

A force of 369 bombers was assembled, including for the last time a major contribution from the training units. Yet again there were Mk IC Wellingtons, flown by crews of instructors and almost-graduated pupils, and the obsolete flying barn door, the Whitley. Of the 41 bombers going down that night, 19 were from training units, a grossly disproportionate number and a heavy blow with all those invaluable instructors and almost-trained aircrew killed or taken prisoner. In among the 11 per cent of aircraft lost were two Lancasters of 9 Squadron. One fell near Düsseldorf and one, S-Sugar, disappeared completely. No remains were ever found of Maurice Buechler and the rest. All that's left of each man is a name carved on the Runnymede Memorial. The RCAF gave Maurice his gunner's half-wings posthumously, on 27 September.

The damage to Essen was the best so far, over 100 fires started and Krupp hit by 15 HE bombs and a crashing bomber full of incendiaries. Dr and Mrs Harry Buechler of Newark, New Jersey, didn't know that. All they had to go on was a letter from Wg Cdr Southwell, the squadron CO: 'Your son was a keen and efficient gunner, who was most popular with everyone in the squadron. His loss is a great blow to us all.'

The CO was trying to do the right thing. Possibly his letter was a comfort to the Buechlers but feeling losses as great blows was not something that happened. It was not conducive to good morale. If aircrew started to feel anything beyond 'Ah well, sorry, but glad it wasn't me', they'd never get in the aircraft tomorrow night. In truth and under the frenzied pressures of war, exacerbated by the problems of adjusting to a new base and a new aircraft, there would be very, very few people on the squadron beyond his own crew who had had the slightest idea about Maurice and who he was. Perhaps, as a fellow American in the sergeants' mess, Andy Storey might have met him and so felt the loss a little. Of the other crew that went down that night, Sgt Hobbs's lot, five were from the Wellington days so they'd be known and missed but, apart from Musselwhite, S-Sugar's boys were all first-timers. Nobody would miss them because nobody had had time to get to know them.

Andy Storey's lads were all sprogs too, and he took them for their initiation to Munich, 19 September. ORB: *The target was Munich, the Nazi shrine. The aiming point, appropriately enough, was the beer cellar. Navigation seemed to be of a high order, for everyone returning had located the target and dropped their bombs.*

The 9 Squadron crew not returning might have hit it too, seeing as they came down less than 10 miles from Munich. The mid-upper gunner survived but the rest, including Plt Off Howard Houston Burton, veteran of 18 operations, did not.

Storey and the rest claimed a good raid, although later reports showed they'd missed the beer cellar but laid waste to large areas of the suburbs. Storey was last by 20 minutes to land back at base, which was pretty good considering an engine had failed shortly after bomb-drop. Coming home safely on three, on your first trip, was bound to inspire in his crew that confidence and respect that had been lacking in his earlier career.

Three days after Storey's first Lancaster op, a large bouncing ball of an American arrived at Woodhall Spa, Lincolnshire, to join 97 Squadron, which had been flying and losing Lancasters since the beginning of the year. J9346 Plt Off Joseph Charles McCarthy was destined for glory and, unlike so many, a long life, but they didn't know quite what to make of him in the officers' mess. His language was colourful to say the least, his attitude go-get-'em professional, his style as unlike that of the understated British Standard RAF Officer as it was possible to be. RAF officers as a rule had not worked as lifeguards at Coney Island. Some of them might be 6ft 3in and 225lb beefeaters like McCarthy but they hadn't been brought up in the Bronx. Like Andy Storey, he was one who would make the adjutant's moustache twitch but for quite different reasons.

At this time of the war, pretty well any squadron leader or wing commander, those officers who led flights and operational squadrons, was regular, pre-war RAF with the typical attitudes of the British Empire officer class. The RAF they had joined had been an Imperial police force, keeping the colonials in order. An officer's distinguishing features were not bravery and self-sacrifice because these were taken for granted, but you might be considered a rotter if you didn't understand the correct, gentlemanly thing to do in all situations.

You didn't crash; you pranged the old kite. You didn't commit a social sin; you put up a bit of a black. And you certainly didn't have a near-death experience under fire; you had a shaky or dicey do. You had utter contempt for the fishheads (Royal Navy), who shot at you because they couldn't tell a Wellington from a stuffed seagull, and for the brown jobs (Army), who were similarly understrength in the intelligence department.

Later, when things hotted up, dead officer's shoes were reoccupied at such a staggering rate that a bomber pilot could go from the most junior rank, pilot officer, to flying officer, flight lieutenant then squadron leader (equivalent to major in the USAAF), and leading a flight of ten bombers, in four months. He might still affect the handlebar moustache and the briar pipe but, when he wondered if a new boy was made of the right materials, he was thinking not of which school had been attended, or whether said new bug could be left alone with the air commodore's daughter, but whether he had the near unbelievable amount of skill, nerve and daring necessary to get to Berlin more than once.

Joe? Well, Joe was born with the necessary on 31 August 1919 in St James on Long Island, then largely a farming community with families going back to earliest American times but also popular as a resort of the rich and famous. Some built mansions there; some took their summer vacations, and names dropped in the General Store, said to be historically the 'most authentic' in the USA, included Irving Berlin, the Barrymore tribe, Myrna Loy, Buster Keaton and many more.

The McCarthy family was neither rich nor famous. Joe's dad, Cornelius Joseph, was a clerk, married to Eve, and soon after Joe was born they moved to the Bronx, to Joe's grandfather's house, No. 438, 136th Street, New York, where Cornelius found a job as a book-keeper at the shipyards. Grandpa Joseph was a deputy sheriff; Cornelius later became a fireman with the City Fire Department as the family stayed together and moved around the corner, with Aunt Annie and Katherine the lady lodger, to 170, Alexander Avenue.

Grandpa was Irish, an immigrant from the Emerald Isle, the whole of which in his time was part of Great Britain. Perhaps this was the link that sent young Joe over the border to Ottawa in May 1941, already equipped with flying experience which was how he came to be in England with No. 14 OTU flying a Hampden to Düsseldorf not much more than one year later.

Lancaster squadrons mostly had training/conversion flights at that time. Big Joe learned his four-engined stuff with 97 and 106 Squadrons in the summer of 1942 and ended up with No. 97. His transfer was noted as that of Flg Off J.C. McCarthy, the only time the 'Scribe of Operations' ever got his name right. For the rest of his stay at 97 he was always, for some reason, listed as J.V.

While McCarthy and crew settled in and went on their cross-countries and Bullseye exercises (night-time over a British city with friendly searchlights), Storey was gardening in the North Sea in the direction of Denmark, at the western mouth of a complex set of fjords, the Limfjorden, more like a series of lakes, which stretch right across Denmark. Mines were dropped by parachute from low level, about 400ft. As they tended to be placed in important shipping lanes, there was almost always heavy opposition from shore batteries and flak ships. This particular aiming point, codenamed Geranium, near Thyborøn, was no exception and bad weather conspired against them too.

Of the seven that went, three missed the primary target and planted their vegetables elsewhere. Positions given for planting put one on the west coast of Denmark where he should have been, and two on the east in the Kattegat where they shouldn't. Of the others, one crew planted in the right spot, one got them near enough while under persistent fire from the shore, and one lost his way entirely and was brought down near Szczecin (Stettin, Poland), all crew killed.

Storey was lost also. *Vegetables not planted. After touring Stettiner Haff, lost position. Now believe flew over Swinemünde at 500 feet. Intense light flak and some heavy. Violent evasive action. Descended to nought feet. One searchlight seen pointing downwards at us.* He'd been nearer Wismar than Thyborøn, 200 miles away. Well, that was the navigator's fault, not the pilot's.

As September ended, 9 Squadron counted their costs. Six Lancasters, six crews, all gone in twenty days. Things were better at McCarthy's 97; only two lost in the month.

Krefeld was next, yet another small/medium city, population 170,000, almost on the banks of the Rhine which would have been a help in finding it if the foul weather from September hadn't persisted. Andy Storey was an educated man. He might have known that the very first Germans to emigrate to America, in 1683, were thirteen Mennonite families from Krefeld. He might have wondered why the place was on the list if it was mainly known for silk weaving, especially for the silk used to make umbrellas, but it was its position as a hub of the railway system that made it attractive to Bomber Command.

On this night, Krefeld's many fine medieval buildings remained untouched. The new Path Finder Force, there to mark the target for the rest, marked somewhere but it wasn't the railways of Krefeld. Of the four crews of 9 Squadron who reached the target area, three said they'd bombed Krefeld on a mix of Gee fixes, ETA and pathfinder flares, while Andy Storey said he'd bombed a town but he didn't know which one. Big Joe McCarthy was there too, flying second dicky with Flg Off C.D. Keir, another destined to see the war out. From No. 97, six went, like No. 9 carrying incendiaries and the 4,000lb cookie, and in the thick ground haze bombed also by educated guesswork. Flight Commander, Sqn Ldr Hallows, complained *Opposition not up to Ruhr standard*.

Three residential streets on the north side of Krefeld took some hits while seven bombers were shot down and another two crashed at home, and the next op was even worse on the balance of payments, to Aachen, or Aix-la-Chapelle, where Germany meets Belgium and Holland. With the pathfinders of little use again in terrible weather, Joe McCarthy on his first trip as captain found his instruments icing up, his wireless u/s and various small but important parts of his aircraft cracking under the strain. He bombed the alternative target on ETA and saw some fires. Storey, on his twelfth trip altogether, believed he'd hit Aachen but with the electrical storms, his intercom u/s and visibility nil, he could not be sure.

The bombing force was 257 aircraft, of which 18 were lost, some due to thunderstorms over Britain, some going off track and being unable to make base, and some due to direct enemy action including, as Joe would have found out next morning, a 97 Squadron Lancaster with a crew mostly of second-tour men. With two DFCs and two DFMs among seven dead, it was a clear demonstration to McCarthy that no amount of experience could guarantee immunity. Nothing was guaranteed, not even, he would have realised, his own death.

Storey was clearly blossoming with his experience and must have been regarded as anybody's equal because he was picked with Stubbs and seven others of No. 9 Squadron as part of an elite group to train in special formation flying. At a time when all their operations were at night, they had to prove they could fly flat out at zero feet, almost touching each other, for hours on end during the day. Of course, nobody told them why they were doing it. It was the same at 97 Squadron, daylight formation flying, but not featuring McCarthy. He was a new boy and so not considered up to it. Next year, when they started talking about dams and bouncing bombs, Big Joe would be viewed differently, but not yet.

Two days before the daylight op, whatever it was, they were sent to Cologne. The Germans lit a large decoy fire, a trick so successful that less than half a percent of the number of bombs dropped hit the city, while enemy action accounted for 19 out of the 289 aircraft on the raid, none from No. 9 but another from No. 97 for McCarthy to notice.

When the daylighters were given their special target, feelings were mixed. They were going to fly right across France almost to the Swiss border, to the Schneider works at Le Creusot, the French equivalent of Krupp in the heart of Burgundy, where guns, engines and armour were made. The factories were to be hit by 88 of the 94 Lancs while 6 bombed the power station. The crews had all heard of the Schneider Trophy, the race for seaplanes first held in 1913 and won outright in 1931 by a floating forerunner of the Supermarine Spitfire. This was fine, only there did seem to be many similarities with the Augsburg daylight raid earlier in the year, when No. 44 Squadron lost five out of six Lancasters and only Nettleton VC came home. No. 9's Waddington base was shared with 44 Squadron, whose members were happy to tell anyone who would listen all about Augsburg.

ORB, 9 Squadron: *Flying at 0 feet over the Channel, ran into sea fog which cleared 40 minutes later with all aircraft still in sight and squadron formation regained by French coast.*

Anderson Storey told the same tale in a letter to his mother, with only a few details blanked by the station censor.

Dear Ma,

You have probably read all about the raid last Saturday [17 October] on the Schneider-Creusot steel works in France. Here is a slightly more detailed account with which I hope the censors will deal kindly.

After a week of fairly intensive formation practice we were informed on Friday that we were all confined to camp that nite, and that briefing would be at 06:00 Saturday.

We were all up at 05:00 and after breakfast went to the briefing. The rest of the morning was spent in working out all the various navigational details and checking over equipment. We had [blank – probably the operational meal of bacon and egg] and were out at the aircraft at [blank – probably 11:00] sharp. [Take-off was around midday; Storey was away at 11:56.] We were soon formed up in squadron V and on our way to the first rendezvous [Upper Heyford, near Bicester, Oxfordshire]. All the way over England we could see other squadrons coming in to take up their positions in the formation [all from No. 5 Group: Nos 44, 49, 50, 57, 61, 97, 106, 207]. We were the extreme right of the first wing V [with Nos 49 and 61 Squadrons]. Soon we were over the sea. Got a bit shaken over the sea. We were flying at about 20–50 feet and kept running into fog. Very frightening too, it is, to see your formation leader disappear into the fog [Wg Cdr Slee, 49 Squadron] and know that the slightest deviation from course, speed or height may mean a crash. At one point I only just managed to swing outside a point of land. Saw my leader [Wg Cdr Southwell, 9 Squadron CO] swing out and followed suit. The next thing I saw was a huge cliff off the wing tip. Another time saw a destroyer loom up out of the fog going full speed in the opposite direction just as we were coming out of another fog bank. He was right in the center of the formation and still had two more wing Vs to go through. Luckily no-one touched anything.

Finally we came into the clear and it was one of the most beautiful things I have ever seen. Forward a bit and to port and aft as far as I could see there were scores of huge aircraft [actually 94] hurtling along in formation, just skimming a very calm and blue sea. I kept thinking how I wished I could come up the Western Way like that [Mount Desert Island, Maine] and then come low over the island [Great Cranberry].

Presently we began to see fishing boats with their red sails as we went over. Then we could see the fishermen gaping up at us. We were all set to shoot any of them up should they have wireless equipment that could give warning of our coming. None had and most of the men waved. One poor old soul stood and saluted as we rushed over him. I hope we were an encouragement to him.

Then the coast came up. First an island with a light which we bypassed, then a little fishing-resort town, white and gleaming in the afternoon sunlight, the red roofs and green grass making lovely color combinations. I couldn't see a soul but my crew told me that there were lots of bathers on the beach.

The flight across France, at about 20 feet, was accomplished almost without incident. We had expected to meet fighters but the only attacks on us were made by some Vichy-minded partridges and pigeons. A partridge flew into my mid-upper turret just as the gunner turned it around to look forward. It bust hell out of the Perspex and several chunks cut the gunner rather nastily about the forehead and gave him a lovely pair of black eyes. He wiped the blood off and carried on damned well. He was unable to get the bird out of the turret because of the slipstream and the fact that the damned thing was wrapped around a stanchion about three times with the legs hanging down.

Storey's gunner, Sgt Fred Cater, was not the only one to be blooded by a bird. Four such incidents were recorded by Lancaster crews on the way to the target, two causing injuries, the other being to Stubbs's flight engineer Tom Parrington, lacerated by Perspex and knocked unconscious when colliding with a seagull.

There were some amusing incidents on the way. There was a herd of seven or eight cows which suddenly metamorphosed into steeple-chasers. They took a big hedge like a bunch of stags. Then there was the old farmer who stood gawping at us while behind him his two oxen dragged his plough across about three fields, through hedges and across ditches with the greatest of ease. All of these things flashed past and were sudden impressions forgotten in the excitement of the next, and only remembered afterwards as part of a kaleidoscopic and changing pattern.

There were some perfectly lovely chateaux. There were two which were perfect dreams. One set on the side of a hill – we were almost on a level with it below the hill-top – which sat ancient and grey in the light of the late afternoon, brooding over a tiny hamlet below, its towers raised like protecting spears above the villagers. And the other, which sat in its own moat which was part of a running stream. Its arches seemed almost to float on the mirror of the water.

Soon we reached the hills and climbing over them we ran into cloud just short of the target. I nearly cried because we were supposed to bomb from a fairly high level and I thought the cloud would obscure the target. The squadron commander thought the same for he went down under it and the squadron followed him. The rest of the formation kept on climbing. The next thing I knew I was playing ring-around-a-rosie in formation through hills which lifted their tops into the cloud [monts du Morvan, some over 3,000ft]. It is a sensation I don't care to repeat.

Suddenly we ran out of cloud and saw the target and away above us the vanguard of the formation. Then the first stick of bombs fell and burst in sudden red blossoms of fire floating in a sea of smoke. Soon there was so much smoke that the target was almost entirely obscured but we could feel the concussions of the bombs bursting and see the occasional glow of incendiaries and it was all over.

No. 9 Squadron was in and out of the target in 2 minutes. Storey bombed at 18:15 from 3,000ft and was one of four who had to fly back home with a thousand-pounder stuck in the bomb bay. One Lancaster seemed to misjudge the height, went in too low and felt the concussions of the bombs bursting with fatal consequences. No. 61 Squadron's Sqn Ldr Corr DFC was attacking the transformer station but went into the houses. The mid-upper, Sgt Turtle, survived; the rest were all killed.

ORB, 9 Squadron: *Buildings were disintegrating in all parts of the factory and almost all bombs fell across the works, creating tremendous damage.* Rolling mills, turbine building works and machine shops *had been well hit and were in flames,* true enough, but 'almost all bombs'? Airborne eye witnesses thought that some of the bombs fell short, onto the housing estate that was at one end of the factory, destroying many civilian properties as well as the target. Post-raid photographs would confirm this opinion.

Storey to mother:

Schneider et Cie of Le Creusot will turn out no more munitions for some time to come. Off we went in the dusk separately to find our own ways home. What a way that was! All went well until the Channel; then we ran into dense cloud and got thoroughly lost. Finally we lobbed down, the happiest crew in England at an aerodrome 12 miles from our own base [Swinderby; four others also landed away from base] after [blank – possibly making a Darky call. Darky was an emergency VHF call made by the pilot to any and all nearby aerodromes, the coded callsign meaning 'I am entirely in the dark as to my whereabouts'].

The last hour had been the most concentrated type of hell I have ever known. The automatic pilot had gone for a Burton and I was so tired I could hardly fly at all, and cloud flying is no cinch, but by the grace of God I made a good landing and so to interrogation and bed. The biggest daylight of all was over and only one aircraft lost. Good show.

Well, I gotta go to tea. If you see anything about the raid in the papers at home send 'em on. I'd like to see the reaction. Give my love to everyone.

Love, Andy.

Storey's fatigue was understandable. There were no servos to assist on the controls of a Lancaster, no equivalents to power steering, and no second pilot to give him a break. There was an autopilot, called George, but it was no use for precision flying, although it would have helped Storey on the return journey. The Lanc was light on the touch for a four-engined bomber but it still had to be flown every inch of the way.

His mother would doubtless have guessed what was meant by 'gone for a Burton', an expression with origins ascribed variously to Burton the tailoring chainstore, Burton the brewing town and Burton the Birmingham Council candidate of 1878, but one definitely not in common American usage.

Chapter 5

THOSE ABOUT TO DIE
SALUTE YOU

The CO of Nick Knilans's new base in Canada was an officer of the old school, a First World War veteran, Grp Capt McBride, known as 'Iron Bill'. The noise of a late-night beer session in the mess, with musical accompaniment, brought Iron Bill to investigate. The only light was one dim bulb. 'Attention!' shouted Iron Bill. Some did as they were told; some, including Knilans, rushed off into the latrines to escape through the windows, forgetting, if they'd ever noticed, that the latrine windows had bars.

After a few moments, all the criminals were assembled before the judge, who was looking around for the duty corporal whose job it was to close the mess at the appointed hour. Iron Bill spied him in the phone booth, deep in conversation. 'Corporal. Get out of that booth,' commanded the group captain, a rank equivalent to colonel in the USAAF. 'Take it easy, Mac,' called back the corporal, 'I'm talking to my girl.'

No one laughed or even uttered a smothered snort, such was the regard in which Iron Bill was held. The corporal just about survived his lecture on correct procedure as regards dereliction of duty and the addressing of senior officers, but would probably take quite a while to work his way back up through the ranks from Aircraftman Second Class. Knilans and the other recalcitrants were marched to the guardroom where they spent the night on benches and floors. The sentence the following morning was two weeks confined to barracks, which they didn't mind too much as the camp fence, not a secure structure, was so near to their back door.

Their next mistake, two weeks later, was to celebrate the official ending of their alleged confinement and, once again, Messrs Molson and Labatt were to blame. The duffel-bag fights would have brought no retribution, and they might have got away with the smashed mirrors in the latrines, but bringing down the central-heating pipes and half the ceiling was more than enough to excite the attention of the RCAF police.

An early hours inquiry produced only the suggestion that the damage may have been caused by mice, but on parade next morning their flight sergeant was in no mood for levity. He strolled slowly up and down the ranks of stiffly attending cadets and stopped beside one who was having trouble remaining still and upright. 'You!' barked the sergeant, at which the poor boy reeled and almost fell. 'You! You were one of them! Well? Were you?'

The cadet, unable to speak properly, nodded and mumbled something acquiescent, at which five more cadets stepped forward to share the responsibility. The refractory half-dozen were marched yet again to Iron Bill's office where Knilans, voted as spokesman by the silence of the others, tried to explain how, accidentally, the barracks came to be wrecked. The sentence this time was 14 hours' pack drill, to be accomplished over 7 days, 2 separate hours each day.

The drill instructors were not happy at the extra duty thus imposed. Some took out their displeasure on the boys, making them run and double up with their rifles and 40lb of sand on their backs. Others quick marched them round the back of the hangar for an hour's fat-chewing and a smoke.

Such unruly behaviour could be tolerated and punished without danger to the main purpose, to produce pilots for the war. There were more severe consequences for endangering aircraft and the civilian population, as Knilans recalled:

I was on a solo cross-country west of Ottawa when I flew across a lake with a small sailing boat in the middle. I thought it would be a good joke to tip it over by flying low across it. The backwash from my propellor should have done the trick, but it was still sailing after two passes. Coming around for a third I noticed another Harvard alongside me, with an instructor in it. He'd be taking my number to report me for low flying so I climbed away and hot-tailed it back to base. One of our American group had already been court martialed and dismissed from the service for low flying so I suddenly didn't feel so good about my little joke.

After landing I had a word with a drinking buddy who was one of the mechanics and he soon had the cowling off and got busy with the innards. Hurrying without rushing, I called in at the control tower and asked the officer for permission to sign the Low Flying Book, considering I'd had engine trouble which made me lose altitude. He looked at me like he'd never heard this story before, except maybe a hundred times, checked through the window to see that my plane was being worked on, and gave me the book to sign.

Back at the flight office to fill in my log, my flight commander called me into his room, and there was the instructor I'd seen, seemingly a bit pleased with himself. 'Did you sign the Low Flying Book, Knilans?' said my CO. 'Yes, sir,' said I. 'All right, dismissed,' said my CO and I left with the instructor gaping like a goldfish.

By the end of the course, some of Knilans's class had been reassigned to other aircrew training through various inadequacies, and two had been killed playing silly fools in a pretend dogfight. Those who were left were divided into two equal lots. One lot was promoted to pilot officer; the others, including Knilans, were made sergeants. Some chose to stay in Canada with Training Command. Most chose combat duty and used their embarkation leave to go home, possibly for the last time.

A few beers and a few tears and I was back on the train for Halifax, Nova Scotia. Our troopship was the *Queen Elizabeth*, with 22,000 aboard. We cruised at 35 knots, changing course every five minutes, with no escort. The PA system played us a broadcast by Lord Haw Haw, the English traitor working for German radio, who said we'd been sunk with all lives lost. We had to keep radio silence so I guess some people believed it for a few days, until we docked at Greenock and got on our train for Bournemouth. We had a parade when we got there, and a Messerschmitt 109 strafed us and killed quite a few.

Three nights later I happened to be having a conversation about the 14-line structure of Shakespeare's sonnets, or something poetical, with a young lady in a hotel bedroom, when the sirens went off and we heard bombs falling. We got under the bed and listened as a stick of bombs marched towards us with increasingly loud explosions. The one that was the loudest turned out to be the last, so we could resume our literary discussion.

So, Nick Knilans had his first taste of war in a genteel seaside resort on the Hampshire–Dorset border. Next stop for him would be twin-engined training at a base near Burton-on-Trent, the Staffordshire brewery town so often said to be gone for in Bomber Command.

The British Eighth Army was about to go on the offensive at El Alamein and so a series of air raids on Italian cities was set up, to reduce the Axis capability of supply to North Africa and to demoralise the Italian population. First on the list was Genoa, 22/23 October, the most significant Italian port and a major centre of naval shipbuilding. It was a long way to Genoa. Taking a light load, only 4,500lb, they still had to expect a round trip of 8 hours or more.

Storey and McCarthy were both on this one. It was a bright moonlit night. They could see the coastline, they could see the town. Pathfinders, the newly specialised target-marking squadrons, put their flares right over the main target, the docks. With virtually no opposition, bombing could not have been easier. Joe reported the docks well alight and his own bombs dropped on the spot. Andy said much the same. They all did. No losses but a long flight home over the Alps to find bad weather and diversions. They'd left around 17:30 and were back around 02:30–03:00.

The weatherman promised 9 Squadron good cloud cover across France for their next trip, a daylight to Milan. They found flak at the French coast and no cloud, so they did a Le Creusot, zero feet to the Alps, hopped over, found cloud they didn't want over the target but bombed successfully anyway. Andy Storey saw railway lines and factories and rated it *A moderately successful trip, very pleasant journey, excellent job on Navigator's part*. Perhaps Flt Sgt Storey was getting the hang of British understatement: zero feet at top speed across occupied France in broad daylight, a 'very pleasant journey'.

Italian defences had been feeble and the citizens astonished. The sirens didn't go off until the bombs were already exploding. A great deal of damage was done by this small force, only 88 Lancasters, including hits on the Fascisti offices and the Caproni aircraft factory. The Milanese complained that a Lancaster came down to skim the rooftops and strafe the streets full of people. This may have been Wg Cdr Southwell, 9 Squadron's CO, who used 7,000 rounds machine-gunning two trains on the Milan–Navara railway and strafing what he said was Navara.

It was an individual captain's decision to do such things. Some wouldn't, some would. Some, even when fully used to bitter and effective opposition from the Germans that reduced their life expectancy to near nothing, could not be so ruthless. Some would point out that Italy was a modern country, at war as the aggressor. Mussolini had been happy enough mopping up the Somalis and Ethiopians. The Italians had air-raid sirens, anti-aircraft guns and fighter squadrons like everybody else. It was up to them to stop Allied bombers skimming rooftops at will.

Storey's and McCarthy's Lancs had an ice-cream cone painted on their noses to represent an Italian mission, where usually the score was shown in little downward pointing bombs. Four other Lancasters could not have Milan thus recorded, largely due to German guns on the French coast, although one went down in Italian waters.

Storey went to Genoa five times in three weeks, mostly in 'his' Lancaster, W4200 WS/U for Uncle. Of his 23 Lancaster ops, 17 would be in the Uncle, and 6 of her ice-cream cones would be his. Genoa at night, 6 November, and Big Joe had his second serious operational wobble in three trips. It wasn't ice and instruments this time but an engine shutting down 600 miles from home. Storey had no such difficulties but a very long op, 10 hours plus, and a surprise waiting for him. Not in bed until 09:00, up again for briefing at 15:00, take-off 17:47, bombing Genoa again at 21:51, home at 02:21 and no work tomorrow, thank God.

What the Italian gunners could not achieve, the RAF could achieve for them. Nobody at 97 Squadron did both those successive trips; they briefed as many as they could for the second op, six crews, but left those to rest who'd come back from Italy that morning. On 9 Squadron, Storey and four others did both Genoas back to back. Of the last 28 hours, they had spent 18 or 19 flying a Lancaster on ops. At home, in the circuit above the aerodrome before landing, two of the five double Genoans collided. Flg Off Ken Mackenzie DFC and Plt Off Arthur Macdonald, both Wellington veterans and very experienced pilots, fell to earth on the southern edge of the airfield. There were no survivors.

McCarthy's early career continued in bumpy fashion with a mining trip to French coastal waters in the Bay of Biscay, by the Gironde Estuary. Only three of them went. The revered Sqn Ldr Hallows said he'd planted his vegetables successfully in the correct position in excellent weather, noting also that the *Route over the French peninsula is becoming rather dangerous. One aircraft* shot down after being caught in cone*

---

* Wellington of 142 Squadron BJ768 QT/Q; all crew killed.

of light flak over Vannes. Flt Sgt Kruger also planted his vegetables successfully in clear visibility, but Joe dropped his mines in haze, somewhere nearby, and was accused of not doing his job: 'On instructions from the AOC No 5 Group this Log Book is endorsed "Carelessness and Bad Captaincy whilst on Operations"', signed by the group captain a month later. Several more months later, Joe had his endorsement endorsed by fellow dam-buster captains Micky Martin, Dave Shannon and Geoff Rice, and Martin's navigator Jack Leggo.

For a change from Italy, Storey and the squadron went to Hamburg, 9 November, in filthy weather. They all bombed on Gee fixes and ETA. Little damage was done but 7 Squadron lost 3 Stirlings, 57 Squadron 3 Lancs, and 10 other bombers went down, 16 out of 213, a loss rate of 7.5 per cent. If career numbers were a first tour of 30 operations, followed after an interval by a second tour of 20, and if losses were to be sustained at 7.5 per cent, the maths said that of 100 aircraft and/or crews starting out, at the end of the double tour there would be 2 left. Meanwhile, aircraft manufacture and aircrew training would have proved unable to keep up and there would have been a severe and worsening shortage of experienced men to provide leadership. Bomber Command would have become a useless rump.

It was also the case that in units suffering an especially high rate of losses, morale slumped dangerously low. For crews to climb back in those bombers night after night, there had to be some hope of getting through, however slim. In the early days of the Handley Page Halifax, for example, when there were many technical problems with an untried aircraft rushed into service, 109 were lost out of 1,770, a sustained rate over 6 months of more than 6 per cent. The crews couldn't do the maths. They didn't have the figures but they could see with their own eyes what was happening. At the rate of losses they had, of 100 Halifax crews, only 4 would finish a double tour. Despite the necessarily optimistic inclinations of bomber crews, morale in those Halifax squadrons was so poor that they all had to be given four weeks' rest.

RAF Waddington was home to two Lancaster squadrons, Nos 9 and 44. Between them, they would lose 73 aircraft on ops in 1942. They shared sergeants' and officers' messes. They knew what six down a month meant but they didn't get any rest.

The Commander in Chief of Bomber Command, Air Marshal 'Butch' Harris, was to inspect RAF Waddington. The day before he was due, there was a rehearsal parade, 11 November, after which a tale swept the station about Anderson Storey. Everyone else was buffed and polished, clipped and snipped and pressed to perfection. A Flying Control WAAF (Women's Auxiliary Air Force), Pip Beck, remembers what Andy Storey did. 'He turned up wearing carpet slippers, claiming Stores had no shoes to fit his long feet. Not only this, but he brought along a very small dog on a very long lead to further confound matters.'

At the real thing, the Station CO announced that it wasn't to be Air Marshal Harris after all but King George VI, and all crews would line up to be inspected royally and His Majesty would speak to all aircrew captains. That included Andy Storey, of course, properly dressed this time. Perhaps the classically educated Storey tried a joke: '*Ave imperator, morituri te salutant*', 'Hail, emperor, those about to die salute you'.

A new American in the 9 Squadron sergeants' mess, William Harvey Penn from Tulsa, Oklahoma, a gunner who had trained at No. 4 School, Fingal, Ontario, was not important enough to shake the King's hand, and Leading Aircraftwoman Beck wasn't in the line at all. She was mounting her own little protest at the use of extremely valuable and scarce aircraft petrol to scrub out the hangar His Majesty was to inspect. Following her night shift, she stayed in bed, and the night after it was Genoa again.

The Italians put up more flak and searchlights than before but it was described by aircrew as very erratic. No aircraft were shot down. Storey had an uneventful trip but Joe McCarthy didn't get as far as Genoa. Flying at 17,000ft 3 hours into the mission, somewhere over the Haute-Savoie, came his defining moment.

A bomber crew had only a general idea of the capabilities of their pilot and captain until he was called on to save all their lives while under attack by a nightfighter. Sometimes one of the gunners would spot the enemy, stalking and making ready for the kill, or occasionally it might be one of the others searching the sky through the astrodome, a Perspex bubble on the aircraft's back. Whoever it was, he was in temporary command of the bomber. In an instant, he would have to decide if the fighter was going to come in and fire and, if so, from what angle. Having decided, he would order his pilot into evasive action, usually by turning into the attack while changing height. So he might, without any warning at all, scream into his intercom 'Dive starboard!' Or he might scream 'Corkscrew port!' If he had more time, he might say 'Enemy aircraft, 600yd, port quarter down . . . prepare to dive to port . . . dive!'

In any case, the pilot's speed and ferocity of reaction would determine whether they lived or died. Quite often they never saw the fighter at all and the first they knew of it was the sight of tracer bullets whizzing past, or the sound and smell of cannon shells thumping into their frail cigar tube in the sky. If the nightfighter pilot had been able to put himself close enough without being spotted, without any reaction from his Tommy, he might aim for the port inner engine where he knew was centred the control system for the hydraulics, and therefore the gun turrets, or he might blast away at the turrets and the gunners themselves. This often happened. The first warning the rest of the crew had, might be the sound coming over the intercom of a gunner dying.

McCarthy's crew were on their fifth operation together and, at the end of it, they could all say they were very pleased to be flying with Big Joe. They saw the fighter, a Junkers 88, and for fully 3 minutes the German followed them through the corkscrew. A more experienced fighter pilot might have hung back and waited for that moment in the manoeuvre when the Lancaster was at the top of one of its climbs, when it was almost frozen in space. As it was, Joe lost his pursuer at the end of the longest 3 minutes any of the others had ever lived through. *Violent evasive action*, as McCarthy reported when they got home, meant that anything loose in the aircraft, such as the navigator's maps and instruments or, indeed, the navigator, would be thrown all over the place.

The gunners would be trying to get a shot in but they were inside a four-dimensional, dynamic conundrum. Trying to work out where the fighter might appear in the next moment was the hardest test for a gunner's skills. In training, they had been able to sign their names with their guns, but then they hadn't been diving, climbing, half rolling and racketing about the night sky at 200 miles an hour.

Anyway, they lost the bastard and were settling back into their various tasks, with McCarthy asking the navigator, Flt Sgt Brayford, to hurry up and get himself organised because a new course was needed for the target. Going by all the lights below, they seemed to have strayed into neutral Swiss airspace. The navigator confirmed that they were indeed over Lake Geneva, and Sgt Radcliffe, the flight engineer, became concerned about the port outer engine. It was overheating.

Soon, it was in flames. Radcliffe operated the fire extinguisher and the fire went out.

Flying over or through the Alps on three could be done, but an engine once on fire could catch fire again. They were miles off track after their fight. They had no choice but to turn and go home, and a slow journey they had of it, 600 miles on three. They kept their bombs until they were over the sea, jettisoned, and landed back on brakes that didn't work, after spending as long in the air as they would have if they'd made Genoa: 10 hours.

There was one more Genoa for Storey and that was the end of it. There was hardly anything left there that was worth bombing and a poll of Genovese would have revealed a decided lack of enthusiasm for this war. William Penn's crew was on the runway for it, their first operation, and they were the one outfit that was cancelled, moments before take-off. The same thing happened two days later, 18 November, when eight were ready to go but they and three others were held back *owing to the prospect of bad weather for the return*. The other four captains, a squadron leader, a flight lieutenant and two experienced sergeant pilots, were assumed to be able to cope.

After a short career including u/s instruments, engines packing up and on fire, fighter attack and mines in the wrong place, McCarthy's men might have wished for order to be created out of chaos, and they were off mining again, their compass went u/s, they got completely lost, missed the target area and landed at Topcliffe in north Yorkshire; DNCO, Duty Not Carried Out. They'd taken off, flown for 6 hours open to attack and landed safely but, like the Lake Geneva incident, it wouldn't count towards their score.

Turin, 20 November, and Bill Penn was away at last, in Andy Storey's Lanc, U-Uncle. This was a successful raid, good results on the city and the Fiat works, and only 3 down out of 232. McCarthy's next, to Stuttgart, was routine by comparison: flew to target through flak, dropped bombs on pathfinder flares, landed at Topcliffe again. Bill Penn was there on his second: *In the opinion of crew, attack should turn out to be a success. A.P. [aiming point] itself could not be seen owing to smoke but the approximate position was undoubtedly in sight.* Yes, well, this was a sprog crew. The pilot's work-experience outing had been to Genoa but this was Germany. None of them would have seen flak and searchlights like it and the adrenaline would have been singing. Not that they were alone in reporting hits, but the truth was that the south and south-western suburbs, 5 miles from the AP, took most of the bombs.

An exception was the railway station. The German report states 'Two bombers attacked the centre of the city at low level and dropped bombs on to the main railway station which caused severe damage to the wooden platforms and some trains.' The report of Sgt Les Hazell, 9 Squadron pilot, states: *We were coned by approx. 20 searchlights on initial run-up. We nose-dived through it from 11,000 feet to 4,000 feet and bombed. Marshalling yard seen in bomb sight. Sudden loss of height caused nose-bleeding and sickness in bomb aimer.*

Bill Penn had a fine view of things from his gun turret on the Lancaster's back. Bombing half an hour later from 15,000ft, he would not have seen Hazell being coned but he may well have noted some falling fireworks around their point of entry and exit in northern France. A total of seven of the ten aircraft lost on Penn's second night went down to fighters patrolling that region.

Excitement returned too for Joe on his following trip, to Turin. About halfway there the port outer engine overheated. This was the same aircraft, R5512 OF/C-Charlie, in which they'd been attacked by the Junkers 88 when the port outer heated up so much it caught fire, and the same one that failed them the time before coming back from Genoa. They turned for home and landed on three at Downham Market. Another 5 hours in the air that didn't count, while Andy Storey at Turin described some of the biggest fires any of them had ever seen, sent 1,000 rounds of .303 machine-gun bullets after his bombs from 1,500ft, and clocked up his twenty-second op.

Storey was among those briefed for Frankfurt, 2 December. Op cancelled when they were in their Lancs waiting to take off. Next night, squadron ordered to stand by for ops; ops cancelled. Next night, Storey among those briefed for Cologne; op cancelled just as they were climbing into the trucks that took them out to the dispersals. Next night, same again, target in the Ruhr, cancelled as they were boarding the trucks.

Late cancellations were not unusual, although four in a row might be considered overdoing it. The effect on crew members varied. With some, the sudden removal of high tension was like a reprieve. Hurrah, we're not going to be killed tonight, let's go down the pub and get sloshed. With some, it had a reverse and depressing effect. All that briefing and mental stress wasted, for nothing, and we're going to have to do it all over again tomorrow. With a few, for whom the tension and danger had become addictive, the disappointment of a cancellation was like an expected drug-fix being refused. These men too might want to go down the pub; same effect, different reason. For another few, whose nerves were already jangling at the outer limits of sanity, four cancellations in four days would be enough to send them over the edge.

Whatever they might have felt, the relaxed and humorous Flt Sgt Storey and his crew were back up to the starting line as ever, 6 December, Mannheim. Penn was there, searching the sky in his mid-upper turret, and McCarthy continued his researches of RAF bases in England by landing at Exeter. The luck was with 9 and 97 Squadrons at Mannheim, although 14 others went down and 30 bombers were lost on the date out of 365, 8.2 per cent, when you include the murderous but successful daylight attack on the Philips plant at Eindhoven.

There were more Turins. McCarthy came back early with hydraulics u/s and bomb doors jammed, Penn was shaken up when his aircraft lost a tailwheel on landing, Storey went there and back without incident. McCarthy and crew went on leave.

Cloud was forecast for 17 December over the Ruhr, which suited the duty for the evening, a 'moling trip'. The idea of these multi-target, small-scale ops was to avoid the big objectives the bombers usually hit and to attack otherwise unimportant small towns to let them know that there was a war on. There were 8 that evening, including Cloppenburg, Nienburg, Soltau, Haselünne and Diepholz, for 27 Lancasters, and at the briefing the crews were told that these were dormitory towns for factory workers. The CO didn't tell them to go out there and enjoy themselves, but that was the sort of attitude – fly low, shoot up the Hun in his bed, come home in the clouds.

There was no cloud, only bright moonlight. For the sake of this daft stratagem, 2 Lancs from No. 9, 2 from No. 97 and 5 more from other 5 Group squadrons were brought down out of the 27, one-third of the attack. Most were hit around the Dutch coast, by flak, fighters or a combination of the two. Bill Penn in ED349 WS/S-Sugar was elsewhere, straying off track and well north of the target area between Varel and Rastede, near the well-defended Bad Zwischenahn aerodrome. This was the largest Luftwaffe base in northern Germany, from which flew *III Gruppe Nachtjagdgeschwader 3* with the radar-equipped Bf110.

While the rest of the crew survived the crash, the body of William Harvey Penn of Tulsa, Oklahoma, was buried at the local parish church at Bad Zwischenahn and later removed to Sage War Cemetery.

The briefing had stipulated flight at 10,000ft, assuming cloud. When the more-experienced captains saw the clear skies over Holland, they went higher, and the more-experienced navigators took account of a different wind from that forecast. They were the ones who came home. Penn's crew had been on their fifth together, as had the other 9 Squadron crew lost that night. To survive, you needed to acquire the first-hand know-how of an old timer; to become an old timer, you needed to survive.

For Storey there were several more late cancellations, then recognition of his seniority acquired through long toil and travail. He had notice that his promotion to officer rank was on its way, and he was given a novitiate, a second dicky, to take with him to Duisburg, 20 December. He was first away at 17:53 and so he and his student didn't see, some 25 minutes later, a particularly horrific demonstration of the dangers in flying bombers. Two Lancasters collided in the circuit above the aerodrome, before setting course, and fell in flames onto Bracebridge Heath, a couple of miles south of Lincoln; all fourteen crew were killed.

Storey's pupil, Sgt Jack Thomas, an Australian, was treated to a trip Storey described as perfect. Got there without trouble, saw the target in the flares and the moonlight, bombed it, saw many fires, saw many others bombing successfully, and got home uninterrupted. Next morning they would hear about the collision, and another crew had gone missing from the squadron too. The chat around the sergeants' mess might have been that the missing crew had had three cancellations, including one so late that they'd been in the aircraft with the engines fired up. Another time, they'd set off on a mining op only to be called back after 45 minutes on route. When at last they'd flown on a fully functional operation, they'd bought the farm.

Jack Thomas, fledgling, would have noted that the pilot of that lost Lancaster had been a sprog, like he was. Andy Storey, with 26 ops on his record, might have been interested to know that the navigator had been on his thirty-first.

Storey described his next trip, to Munich the following night, as *rather a wasted effort owing to cloud*, cloud that didn't seem to be anywhere else apart from over Munich. He'd bombed on a timed run from the Wurm See as briefed, confirming his position by sight of the anti-aircraft guns firing at him. McCarthy, back on the job, came home on three yet again.

Rather a wasted effort? Alas, it was worse than that. There were 137 aircraft on the raid; 110 claimed to have bombed Munich but almost all the bombs fell in fields and woods outside the city, and 12 bombers were shot down, mostly by nightfighters over France and Belgium. One was a 9 Squadron Lancaster felled near the target; another squadron sent nine Stirlings and lost three of them in France. Overall loss rate was 8.8 per cent, unsustainable, but help was on its way.

German nightfighters operated a cell system. Each pilot was given an area of sky and a dedicated ground radar station to guide him to within a mile or so, when the second crew member, the wireless operator, took over with his air-to-air radar, the Lichtenstein device. There were enough of these little teams to cause savage losses when bombers were flying through in streams of 200 or so. The lower and slower Wellingtons and Stirlings were prime meat for these predators. One answer had to be more Lancasters and Halifaxes flying higher and faster in much greater numbers. They would swamp the enemy's defences and carry far more bombs while they were doing it.

To redress the imbalance of losses against hits on targets, much, much better navigation was needed, and a new bit of kit was about to make life much, much simpler. Oboe was a similar kind of navaid to Gee, now being jammed routinely by the Germans, in that it was based on ground stations in the UK transmitting radio signals to aircraft, receiving signals back and calculating where the aircraft must be. Its selling point was that it could be accurate to 300yd but, like Gee, it worked in a straight line. The signals didn't bend around the earth, and it required a dangerous amount of straight and level flying to get an accurate fix. Oboe therefore needed a high-flying, very fast aircraft to carry it and be a pathfinder for the rest, and the answer came in December 1942 when it was fitted into the de Havilland Mosquito.

Now they could find the target more quickly and more accurately, and could soon expect to be there in really large numbers with big loads of bombs. But what they still needed was a proper target-marking system, and this came with a development by the British firework industry, a 250lb bomb called a Target Indicator, packed with pyrotechnics that were set off at given heights by barometric fuse. These war-class Roman candles then cascaded to the ground in red, green or yellow, highly visible and difficult for the Germans to falsify.

Add all this together, plus other devices that would cause some disruption to the nightfighter system, and Bomber Command was being transformed. It was bigger and better. It could begin to do the job that it had been given but had been quite unable to perform satisfactorily so far. The new year, 1943, was going to be great.

On the other hand, the average losses over the whole of Bomber Command in 1942 had been 3.8 per cent. Statistically at that rate, three out of ten crews would survive their first tour, and less than half that many would get through their second one.

The laws of probability increased the chances of surviving each trip as the number of trips survived increased. At a loss rate of 3.8 per cent, as you climbed into your aircraft on your first trip, you had a 14 per cent chance of climbing out at the end of 50 ops, roughly odds of 7:1 against. If you got as far as 30 and had your well-earned rest, your chances then of finishing the last 20 were almost even money. So that was all right, then.

Experience gained also had a beneficial effect for individual crews. Ignoring that, the chart shows how it went statistically. Possibly only the navigator of any crew could have worked this out. Navigators always said they were the ones who could read and write.

Regardless of percentages and odds, in hard numbers it meant finding ways to replace, and more than replace, 1,846 aircraft lost on ops in 1942, a further 725 on training and other non-operational flights, and 33 more destroyed on the ground. In the year coming, with a massive offensive planned against the Ruhr, could they expect to lose fewer, or more? What would aircrew have thought had they known that Bomber Command on operations would lose, not 1,846, but 2,841 aircraft and crews in 1943?

Pip Beck knew Flt Sgt Storey's name and voice from her work in Flying Control, bringing the bombers in to land. Like everyone else on the station, she knew which was he, the gangling, slightly unco-ordinated one who stood out in any military company, the one who'd turned up for the King's rehearsal parade in slippers with a very small dog on a very long string. Beck on Storey: 'One could hardly miss him

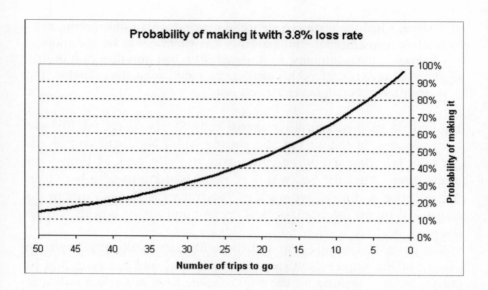

since he was six feet four and towered above his crew like a mountain above foothills.' In the sergeants' mess at the dance on New Year's Eve, she met him:

Everyone who wasn't commissioned went. They were good, the dances in the sergeants' mess. There was a band, playing Glenn Miller and all the popular tunes, and the bar, and lots of tiddly blokes wandering around. This very tall, non-tiddly man asked me to dance and we did.

It was a Viennese waltz, and with the great difference in our heights I wondered how we'd manage but he swept me around with assurance and ease. He was a graceful, gallant partner. We were sitting later with a drink and he was telling me about his life in America, which astonished me as there was nothing about him, in accent or looks, which suggested 'American' as we then thought typical. One of his gunners came up and grabbed his leg and gave it a twist, and ran off. It must have happened regularly. Andy just said that he was big but not very well put together, and that there would be no more dancing. He hobbled across to the bar for more drinks and that was the way the evening went. He told me about his family, his school days at Deerfield and college days at Harvard, and his love of classical music. I was seeing a different side to the man with the long shambling stride, the clown with the scruffy appearance.

Once, I had the eerie experience of dancing with a quiet, pleasant Scottish sergeant pilot, and suddenly knowing he was for the chop. I knew it with a certainty. I wondered if he had any suspicion of it himself. Sure enough, on his next op, he didn't come back. Though I scarcely knew him, it made me very sad.

Pip had no such premonition about Andy Storey. There might have been romance in the air but she already had a boyfriend and Storey perhaps felt that a bomber pilot was not the best of long-term propositions. After the ball was over, he walked Pip back to her billet. 'He whistled a tune as we walked, "Bach goes to Town", dropped a chaste kiss on my forehead, stroked my hair and turned quickly back to the road.'

Sometimes, in private, Pip and those like her might give in to the ever-recurring sadness and weep for the young and the dead, but in public, on duty, waiting for the boys to come back as she did in Flying Control, no such softness could be allowed to interfere. The scene was described in a radio message from London to the USA by Martha Gellhorn (then Mrs Ernest Hemingway), later appearing as an article in *Collier's Magazine*.

At four o'clock, or around then, you go to the control tower. The operations officers walk about and smoke pipes and say casual things to one another and the waiting gets to be a thing you can touch. Then the first plane calls in to the control tower.

Two WAAFs who have been up all night are still looking wide awake, and wonderfully pink-cheeked and they are not frozen stiff. They begin to direct the planes in. The girls' voices, so poised and so neat, begin. 'Hello George. Pancake. Over.' In the glassed-in room, you hear the pilot answer. Then the girls again, 'Hello Queenie, aerodrome, one thousand. Over.' 'Hello Uncle, aerodrome, twelve fifty. Over.' This means that the plane U for Uncle is to circle the field at 1,250 feet until told to 'pancake' or land.

The more planes that come in and are marked up on the blackboard, the worse the waiting gets. None of this shows. No voice changes, no one makes a movement that is in any way unusual. The routine proceeds as normally as if people were waiting in line to buy theatre tickets.

Finally, all the planes were in except P for Peter and J for Jig. They were late. The job was a piece of cake. They should be in. They would, of course, be in . . . obviously . . . any minute now. No one mentioned the delay.

We started to go down to the Interrogation Room, and the group captain remarked without emphasis that he would just stay up here for a bit until the chaps got in. The crews of the planes that had returned were coming into the basement interrogation room for questioning. They all had mugs of tea, huge shaving mugs filled with a sweetish, ghastly warm drink that seems to mean something to them. They looked bad around the eyelids and the mouths and the lines under their eyes were deeply marked.

The crews sit on a wood bench in front of a wooden table, and the Intelligence Officer behind the table asks questions. No-one liked this trip much. It had been very long, and the weather had been terrible; the target was small; there was a lot of smoke; and they hadn't been able to see the results well.

The group captain in command sat on a table and spoke to the crew members by name, saying, 'Have a good trip?' 'Fairly good, sir.' 'Have a good trip?' 'Not bad, sir.' 'Have a good trip?' 'Quite good, sir.' This is the way it is. This is the way they talk and behave, and this is the way it is. Everyone was tired, anxious to get through with the questioning, back to the mess, back to the famous fried operational egg, the fried potatoes, the margarine and marmalade, and the bread that seems to be partially sand. And then to sleep.

Happy New Year, everyone. At the start of that year of 1943, there were 12 experienced crews on 9 Squadron including Andy Storey's. During the month of January another 14 new crews would arrive, 2 of them led by Americans. Of those 26 little bands of 7 brothers, only 15 would be left to start February.

New Year's Day 1943, ORB: *Two crews 'B' (Flt Lt Lonsdale) and 'U' (Flt Sgt Storey) were detailed for a WANGANUI operation on Essen. This type of operation was at the moment experimental and for use on nights of 10/10 cloud. The weather was the cause of cancellation at 1645 hours.* Wanganui was another new type of target flare, a skymarker for use when it was impossible to mark the ground. The op was cancelled again next day, presumably because the weather was too fine, and on 3 January it happened. It was a small, special-purpose trip with 3 Oboe-carrying Mosquitos to drop the flares and 19 Lancs from various squadrons in 5 Group with incendiaries and 4,000lb cookies, the blockbusters. Storey thought the marking not so good: *Release point flares considered to be rather scattered. Estimated 6 miles between first and last.* He bombed from 21,500ft through the cloud and turned for home.

Safety from the nightfighter cell system lay in numbers, a truth that was amply demonstrated this night. The superfast Mosquitos were fairly secure, so in effect the only intruders in the whole of enemy airspace were 19 Lancasters, and fighters got 3 of them over Holland. Unteroffizier Christian Költringer spotted Lonsdale's kite and down she went, all crew killed. Flt Lt Douglas Herbert Scott Lonsdale DFC, aged 31, could hardly have been more experienced, just a few away from the end of his second tour. Andy Storey, thinking about the end of his first tour, came back to Waddington with 28 on the clock.

Two to go. He went mining in the Baltic, 8 January, flew through ten-tenths cloud all the way there, searched the area at 2,000ft for 7 minutes, gave up and came home with his veg still aboard. Pip Beck: 'I met Andy Storey around the camp sometimes, stopping to exchange news but nothing more. His tour was almost complete. I asked him one day if he'd take me up in his Lanc. He promised he'd take me for a flip when his tour was finished. I had a 48 due [48-hour leave pass]. When I got back, Andy would almost certainly have done his last op.'

There was to be a record night, 16 January. The force going to Germany, including 12 from 9 Squadron, amounted to the largest number of Lancasters – 190, plus 11 Halifaxes – in one raid so far, and it was the first all four-engined raid, the first use of the new target-indicator firework bombs, and the first raid on Berlin for over a year. ORB: *The target, Berlin, was received with delight by the squadron. Met forecast good conditions over the area and crews very satisfied with the prospect after so many Wanganui trips.*

It was a long way, the Big City, the target with more flak guns than anywhere else in the world. The squadron might have expressed even more delight if they'd known that, tonight, something like half of the Berlin flak gunners would be off duty on a training course.

Wilkinsburg, Pennsylvania, was founded on a tavern in the late 18th century, became a religious centre, acquired the alias 'The City of Churches', was briefly part of Pittsburgh before reasserting its independence, and forbade all bars and taverns. The original taverners named their hamlet Rippeyville, then it was McNairville, and finally the Wilkins family, a favoured scion of which became Minister of War under President Tyler, made it their own. An additional claim to fame was as the town containing the domestic garage in which the world's first commercial radio station was set up, in 1919, at about the time that Mrs Frances C. Wilks Nelson gave birth to her son Frank Goheen Nelson, named after his father.

He was No. 9's newest American pilot and, whatever he had in the way of feelings of delight, Flt Sgt Frank G. Nelson of Wilkinsburg, PA, was down to fly to Berlin as second dicky with Sgt Arthur Hobbs, who was two years younger by birth but a goodly number older by experience after so many German ops.

Berlin was way beyond Gee and Oboe range so the Pathfinders couldn't see through the unforecast cloud and haze any better than the crews they were guiding. Hobbs: *Believed Berlin, 2010 hrs, 16,500 ft. Red flares seen (Neuwerp). Dead reckoning run to target. Fires below cloud. Impossible to tell whether target or dummy. No results seen although fires appeared where incendiaries dropped. 60 x 4lb incendiaries hung up and were brought back. Starboard inner engine oil pressure failed at Danish coast. Feathered* [Feather – to turn the propellor blades edge on, to minimise drag].

Joe McCarthy, now made up to Flying Officer, was there too, with an 8,000lb double-blockbuster: *Aircraft would not climb so bombed at 14,000 ft, believed Berlin. Several lakes and flares seen.*

Berlin flak at half strength was still deadly enough, and more so at 14,000ft when everyone else was much higher, but the surprise of the attack after all that time, plus a failure in the German air-raid warning system, meant that only one Lancaster was lost. Did anyone at head office wonder how it could be that Berlin had become a piece of cake in raiding terms, easier than an Italian target? Did anyone say, hang on a minute, there's something wrong here?

Next night, they sent a slightly smaller force, 170 Lancs and 17 Halifaxes, on exactly the same route but half an hour or so later. A doubtless equally delighted gang of bomber crews had another record night, and this was a record that would stand through the next half year, through the whole of the coming Battle of the Ruhr, which would not be broken for seven of the busiest bombing months of the war: largest number of Lancasters lost on a single op.

As on the previous night, there was no serious damage done to Berlin, whatever Flg Off McCarthy thought: *Own bombs seen to straddle marshalling yards. Fires observed over large area. No help from PFF [Path Finder Force] who apparently failed to locate target. Completed return journey with three engines.* The large area certainly wasn't Berlin, where no building was destroyed or even classified above 'lightly damaged', while eight people were killed.

It would be decided that the experiment, of a smallish force with a troop of four-engined bombers trying to mark a faraway target without effective navaids, would be discontinued. The reason for that decision lay on the ground in Berlin, other parts of Germany and occupied Europe, and in the sea. There were 19 Lancasters and 3 Halifaxes down with 132 out of 154 crew killed. Another flak-damaged Lanc crashed at home, no casualties, and one ditched off Flamborough Head, one man killed, making aircraft losses of 13 per cent on the night.

Contrary to tradition for a last op, Anderson Storey had been 9 Squadron's last away at 17:20. Two of the squadron's contingent of 11 had proved lucky; they'd had technical troubles and returned early. That left nine for the Flying Control staff to wait for. The Kiwi pilot Bill Cowan had the new Yankee boy Frank Nelson on his second passenger flight: *Very scattered effort. Some fires appeared to be in the nature of decoys. Starboard outer engine failure.* Nelson would be captain next op.

Four more of the nine did get back; four didn't. One crashed about 25 miles from Magdeburg with some surviving. Nothing was heard and no trace was found of two more. Pip Beck, away from Waddington on her 48 and so not at her post on that dreadful night of endless anxiety, would not have her flip with Anderson Storey. His old Lancaster, W4200, U-Uncle, had been transferred to 97 Squadron on 13 January. Why hadn't he been listed to complete his tour the night before, when almost everyone came home? Instead, on the way to Berlin, a nightfighter found him and he and all his crew died when they fell to earth outside the railway station in the small town of Klein Kummerfeld, near Neumünster, Schleswig-Holstein. That was 24 aircrew of 9 Squadron dead on one night.

Life had to go on, and while there was life there was a modest quantity of hope. Some new Mk III Lancasters arrived at Waddington, which were identical to the Mk I except they had American-built Packard Merlin engines, slightly more powerful but as the Lanc was expected ever to carry more and do more, the extra power didn't signify. Still, they were new, fresh from the factory, which was good.

Doubtless Frank Nelson, promoted to Warrant Officer Second Class, felt more than a modest mixture of hope and anxiety when he was told that he, the captain, and his crew and one of the other freshman outfits were going on ops. Perhaps he'd have one of the new aircraft and he'd come home with all four engines going, for a change. The trip was cancelled almost as soon as notified.

The typed sheet of foolscap paper called Battle Order, pinned up on 27 January by a WAAF on the mess notice board, showed that Nelson and two others were going gardening while six crews were off to Düsseldorf, including Sqn Ldr Fry with a second dicky called Van Note, another American. That was changed later in the day to eight crews for Düsseldorf, including Nelson's. They were indeed in one of the new Lancs, untried apart from local air tests, ED481 WS/N.

Seemingly unremarkable in itself, with only 162 Lancs and Halifaxes going, this op was a turning point in the war. It was the first of the 'modern' raids which were to become so efficient and so deadly. Instead of being yet another Ruhr miss in cloud and haze, with a grinding imbalance between bomber losses and bombing effect, this one worked. The Oboe-carrying Mosquitos were switched to the new, cascading, ground-marking target indicators instead of the old parachute flares.

PFF technique worked well. Flares as expected appeared on time, said one 9 Squadron skipper. *PFF flares roughly on time. Reds and greens seen cascading and in bomb sight*, said another. *Warning flares and red and green incendiaries seen and in bomb sight. Burst of own bomb and two large and one small fires observed*, said WO2 Nelson, still listed as a Flight Sergeant. Overall losses were six bombers, 3.7 per cent. Effects included 31 industrial firms hit, 15 public buildings, almost 500 houses destroyed or seriously damaged, another 2,400 lightly damaged, and almost 200 Wehrmacht soldiers killed or injured when the railway station was flattened.

The next raid, on Hamburg, 30 January, should have been another great leap forward. The pathfinder Lancasters had H2S for the first time. H2S was an early form of ground-scanning airborne radar with a large and complex transmitter in the belly of the aircraft connected to a screen, a novelty called a PPI (Position Plan Indicator), the small, circular, clock-hand display seen in all the war films. The big thing about H2S was that distance from home was no longer a factor, as with Gee and Oboe.

The system had disadvantages, including the necessity for a kind of second sight in its operator who had to decide what the flickering shadows on the screen meant in real terms. In bombers, if it was working, the technology would reveal a coastline, a big river, a city, but any more had to come through interpretation by an intuitive and experienced human.

H2S had been a long time coming. The first set had been tested almost a year before, but a mid-summer crash had destroyed much of the good work and several of the scientists doing it. Introduction had also been delayed by a concern that its heart, the top-secret cavity magnetron, would fall into enemy hands, and so a different but inferior device, the klystron valve, had been tried and tried again for too long. It would be a while before there were enough H2S sets but it was a start.

Hamburg was a good target to try out H2S. It had obvious features – a river, near the coast, not part of a vast urban sprawl – but the marking was nothing special. Most of the bombs fell harmlessly but some damage was done and fires started, and the losses were only 3.4 per cent.

For 9 Squadron, however, it was a nightmare. They sent 11 Lancasters, of which 5 came back early with various troubles. Such was the lot of bomber crews in winter: *Unable to maintain height due to severe icing. Mid-upper turret failed to operate. Visibility nil due to frost on Perspex inside and out. Intercom u/s through cold.* Four crews got to Hamburg, bombed and came home. Andy Storey's second dicky, Australian Jack Thomas, strayed many miles off track and fell near Vechta in Lower Saxony, when he should have been off the Danish coast.

Frank Nelson had reached Hamburg, bombed and was off track too, but not so seriously, just some way north as he approached the English coast. He had engine trouble and so was diverted to a base nearer than home, Leeming in north Yorkshire. He was in touch with Topcliffe, a training station not far away, as they flew over the bleak and lonely North Yorks Moors. Before the safety of the Leeming aerodrome in the flatlands of the mature River Swale, nature had placed one final obstacle, the Hambleton Hills, and they crashed straight into one, Hawnby Hill, and all were killed on their second op together.

In this month of January 1943, No. 9 Squadron lost ten Lancs and crews. New crews arrived as fast as they could be trained, like the ones led by Flt Sgt Howard Clark Lewis, from Ann Arbor, Michigan, and by Plt Off Robert Van Note, from Boulder, Colorado, but of the January ten lost, seven were new anyway.

Chapter 6

NOW ALL THE YOUTH OF ENGLAND ARE ON FIRE

Charles Owen Van Note, a builder by trade, came from Warrensburg, Missouri, via Iowa and Las Vegas (New Mexico, not Nevada) to Boulder, Colorado, in 1906. According to a later report in the local paper, the *Daily Camera*, he was impressed by the rivulets of irrigation water that flowed on either side of Pearl Street. He saw street cleaners depositing rubbish in the streams, to be carried to the main irrigation ditch. Frequently he saw apples going down the stream.

Another attractive sight was the four-in-hand carriages taking tourists to the mountains. There were three livery stables in Boulder at that time; one was displaced by the post office, another by a filling station at 15th and Pearl, and a third stood west of the fire station, also Pearl Street.

Pearl Street was paved in 1917, the apples stopped flowing down the gutters and Charles O. and his wife Amy Grace set about raising a family and making a name for themselves. They lived at No. 789 15th Street with eldest son Charles O., daughter Helen and the youngest, a boy they called Robert Owen, born in 1919. By 1932 they had moved to 1029 University Avenue. Grace died in the April, when Robert was in the first year of junior high school, and in 1941 father Charles married again, to Mrs Elizabeth Gilmore of Denver, lately of Boulder:

> The bride will wear a floor-length blue crepe gown, fashioned with an Eton jacket. She will wear silver slippers, a headdress of rhinestones, and a locket-style watch that is an heirloom in her family. Her bouquet will be of valley lillies and Joanna Hill roses tied with silver ribbons. The bridegroom's son, Robert Van Note, who attends the University of Colorado, will be best man.

In days when local newspapers were full of such matters, thus did the *Camera* announce the forthcoming wedding of widower Van Note to

79

Robert's stepmother, a lady who was 'prominent in White Shrine, Eastern Star, Woman's club and social circles'. The White Shrine of Jerusalem and the Eastern Star were, and are, Christian organisations linked to the freemasons. Father Charles was a leading figure in the Church, too, and had built at least one. 'The couple will live at 1400 Gilpin street, Denver, until a suitable place can be found in that city to erect a new home. Mr. Van Note will start remodelling his home here, 1029 University avenue, into apartments.'

Robert had already been a best man, for his brother Charles, when the bride wore ivory satin cut in the princess style and Helen Van Note, as matron of honour, wore a raisin red moire period gown with sweetheart neckline, elbow-length leg-o-mutton sleeves, bouffant skirt and ostrich plume hat in robin's egg blue. Robert's own wedding wasn't thought about. He didn't have a sweetheart. He had decided he was going to be a pilot and he was going to fly in this war.

Entry requirements for the US Army and Navy air forces included a college degree and an especially thoroughgoing set of physical standards. Van Note couldn't get in, so he applied to the RAF and joined a mixed group of British and American trainees at the Spartan School of Aeronautics in Tulsa, Oklahoma, one of five flying cadet schools in the USA set up in wartime 'for the training of British civilian pilots'.

Having thus trained, Robert reported to the RCAF at Ottawa, 28 March 1942, and was soon off to England, 23 June, and the *Camera* was able to inform its readers of the luxurious treatment a young American volunteer officer could expect over there while building up to risking his life:

Pilot Officer Robert O. Van Note writes from England that he has been appointed a squad commander, and as such has to see that sergeants and officers get to lectures and attend to all their other work. He is making fine progress in flying and enjoying it; that the mess is good; that the WAAFs are taking good care of him; that the flying field has a comfortable lounge and that he spends much of his leisure time in it since there are no nearby towns to go for recreation.

He made a trip to London, which is a three and a half hour bus ride away from his camp and stayed at the American Eagle club [28 Charing Cross Road]. Bus rides about London acquainted him with the city. He plans more trips to London but will stick close to camp in order to learn everything that is to be learned about flying ships.

One of the things to be learned was studied at a conversion unit. 'Robert Van Note, 23, writes his father that he has passed all his RAF tests in England and likes the service. He has not yet engaged in combat raids across the channel. He has been piloting four-motored fighting planes' (the *Camera*).

Father wrote back: 'I am glad to hear that you are happy in your new surroundings. I always listen to the broadcasts from the American Eagle Club in London. Perhaps some day I will hear you speak from there.' His wish was not to be and he may have known it, having suffered from a bad heart for the whole of that year. His second wife was already dead; he died at the Community Hospital only a few weeks before the orphaned boy Robert flew his four-motored fighting plane for the first time over Germany.

Bad weather, cancellations and the arrival of the Lancaster Mk III had meant no operational flying for 9 Squadron between Storey's death and 27 January 1943, when Van Note saw his name up beside that of Sqn Ldr G.S. Fry DFC. Fry was well into his second tour and the RAF officer par excellence, fully equipped with moustache and pipe. Known everywhere as Tubby Fry, there could not have been a better mentor for the young man from Colorado. They bombed through cloud on the new pathfinder markers and came home.

Van Note, crew and Lancaster A-Apple were listed on 29 January for a solo flight to Lorient, where the U-boat pens were. It was cancelled but they didn't have long to wait for their debut. Cologne, 2 February, was another trial for marking techniques, with 151 Lancasters and Halifaxes shown the way by 2 Oboe Mosquitos and 8 Stirlings with H2S. From Waddington, 44 Squadron took off around 18:15 followed by the seven of No. 9, with Van Note first in line at 18:26.

The marking was scattered and so was the bombing. Only 15 of many 4,000lb cookies fell in the target area. There was the double explosion of two bombers colliding over Holland, and three more were shot down by nightfighters. Perhaps Van Note saw some of that, or perhaps he saw nothing. Back at home he would learn that a 44 Squadron Lanc had failed to return, but only a very select and high-up few would be told that the Germans might well have got hold of an H2S set, three days after its introduction.

A nightfighter had shot down a pathfinder, a 7 Squadron Stirling, in Rotterdam, but the screen disappeared in the crash. What was left was certainly a big bundle of wierd looking kit, and everybody knew what wizards the British were at electronics, but what was it for? The Germans spent months puzzling over the 'Rotterdam device' and didn't work it out entirely until they got another, with screen, but by then had done quite a bit of work on Naxos, a device for nightfighters that enabled them to home in on H2S aircraft.

The Rotterdam fighter in question was piloted by Oberleutnant Reinhold Knacke, Knight's Cross with Oak Leaves, and that Stirling was his forty-fourth victory. Too bad for him, after landing, refuelling and going into battle again, he also was shot down and killed.

Joe McCarthy was on that one but he and Van Note were not required on the Hamburg raid of 3 February. Their squadrons went and all came back, but 16 others didn't, almost all shot down by nightfighters, mostly over Holland. Losses of 6 per cent made for a poor investment: scattered marking made for scattered bombing, with no serious industrial damage done. Considering that many of those who set out on the raid had to come back early because of the weather, losses as a percentage of those who reached enemy territory were about double that figure.

Turin was a different story entirely. Joe went, Bob went, and they smashed the place. Two Lancs fell, one due to engine failure and one flew into a mountain. Van Note, having flown over the Alps in the moonlight, had another new experience if more mundane, when he was diverted to land at Middle Wallop on the Hampshire–Dorset border. This was a fighter base, with a grass runway meant for Spitfires and Hurricanes in the Battle of Britain. They were shortly expecting the arrival of the USAAF 67th Tactical Reconnaissance Group and their Mustangs, but not an American in a Lancaster at night. Well, they got down all right, they'd hit the target with bombs and leaflets, it had been a good trip and a long one.

Next day, when they flew back to Waddington, they heard that a new 9 Squadron crew, just like them except without the benefit of an operation yet, had crashed on an air test, only one body found. That was life in the air force, seemingly. You joined, you trained, you came up to the starting line full of hope and trepidation, and you died before the gun went off. Or not, like Joe and Bob.

Wilhelmshaven, 11–12 February, Flg Off McCarthy: *Much larger glow observed when aircraft was 80 miles away*. That was the naval ammunition dump blowing up, which wrecked dockyards and town buildings across 120 acres. Skymarkers had been dropped on H2S readings, not normally the most reliable target indication but this time it worked. It was blind bombing, through cloud at night. The holy grail of bombers had been found, or so it seemed.

Sir Arthur Harris, Bomber Command C-in-C, was keen to use his new abilities on the industrial core of Germany, the Ruhr, where smog and cloud had always prevented accurate target finding, but he was ordered to switch his attentions to the U-boat bases on the French coast. This, to Harris's mind, was pointless. The U-boat pens were bomb-proof, massive structures of reinforced concrete cunningly designed to repel all forms of airborne attack known at the time, and they were well defended. The Lorient pens, for instance, were surrounded by more than 300 anti-aircraft guns.

Even a C-in-C has to take orders from above and his were clear enough, with priorities stated in an Air Ministry Directive: 'The effective devastation of the whole area in which are located the submarines, their maintenance facilities, and the services, power, water, light, communications and other resources on which their operations depend.'

Harris did as he was told. Bomber Command went several times to Lorient; Van Note was on two of the ops. They went with 4,000lb cookies and incendiaries and, by the last one, 16–17 February, the town had been flattened and the citizens had fled. There had been very few losses – no German nightfighters were going to be deployed to defend a French town with an indestructible target – and just about the only buildings left intact were the U-boat bases, still working as normal.

In 1926 on Washtenaw Avenue, a little outside the city limits of Ann Arbor, Michigan, a mock-Tudor mansion was built, later given the number 2020 but then given only a name, Hilldene Manor. Inside were six spacious, luxury apartments, plus quarters for a caretaker. The man who took that job was Roy F. Lewis of Ypsilanti. He had a wife, Amy, and a son, Howard Clark, born 1922. By the end of 1942 that boy had trained for the air force in Canada and was in England, converting his recently learned skills to four-engined bombers.

By 20:30 hours, 18 February 1943, he was standing behind the pilot in the cockpit of Lancaster ED495 WS/Y, approaching Wilhelmshaven. Visibility was good so Flt Sgt Lewis would have been able to see the target indicators going down and the flak in all its glory coming up. In a few days' time this same Lanc would FTR, shot down over Nürnberg.

Lewis's work-experience tutor at Wilhelmshaven was Flt Lt Jim Verran. He had already survived 35 operations with 102 Squadron in the Whitley bomber, the flying barn door. Next week he would live through a flaming Lancaster crash at home, with some crew killed, and undergo a great deal of surgery at the hands of the legendary burns man Sir Archibald McIndoe. Later, as Sqn Ldr Verran in No. 83 Squadron PFF, he'd be shot down by a nightfighter, most of the crew killed, but he would parachute, get stuck in the bomb bay of his burning, falling aircraft, free himself, land, suffer more surgery but German this time, and end up as a POW. In Bomber Command, though, for every one or two Verrans there were seven or eight Lewises.

Van Note was doing well. That same Wilhelmshaven trip was his fifth as skipper, plus one as a second dicky gave him a certain seniority. The sprog Lewis, it was decided, needed another passenger trip before he could be let loose, and what a trip they gave him. Captain was the squadron CO, Wg Cdr Southwell DFC, and he put Lewis in the flight engineer's seat. Apart from the tail gunner, the rest of the crew were officers and the top men, department heads, the squadron's navigation, wireless and gunnery leaders, men who had seen and done it all.

The pathfinders were late with their marking but everything else seemed to go well in middling weather. The squadron's Lancs were over the target together, bombing around 23:25, so Clark might have seen one hit by flak and set on fire. He might have seen it tumbling to earth, not knowing it was the aircraft he'd been in to Wilhelmshaven. The squadron had another loss too that night; 2 gone out out of 12, 1 with an older, experienced pilot, 1 with a young Canadian on his first. What sort of odds were they, Howard?

Being taken on a trip by the best team was a privilege, surely, but it was no guarantee when they made you captain of your own ship, which they did on the last day of February, U-boat pens at St-Nazaire. It went fine. Lewis saw *A number of big fires well in the target area*, and McCarthy likewise: *Several large explosions observed. Many good fires burning in town.* That was quite right. Two-thirds of the place was dismantled, with few casualties because almost everyone had left, and no damage whatever was done to the U-boat pens.

Van Note came back from leave, the usual time off after half a dozen or so ops, to find himself listed for Berlin, 1 March. C-in-C Harris, and many others above him, had the notion that destroying Berlin would end the war but all knew that Bomber Command was not yet strong enough to do such a job. Raids so far had been good propaganda, proof that the RAF could bomb the devil in his lair, but with heavy losses to set against causing only minor inconvenience. This night, although not part of a major campaign against the Big City, was to prove the best yet.

Van Note bombed at 22:17 from 19,200ft. He saw his bombs burst beside the green markers: *approx. 40 fires already burning. Own bombs fell on fires and added to them. Some bombs seen dropped outside the target area.* The attack had drifted away to the south and west of the city but still destroyed over 1,000 buildings including 20 factories, one of which was the Telefunken laboratory where the Germans were analysing the 'Rotterdam device'. With a marvellous piece of luck, a bomb blew the lab and the captured H2S set to bits.

A few hours later, a No. 35 Squadron Halifax, W7877 TL/O, was spotted on its return journey by Lt August Geiger of III/NJG1. This Halifax was unusual in several respects. Its skipper was Sqn Ldr Peter Elliott DFC, a pre-war regular on his second tour; its flight engineer was Flt Sgt Stanley Watts AFM, who had joined the Royal Naval Air Service in 1916 and so became a founder member of the RAF in 1918; and it had on board a fully functioning H2S set. When it crashed near Goor in Overijssel, all the crew were killed except the navigator but the H2S stayed intact, so there was hardly a pause in German research. Geiger would go on to a score of 53 victories until he too was shot down in the September and drowned in the Zuider Zee entangled in his parachute.

For Lewis and No. 9 Squadron there was now a run of German targets, starting with Hamburg, 3 March. Most of them missed, wrecking the small naval town of Wedel instead, but the next raid, Essen, 5 March, marked the opening of a new and prolonged campaign, the Battle of the Ruhr, which crippled the German war machine and did as much to defeat the Third Reich as any other Allied action, or possibly more.

Lewis and Van Note were among the 444 captains of bombers heading for Essen. Of these 2 crashed on take-off and 53 turned back for various reasons, as well as 3 of the marking Mosquitos. The flak and the nightfighters collected their usual tribute, another 14 bombers, but the remaining 5 Oboe Mosquitos did a superb job of blind marking in the industrial haze. Between the Krupp works and the city centre, 160 acres of Essen were razed in 40 minutes, including more than 50 of Krupp's workshops and offices. Returning, Lewis could still see the glow of the fires 120 miles away.

It was a long way to Nürnburg, 8 March. Van Note and the rest made it a 7-hour round trip, although Lewis, last back by some distance, did almost 8. Out of the range of Oboe, marking had to be done by a combination of the newfangled H2S and the oldfangled eyeball. Ground haze negated the eyeball and H2S was not yet completely mastered, so marking was scattered, bombing likewise, partly as a result of the phenomenon known as 'creep'. Once over the target, it was a natural desire in most bomb aimers, and everyone else in the crew, to get rid of the load as soon as possible and get away. Some of the first ones there might drop slightly short of the markers and fires would start. Later arrivals might drop slightly short of those fires, and so on, and the attack would creep back, in this case for 10 miles. Even so, MAN, Siemens and the railways all took hits.

Munich was 9 March for Lewis when the BMW factory was hit, and Stuttgart was 11 March for him and Van Note. Bob Van Note had now done a round dozen and was due some leave. So was Lewis, who had done six plus two second dickies, but he didn't get any. Instead, he and one other, the long-timer Sgt Arthur Hobbs, set forth in the deep dusk on a mining trip. Vegetables were to be planted in that part of the garden reserved for Spinach, which is to say an area of the Baltic Sea off the large and modern port of Gdynia, designed and built by Poles, occupied by Germans. Almost 10 hours later, Hobbs came back saying he hadn't been able to find any Spinach because of a sea fog, and so had dropped his mines in another district. What Lewis found, no one will ever know. That was the usual thing with losses while gardening. You went into the sea. You were lost without trace. You were destined for Runnymede.

Nick Knilans wasn't lost but he was in a ditch with an injured elbow, having fallen off his bicycle on a night ride back to camp from Burton upon Trent. He blamed his accident on his lack of experience in cycling, an art only recently acquired under the necessity of finding some means of getting to pubs, and on the meagre light offered by his blackout-shaded bicycle lamp. Another contributory cause was the evening spent at the Bass brewery.

After a rapid tour of the production facilities, a group of gallant airmen had been shown into the sampling room and offered vintage ales at pre-war strengths. While the actual bottles of Red Label seen in the foreground of Monsieur Manet's *A Bar at the Folies-Bergère* were not among them, their dusty and straw-wrapped equivalents were plentifully supplied and gratefully received. Wartime beer in Britain was weak, warm and watery. Americans and Canadians could not understand it. Ah, but this, this Bass of the golden years, this was something to revel in. The day, or the evening, had to be seized.

Knilans's bicycling accident took him off flying duties for a fortnight. Morning treatment sessions with nurses at the local hospital gave him ample opportunity to elaborate on the topic of Elbow as War Hero, and afternoons were spent investigating the life histories of female bar staff. A mended and more knowledgeable Knilans went back to training and next stop was a long way from the fleshpots of Burton. The grass airfield of Balnageith, a mile to the west of the ancient Royal Burgh of Forres on the Moray Firth, was home to No. 19 OTU. Forres, one of Scotland's oldest towns, down the road from Cawdor and the setting for the opening scenes of *Macbeth*, offered only limited opportunities for personal research and development, which, considering they were flying Whitleys, was a cause for concern.

Beer was provided by the RAF at a ritual new to Knilans, called 'crewing up'. Near-qualified apprentices to the various trades – pilots, navigators, bomb aimers, wireless operators and gunners – were assembled at a kind of party-cum-group exercise, the idea being that they would gravitate into mutually acceptable teams. The notion of a settled crew had always been promoted but, earlier, crews had been allotted to captains more or less at random. The modern theory was that men who had a say in their selection were more likely to knit into a fighting unit whose members looked out for each other, and so was more likely to survive.

Nick Knilans had ridden up from Edinburgh on the Inverness train in the same compartment as a wireless operator, Les Knell, and they'd got on well. Two gunners who were already mates, a big Aussie called Roy Learmonth and a Scot, Gerry Jackson, were the next on board, and a schoolteacher from north Yorkshire, now bomb aimer, Robin Tate known as Joe, seemed to fit in.

Knilans: 'The evening was getting on and I still needed a navigator. Harry Geller, a jolly fat Jew from Toronto was having a good time but hadn't been accepted by the other pilots. I thought he was being discriminated against.' Nick, the judge of human nature, saw a highly intelligent fellow who enjoyed the good things of life, which he equated with the brains necessary for navigation plus a deep-seated wish to get home alive. Harry Geller joined the crew.

Next day, they went up in a Whitley for 2 hours with an instructor and then they were on their own, mostly on day and night cross-countries. Knilans:

We only had two disturbing ones. The first was over the North Sea, climbing up from 2,000 feet through cloud. We got to 10,000 when rime ice started forming on the wings, which slowed us down, so I increased the throttles to maximum. We just about made it into clear sky. We were in and out of the cloud tops and sunshine but the ice kept building up. If we got too much the aircraft would stall and we'd be heading for the drink.

So, down we went, and out of the cloud base we popped at 2,000 feet again with the ice breaking off, and we were being shot at. Heavy flak. Shells bursting right in front of us. Away to port we could see a large convoy of freighters, and three destroyers peeling off from escort duty towards us. We could see their curving white wakes in the sea as they turned our way at full power, guns blazing. There were yellow dots blinking on the ends of their guns as they fired, which turned into black explosions in the air getting nearer and nearer to us. Joe said 'Oh, they must think we're a Dornier', because the planes were a bit similar, but I wasn't really listening as I climbed and turned hard a-starboard and back into the clouds. I learned later that aircraft recognition was not considered a necessary attribute in Royal Navy gun turrets.

The other incident was at night, over the Moray Firth:

We had a fairly primitive type of air-to-air radar called Monica, which was supposed to warn us of near-by aircraft. Les, our w/op came on the intercom and said he'd got a blip and it looked like it was coming up fast. I changed course and height pretty rapidly and asked Les what there was now. 'He's changed course and altitude, same as we did,' said Les. So I changed back to our original course and climbed 500 feet. 'He's 300 yards behind us, and steady,' said Les.

Of course we all thought it was a long range nightfighter, like a Junkers 88. They used to prey on training units, hanging around looking for easy kills. Thing was, our guns were not loaded. I turned 90 degrees and dropped 1,000 feet like a stone. 'Did he follow us?' I asked Les. 'Sure did,' was the reply. 'Hang on to your hats, boys,' I said as I let down to nought feet and wave-hopped flat out for base. 'Where's the so-and-so now?' I said. 'Gone,' said Les. I reported the story to our CO and he called me in two days later. 'Remember that nightfighter, Knilans? It was one of ours. They've got some new kit for intercepting bandits and they were trying it out on you. But don't forget. Next time, it might be a real German.' 'Thank you very much, sir,' I said. 'Will that be all?'

Flying training seemed to be getting better and better. The bigger and heavier the aircraft, the more it suited the chunky farmer's boy Nick Knilans. Soon he would be converting to Lancasters but there was a 48-hour pass to spend in Inverness first:

We'd made good friends with one particular crew and we went off to Inverness together. Ken McLean, the Canadian pilot, said he'd discovered a new drink called a Torpedo. It was a measure of Scotch, a measure of gin, and half a bottle of port in a pint glass. 'Two torpedos in your hold would cause you to sink,' said my friend, known as Mac. In fact, what it did was remove all inhibitions when taking part in Scots reels and jigs and the Dashing White Sergeant. We learned that the famous Highland Fling was when some little old Scots lady tried to fling you out of the window on a fast turn.

We finished up having a mock Western shoot-out in the hotel bar, drawing imaginary six-guns and trying to pretend that our staggering around was all play acting as we fell on the floor. Anyway, the management suggested that we should leave which, somehow, we did.

By mid-April, Van Note was up around the 20 operations mark. An old hand from No. 44 Squadron, Flt Lt 'Red' Wakeford joined No. 9 with a crew of freshmen which included navigator Flg Off Jonah Bruce Reeves, a 20-year-old graduate of No. 8 Air Observers School in Canada, class of August 1942. He was from Oneida in Madison County, New York State, a place of creeks and lakes and country pleasures known as the Leatherstocking region, after the deerskin boot-cum-overtrouser worn by the pioneers of the 18th century.

His parents, Jonah B. and Ora Grace Reeves, were living at 446 Stone Street when Jonah Junior was born. He went to Oneida High School, graduated in 1940 and, being a brainy and highly promising fellow, on to the first year of the exclusive and expensive Hamilton College, Clinton, New York. His parents divorced and his mother took her son to Canada; his father, a carpenter, moved up the road to Durhamville where he had family. In November 1941, a month before Pearl Harbor, Jonah volunteered for the RCAF.

Reeves came to a squadron reeling from its losses: eight more Lancasters, eight more skippers and crews, no survivors, between 3 and 10 April. What was left had to move, down the road apiece to a new base at Bardney, which they did on 13 and 14 April under the direction of a new CO, Wg Cdr Burnett, who had arrived on 12 April. The first op from Bardney, 14 April, sent only five Lancasters to join in at Stuttgart. Of these five, four, including Bob Van Note's, took second dicky sprog pilots. One didn't because he was only on his first op himself. The effort and determination, while faced with devastation in staggering ratio to resources, can only be marvelled at.

Jonah Reeves's first was to La Spezia on the north-west coast of Italy in Liguria, one of the most important Italian military targets and a major naval centre. The squadron was briefed to attack the docks, the naval barracks and two battleships reportedly at anchor there. It was a long haul – up at 21:08, down at 06:45 – but a successful one. Nobody saw any battleships but they pasted the docks with little opposition. The only bomber lost out of the 186 on the raid was shot down off the French coast.

Wakeford, Reeves and co. were not required for the next three ops but went gardening on 28 April, the second of two very big mining nights involving over 350 aircraft. The other trip had been to the French coast and the Frisian Islands with one bomber down. This night it was more dangerous waters around Heligoland, the Elbe Estuary and the Danish coast, AKA Nasturtium, Verbena, Spinach, Forgetmenot, Radish, Sweet Pea, Quince, Rosemary and Silverthorne. Kriegsmarine flak and nightfighters, presumably unaware of their floral reclassification, did for 23 Lancasters, Stirlings, Halifaxes and Wellingtons with only 4 crewmen surviving out of 149. Van Note and Reeves survived all right but at least two of the dead were Americans, 158 Squadron wireless operator Flt Sgt William Priddin, a married man from Saugus, Massachusetts, and 419 Squadron tail gunner Flt Sgt Robert Gourde of Longview, Washington.

Essen was next. They left around midnight and bombed through the cloud at around 03:00. Van Note: *No results observed over target but at 0333 explosion seen from 23,000 feet which lit up whole sky for at least five seconds.* Reeves's crew couldn't see their own bombfall either but, for a cloudy night with sky markers, the raid was remarkably successful. Over 400 buildings in Essen, including some of Krupp's, were knocked down or severely damaged. Bombs also fell on ten other Ruhr towns, especially Bottrup, which was off target but not entirely off purpose.

The night of 4/5 May saw the biggest raid of the war so far, apart from the three 'Thousand Plan' efforts in 1942. This time, instead of collecting together just about anything that could fly and carry a bomb, a much more powerful and professional force of 586 Lancasters, Halifaxes, Wellingtons and Stirlings went to Dortmund for the first major operation against that city. It was another raid illustrating what might have been if only the target marking were spot on. Roughly half the bombers missed, aiming at decoy fires and inaccurate flares, yet the rest destroyed or badly damaged 3,350 buildings including the steel works and the town hall. Van Note saw 40 or 50 fires and smoke covering the target up to 5,000ft, and he came home to say so, as did Jonah Reeves, unlike a 22-year-old gunner, Sgt Martin Davis of 101 Squadron, son of Martin and Cora, of St Anthony, Idaho.

Sgt Davis was one of many that night. Including the 9 aircraft lost in accidents arriving back in bad weather, 42 bombers was the score against, 7.2 per cent. While Dortmund could not withstand many more attacks like this one and still function, the same could be said of Bomber Command.

Reeves, studying his maps in his dimly lit miniature flying office, could not see as much as some of the others. He couldn't see all those bombers going down in flames, but he would hear all about it, and the next op to Duisburg was the same. The bomber force was 562 including some pathfinder Lancasters, plus 10 Mosquitos. The town centre, the docks and the ships in them were so thoroughly smashed up that Duisburg was struck off the list for the time being. In an attempt to reduce losses from flak, 9 Squadron and others were bombing from greater heights. Van Note was among those saying that being at 20,000ft helped bombing accuracy because, being less disturbed and pushed about by the flak, he could concentrate on a longer and steadier run up to the target. By accuracy he meant a general observation on the proportion of bombs seen to explode near the target indicators. If the TIs were right, as they were here at Duisburg, the bomb aimers could do the business at that height. While the business of the flak gunners was thus made more difficult, it was not made impossible. There were 38 bombers lost, 6.8 per cent.

The Skoda works at Pilsen, now an important part of the war machine, had been attempted a number of times, always proving hard to find and mark properly. The night after Duisburg, navigator Reeves was one of 120 such trying again, this time with the help of no fewer than 48 Pathfinder aircraft. In Reeves's own Lanc they noted that the bombing was well concentrated but was not causing many fires. This was because almost all the bombs of this raid fell in open countryside, north of the factories, while the nightfighters got seven, two more were lost without trace and one was written off crashing at home with bad engine trouble, 6 per cent.

Such wounds could be rested for a while as it was the full moon, which called off the bombers except for a few minor outings to French airfields and the like, and one to the dams.

The day Reeves took off for Pilsen, 13 May 1943, was the day the *London Gazette* announced the award of the DFC to Joe McCarthy:

> On many occasions this officer has attacked targets in Germany. As captain of aircraft he has participated in sorties to the heavily defended objectives in the Ruhr and took part in the successful raid on Essen on a night in March 1943. He has also attacked Berlin three times and Italian targets on five occasions. Throughout his whole career, his conduct has set an example of high courage and efficiency to other members of the squadron.

Three days later, efficiency would not be the first word on Joe McCarthy's lips and this officer would have attacked every man responsible for servicing his Lancaster, had he found any on the occasion. A fortnight later, he would become the only American airman to be awarded two of the RAF's biggest gongs in the same month.

Chapter 7

DAM BUSTERS

Plt Off Henry Melvin Young, down from the varsity with his pal Leonard Cheshire, turned up at RAF Driffield in the East Riding of Yorkshire, home of 102 Squadron, in June 1940. Young had an American mother, Fannie Forrester Young née Rowan, from Los Angeles, California, sister of a well-known architect and used to moving in glossy social circles. She was a graduate of the Marlborough School for Girls in Los Angeles, and of the Mount Vernon Seminary in Washington DC. She married an English lawyer, Henry Young, in California in 1913 and moved to London with him; Henry junior was born in 1915. The family split up briefly in 1928, Fannie moving back to Los Angeles with young Henry and putting him in the Webb School and later the Kent School in Connecticut and Pomona College, Claremont, California. Father Henry came out to join them but by 1933 his career in American law had not prospered, so he took the boy away to London again.

By 1938 that boy was a student of Trinity College, Oxford, and rowing at number two in the university Boat Race, rowing weight 12st 12lb. After 4 miles and 374yd, or 20 minutes and 3 seconds, of supreme physical effort the Oxford crew crossed the finishing line two lengths ahead of Cambridge and a thousand hats were thrown into the air, seen for the first time on television by the very few people who had receiving sets.

At 102 Squadron in 1940 they were equipped with the Whitley. Earlier versions of this aircraft had been barely able to reach 200mph in level flight unladen, and carrying their 7,000lb bomb load they cruised more around the 130mph mark. By this time they had Rolls-Royce Merlin engines and could make a better effort, although were still very slow and cumbersome compared to the German fighters.

Relatively the opposite on the road was Leonard Cheshire's car, a Bentley Speed Six, 6.5-litre engine, top speed 84mph, one of the marque that, according to Ian Fleming, a certain Mr Bond, James Bond, had put in store for the duration. As Cheshire and Young disembarked, among the small crowd of admiring officers around them that afternoon was Plt Off Geoff Womersley (later Group Captain DSO, DFC) who, as well as flying regular ops, was responsible for getting the squadron's new boys' flying up to scratch.

Later in the war, pilots would arrive on squadron with 450 hours in their log books flying single-, twin-, and four-engined aircraft, plus another 50 or so on the Link flight simulation trainer. RAF Bomber Command in 1940 was not quite so fussy, especially if the chaps were the right sort.

Womersley commented: 'Young and Cheshire arrived with about 50 hours each on Tiger Moths. I was the squadron instructor and these were the first pilots sent to us from the university air squadron. They'd had no twin-engined training at all,* so I took them up in our Whitleys for day and night flying.'

Henry Young's flight commander on operations was Sqn Ldr O.A. Morris:

We were attached to Coastal Command for a while in September and October 1940, hunting for U-boats and protecting convoys, operating out of tents at Prestwick with packing cases for furniture. It was not a popular posting. We had no training for a maritime role and no instructions about what we were supposed to be doing. Our Whitleys were not suited to the job either. For a start they wouldn't take the standard depth charge so had to be modified, and we soon found out that low flying over the sea made the engines liable to fail.

One chap who could certainly vouch for that was Flg Off Young, who was well out in the Atlantic when his engines stopped. After a considerable time in the little dinghy they issued you with, the crew were picked up by an American destroyer, one crossing the ocean on the lend/lease scheme. Anyway, it had a photographer on board from *Life* magazine and this was just the ticket for him, and a well illustrated feature subsequently appeared.

It happened on 7 October and they had been in that little dinghy for 22 hours before Town Class destroyer HMS *St Mary*, ex-US Navy, picked

---

* It wasn't quite as bad as Grp Capt Womersley remembers. They had had two whole months on twin-engined aircraft at No. 10 OTU.

them up. After the maritime interlude, the squadron moved back to bombing duties at RAF Topcliffe, north Yorkshire, a new station but still a grass field where bad weather caused many problems with boggy take-offs and landings.

Sqn Ldr Morris:

Each captain [such as Henry Young] planned his own route to the target. Bombing tactics likewise were delegated. A take-off time was laid down but if you were delayed you still went so long as you had enough time to come back over the enemy coast before daylight. Because there were no navigation aids it was all done by dead reckoning and looking at the ground, and so navigation was poor. Some captains distrusted their observers and decided on course alterations themselves. The result was a great many losses due to running out of petrol while many miles off track on the way home.

At the interrogation when you did get home, the intelligence officers didn't like it if you admitted you were not sure if you'd been to the target laid down. They gave you a black mark. Tired and jumpy crews got wise to this and said 'Oh yes, hit the jolly target bob on', and slid away to bed early.

Henry Young and six others set off for a raid on the Fiat works at Turin, 23 November at around 13:45 hours, landed to refuel and eat a meal at Horsham St Faith (now Norwich International Airport) and, at about 17:30, began their long, long, slow trip. They flew all across France, saw the lights still on in Switzerland, and came to the Alps. Three of the captains decided they were not going to make it and turned home. But four, including Young, wove their way through the Alps, not over them. At Turin they dropped their bombs without opposition and set off back into thickening cloud which eventually became ten-tenths.

With no reference points, no stars, no landmarks and unable to get a wireless fix from anywhere, they were like mountaineers in a white-out. They had to keep going, with no idea in which direction. One crew force-landed in a field, out of petrol, and were simultaneously amazed and joyful to find themselves on home ground, near Brighton. Another, Sgt Rix and crew returning in Q-Queenie, dipped below the cloud to see what they could see, were hit by a barrage of flak and assumed they were over France, although in fact it was Portsmouth. Hit again, they flew away from their attackers, searched for somewhere to land, but ran out of petrol. Bailing out and floating down into what they believed to be enemy territory, they also were amazed to land in various bits of Sussex. Nobody was hurt, nor did they get as wet as another crew, 45 minutes later.

Low on fuel, off track, F-Freddie was struggling to make what Henry Young hoped would soon be England, since his fuel gauges had been showing empty for some time. Whether the coast watchers on Start Point would prove better at aircraft recognition than those at Portsmouth became an irrelevance as both engines conked out. Land was out of the question. Flg Off Young once more issued his instructions for ditching, off Torcross.

To survive one ditching in a 1940 RAF emergency dinghy was fortunate. To survive two was bordering on the miraculous and Henry Young, Oxford rowing blue, *matelot extraordinaire*, would be saddled with the nickname 'Dinghy' for the rest of his life, which included a posting to the RAF Delegation in Washington DC, on temporary duty with the USAAF, in the summer of 1942. This was when he married his long-time American sweetheart, Priscilla Rawson, of Kent, Connecticut, where he'd been to school.

The RAF took him back in February 1943, decided he had better learn to fly a four-engined bomber, which he did in five weeks at 1660 and 1664 Conversion Units, posted him to 57 Squadron, Scampton, Lincolnshire on 13 March and immediately reposted him to X Squadron at the same base. Who or why or which or what was X Squadron, nobody knew, except a very few of the topmost brass.

Its CO, Wg Cdr Gibson, didn't know. All he had been told was that it was his job to assemble a new Lancaster squadron for a special duty, recruiting only experienced captains, preferably tour or double-tour completed and, where possible, experienced crews. Gibson himself had done three tours. He took on Dinghy Young as his second in command and wondered what the 5 Group circular, asking for volunteers, might bring in.

Joe McCarthy had had a highly active last few weeks. Since Wilhelmshaven, 11 February, he'd operated on 21 February – Bremen, 25 – Nürnberg, 26 – Cologne, 28 – St-Nazaire, 1 March – Berlin, 3 – Hamburg, 8 – Nürnberg again, 9 – Munich, 11 – Stuttgart, 12 – Essen. He'd also been on low-level formation flying practice for three days, then it was St-Nazaire again, *an uneventful trip* to the U-boat base when the port was wrecked but not the U-boat pens. That was 22 March and McCarthy's thirty-third op according to common sense but thirtieth according to the RAF, with those DNCOs not counting. He could have packed it in, got a desk job, something in liaison, maybe, with the USAAF but it didn't happen. Joe and his crew had done very well in the low flying, and they went with David Maltby and New Zealander Les Munro and most of their crews from 97 Squadron to RAF Scampton and X Squadron, 25 March. Nobody had a clue about what they were in for.

They could presume that their experience and luck in lasting so long had had something to do with acceptance for this hush-hush posting, which impression was confirmed when they looked around at their new colleagues in the officers' mess: a higher average age than usual, a lot of premature grey hairs, and a great many tunics with DSO and DFC ribbons. One tunic had both, and Bars to both, and that belonged to their new CO, a small but belligerent fellow, Wg Cdr Guy Penrose Gibson.

Gibson couldn't tell them much. They were to be a new squadron, as yet unnumbered, and they were to train intensively in night-time low flying for one special operation. Security had to be tight as surprise was essential to their success.

There were no fools in that room, listening to Gibson. This was to be a hit-and-run raid, obviously, not part of a mass attack, hence the low flying. It would be unescorted by fighters, equally obviously, being at night, although they might hope for feints and diversions elsewhere. Likewise obviously, it was a highly valued objective, so they could expect the Germans to be keen on its preservation. And it would have to be a target never attacked before because it was too dangerous, or one that had been attacked but which had proved too difficult for conventional bombing.

It all sounded very hairy. They wondered if they were going to try to sink the *Tirpitz*, sister ship to the *Bismarck*, holed up in a Norwegian fjord out of normal range, attacked dozens of times and apparently invincible. They wondered if it might be the Dortmund–Ems canal, main artery of Germany's transport system, well defended and never yet breached.

It could have been one of those. They were on the list compiled by the Air Ministry of targets to be hit before any Allied invasion of

Germany could be launched with confidence. Arthur Harris did not believe an invasion would be necessary because Bomber Command would force Germany to give up, but he could see that, if there were to be an invasion, it would have a far better chance if bombers could inhibit the Germans' ability to bring up reinforcements of men and weaponry, which meant hitting the transport system. Also, the war would end sooner, with fewer casualties, if most of the enemy's naval power could be removed and, clearly, the means of production could be destroyed, which he was doing anyway.

The Air Ministry's list of targets was:

- The battleship *Tirpitz*, which threatened the Murmansk convoys and therefore the ability of the Soviet allies to survive.
- U-boat pens on the French coast and elsewhere.
- E-boat pens ditto.
- Dortmund–Ems canal.
- Mittelland canal, including the Rothensee shiplift at Magdeburg.
- Major railway routes, especially tunnels and viaducts which would take months to rebuild.
- Möhne and Sorpe dams, which controlled the greater part of the water supply to the Ruhr and therefore the Germans' ability to manufacture steel.

There was information also on secret weapons that could destroy London – rocket bombs, ballistic missiles, in deep, impregnable silos and massive *blockhausen*, built by slave labour.

Among the problems with these objectives was one which, it was hoped, technology would soon solve. There was no weapon yet which could knock a serious hole in a U-boat pen or a *blockhaus*, nor was it clear how the canals, tunnels and viaducts could be damaged sufficiently to make a difference. The Rothensee shiplift, for instance, seemed impregnable. Completed in 1938, it was a marvel of German engineering that linked the Elbe–Rhine–Mittelland–Dortmund–Ems network at its centre and made them in effect one great 7,000-mile system.

As for dams, well, the simplest method of dealing with a dam would be with deep-swimming torpedos dropped from the air, but they had anti-torpedo nets. A conventional bombing raid would be hopeless.

Even if anyone could hit the dam wall it would only damage the top and that superficially.

There was a weapon that could split open a dam or, at least, there might be, if a way could be found of delivering it satisfactorily. Barnes Wallis, designer of the airship R-100 and the Wellington bomber, had had an idea that could work. If you dropped a depth charge onto a reservoir's surface at a certain speed and angle, it should bounce along like a ducks-and-drakes stone. It could, therefore, hop over the torpedo nets. It must not bounce too high, or it would hop right over the dam. When it hit the dam top it should sink, clinging to the wall, so it could explode close up at the best depth, making a fissure in the masonry where the mass of dammed water would be the greatest help in pushing that fissure open. It would also have to be a big explosive charge, very powerful, which meant heavy.

The Germans were perfectly aware of their invulnerability to conventional weaponry and were confident that the Sorpe in particular could withstand anything then known about, but they also foresaw that the Allies would probably try something. The dams therefore had defences against aerial attack but they were adequate rather than awesome.

Once Barnes Wallis had convinced the planners that his skipping depth charge could perform, a scheme was drawn up. Number one priority was the Möhne, the most important dam for the Ruhr and one built of stone blocks, so more susceptible to Wallis's depth charge. The Sorpe, a massive earthwork on a concrete core, was only exceeded in importance by the Möhne but it was probably not breachable, so it was relegated to number three priority. Number two would be the Eder dam, not a supplier to the Ruhr but stone built and able to cause a lot of damage if it flooded.

Experimental parameters had been decided. The charge would be given back-spin as it was dropped, helping to keep the bounce low and giving it a tendency to stick to the dam wall as it sank. It would have to be dropped at a precise speed, at a precise height, and at a precise distance from the dam wall. The assumption was that the aircraft would be under fire while doing this, and they would be doing it at full moon, in May when the water behind the dams would be at its highest.

All this was planned, the squadron was assembled, the op had a name – Operation Chastise – it was the end of March, but much of the technical detail had not yet been worked out. How do you fly over calm water at exactly 60ft? You can't judge it by eye and no altimeter was accurate enough. How do you get up to the required speed to drop the depth charge, a 4ft by 5ft drum, when it's hanging outside a heavily loaded aircraft causing a great deal of drag? Assuming you can make the speed at the height, can you keep the aircraft perfectly level so that the drum hits the water flat, rather than at an angle, the slightest tipping to the side being enough to send it off course? How do you get the job lined up when you have to fly through hills and vales to get to the reservoir in the first place?

Low flying was the first thing. They would have to fly over a large tract of enemy territory as low and as fast as possible, on routes that kept them away from the flak guns and below German radar. The new squadron had the necessary for that, Lancasters. They began training in earnest in early April, flying complicated routes through upland districts and over lakes and reservoirs, requiring perfect navigation and a lot of nerve. Such low flying was normally banned as a serious disciplinary offence. The pilots loved it; not all crew members had quite the same sense of adventure.

The only way they could attach the depth charge, codenamed Upkeep, to the aircraft was to fit it in a rack outside the bomb bay. It would be connected to a motor inside, which would get it spinning at 500rpm before release. These charges weighed over 4 tons and were quite the opposite of streamlined. When they tried flying with dummies in the racks, they found such an adverse effect on aircraft performance that, level at very low altitude, the correct speed for dropping, 220mph, could not be reached. The answer was to come in to the reservoir at a fast dive before levelling out, expecting to be at the right speed at the release point, no more than 475yd away from the dam wall and no less than 425.

The mid-upper turret was removed to save drag and weight, and the gunner put in the front turret, which would probably be more use against the dam defences anyway. Fuel was heavy; they couldn't take luxuriously spare amounts.

The height-measuring problem had been solved by fitting two spotlights beneath the aircraft at an angle to each other. When their two circles of light on the water touched, the Lanc was at 60ft.

Came the day, 16 May 1943, after 2,000 hours of training and 2,500 practice bombs. The skippers in their sections were:

- Gibson, Hopgood, Martin;
- Young, Maltby, Shannon;
- Maudslay, Knight, Astell;
- McCarthy, Byers, Barlow, Rice, Munro.

In reserve were Townsend, Brown, Anderson, Ottley and Burpee.

At the operational briefing in the afternoon, the crews and most of the captains heard for the first time what the targets were to be and examined models of the Möhne and the Sorpe. Those crews going to the Sorpe had a longer, diversionary route to the north of Holland and so would take off first, but the first to attack would be the Möhne wave. Once this dam was breached, those crews still with an Upkeep would fly to the Eder and possibly on to other targets as directed by radio from base. The third wave would arrive later and be ready to finish any busting not completed.

All were to follow complicated routes of easily recognisable pinpoints but avoiding flak concentrations. Apart from a few Mosquitos dropping flares over German cities in dummy raids, these were the only Bomber Command aircraft flying over Holland and Germany that night. It was hoped they'd be taken for minor intrusions, low priority. Quite rightly, fighters were not expected to cause any trouble. They would not be looking for heavy bombers so far below them.

Things started badly. McCarthy found his aircraft, Q-Queenie, unserviceable with coolant fluid leaking from an engine. T-Tom was the spare, a new Lanc arrived on squadron that day. They'd had time to fit it with a bomb but not with the spotlights. That didn't matter for the Sorpe; they were using a different method. Joe and his boys ran over to it. In the cockpit of every bomber, and never supposed to leave it, was a card on which was written essential information for the pilot. It gave the deviations calibrated for that aircraft's compass. When the navigator called the course, the pilot adjusted it slightly according to the data on the card. T-Tom's card wasn't there.

Calling down the wrath of all the gods onto instrument technicians everywhere, McCarthy climbed out and set off for the instrument section, letting everyone know in loud and universal terms what he thought about erks and jerks. Flt Sgt 'Chiefy' Powell, the senior squadron NCO, found the missing card and placated the fuming McCarthy with it, also providing a replacement parachute for the one that had opened by itself and which Joe had been quite prepared to fly without.

Meanwhile, the rest of McCarthy's Sorpe section had taken off – Barlow, Munro, Byers and Rice, followed by Gibson and the rest of those Möhne bound. McCarthy and crew got going at last, on their own, something like 30 minutes late, and as they flew over the sea the first score went to the enemy. Light flak in Holland did such damage to Munro's kite that the crew had no intercom, the skipper had no VHF to speak to the rest of the raiders, the rear turret wouldn't work properly and neither would the compass. They had no choice but to turn back.

A few minutes later, Rice flew so low that his props touched the sea. Trying to climb out of danger he dipped his Upkeep in the waves, lost it, and scooped up gallons of water through the hole torn in the fuselage floor. With his rear gunner thinking he might become the first airman to drown in a flying Lancaster, Rice too turned for home.

Flying at zero feet assumed perfect navigation. If they didn't fly over the correct pinpoints, they couldn't see anything else to identify where they were. Byers, in uncertainty, climbed to try and spot something that would confirm his position and the flak got him. No survivors, only one body found. McCarthy, now about 20 minutes behind but on the right track and so low he was at one point between two sand dunes, found the flak gunners fully awake to this mysterious incursion but unable to do more to him than one hit on the retracted undercarriage.

Following take-off 2 hours and 20 minutes earlier, Barlow flew his Lancaster into Germany, across the Rhine and into some power cables. All were killed. Astell of the Möhne wave, possibly damaged by flak, got as far as Borken before he too flew into cables; all killed.

Coming in to the reservoir, the Möhnesee, the attackers had to dive to get up speed and level out at the approximate height, when they had something like 10 seconds to make the exact height and the exact direction. Gibson was first in against the Möhne dam and his bomb exploded very close to the target. Hopgood, possibly injured and with a flak-damaged Lanc, was terminally shot about as he came in. His Upkeep bounced over the dam and blew up the power station below.

Alfred Lengherd was an anti-aircraft gunner at the Möhne dam, a cushy number for a soldier as no aircraft were ever expected to try bombing in this ridiculously difficult terrain. Alfred spent his days and nights when he was on shift reading, playing cards, chatting to his mates, and he lived only 20 miles away in Dortmund where he was far more likely to be bombed than at his place of work, as had been demonstrated only ten days previously:

On the moonlit night of 16 May, I was at my gun post inside one of the towers on the dam. A bomber came straight towards me at zero feet; there seemed to be no space between the bomber and the water. There were two spotlights shining from the bomber onto the surface, which I could not understand. The night was so bright I could read my newspaper, so why did they need spotlights?

Then I saw it coming towards the dam, something that looked like a big ball, skipping across the water. It jumped over the nets [anti-torpedo defences], hit the wall and sank. A few moments later, the dam shook. I also was shaking. I had never seen such daring nor anything like the rolling mine that hopped over the water so easily.

We were now busy returning fire. More bombers had come and their gunfire was greater than ours. They shot the roof right off our tower. I could see flashes from our guns hidden in the hills. The sky was alight with tracer and fragments of stone were flying everywhere. One bomber was hit by our guns. We knew he was in trouble and watched him crash 20 or 30 kilometres away [Hopgood]. Then the raid was over, but we could still hear the drone of the bombers.

Martin bombed, was hit by flak and missed with his Upkeep. Dinghy Young did a perfect run, also Maltby, while Gibson and Martin flew about with nav lights on to draw the fire from the dam's defences. Each bomb produced a great tower of water and a flood over the top of the dam, but when everything settled down the dam was still there. As Shannon was about to go in, it split open. Young's bomb had weakened it so severely that it may well have gone anyway, but Maltby's sealed its fate. It was breached.

Lengherd: 'We heard this noise, like a giant tree being split in half. There was 160,000,000 cubic metres of water pressed against the dam, and out came the water. Incredible was the sound, and spectacular the effect. The valley was soon flooded and we saw the power station had gone.'

Gibson sent Martin and Maltby home and, with Young accompanying as deputy leader, ready to take over direction if Gibson went down, flew with Shannon, Maudsley and Knight to the next dam, the Eder, where there was no flak at all because the Germans were certain nobody could get a bomber in there. Shannon made five runs in fog, almost crashing each time, without dropping. Maudsley bombed and seemed to suffer in the blast. Shannon tried twice more and did bomb, and hit. Knight hit on his third run and that was enough. The dam collapsed and the codeword 'Dinghy' was transmitted home.

This was the first example of a bombing-management technique that later became standard practice. Raids would have a master bomber or master of ceremonies who would direct the attack, which was what Gibson had been doing and what Young would have had to do. When Joe McCarthy, the blond bear from Brooklyn, eventually reached what his navigator told him was the Sorpe reservoir, he had nobody to please but himself. He didn't know his colleagues had been killed or gone home. He was late, there was nobody else about, and the dam, if it was there, was hidden in the mist.

Skimming the water on a dummy run to investigate, there was the dam. It was the right one, too, from his memories of the model at briefing. He had the same difficulties as the others finding a way in at sufficient speed and with enough time to find his height and direction, and it took him a number of runs before he could drop his charge, without spinning it and taking his line from a church steeple. It hardly bounced, hit, exploded, and knocked down some of the upper works, but bust the dam was not. Some 18 months later, 9 Squadron would go to the Sorpe with 18 Lancasters, 1 captained by American Ed Stowell, armed with Barnes Wallis's Tallboy, the earthquake bomb, and, despite 2 direct hits, also fail to shift it.

The reserve force was directed to the Sorpe and other dams. Burpee was shot down near Gilze Rijen airfield in Holland, on his outward way. Brown made ten runs before dropping, and hit but to no effect. The target was invisible in the mist when Anderson arrived, so he turned away. Ottley was shot down near Hamm, heading for the Lister dam.

Dinghy Young had done his bit and was tearing back to base as fast as his low altitude would let him. The route took him around and between gun emplacements on coastal Holland, especially wanting to avoid the well-defended area by the Ijmuiden E-boat base. He strayed a little, got himself in range of the Ijmuiden guns at Castricum-aan-Zee, and they had him and all his men.

The dams raiders were among the most daring and brilliant airmen of the war. No praise could be high enough for their courage, determination and skill. Their exploits were met with great acclaim, giving a huge boost to civil morale and the Bomber Command image, and a new phrase to the language, Dam Busters. The actual results, the real damage to the German war machine, turned out to be rather less hurtful than had been forecast, mostly because the indestructible Sorpe could keep the Ruhr supplied while the Möhne was repaired.

Of the 19 Lancasters that went to the dams, 11 came back. Out of those eight crews lost, only three men parachuted into imprisonment. That was 53 men killed, a heavy price, but what remained of the squadron was special. The dams raid produced 33 decorations for 617 Squadron: a VC for Gibson, DSOs for McCarthy and 4 others, bars to DFCs for 4, 10 DFCs, and 12 DFMs, many of them posthumous.

Air Chief Marshal Harris had never been keen on the idea of attacking what he called 'panacea targets', by which he meant key pressure points identified by the boffins and mandarins of the Air Ministry, destroying which was bound to set Hitler back by years but which always expected excessive sacrifices by his bomber crews. Harris had seen the dams in something of the same light, and summed it up thus: 'The successful breaching [of the dams] . . . was merely one outstanding incident in what must have been a period of indescribable strain for the three million inhabitants of the great industrial region of the Ruhr.'

For a while following the dams raid, nobody seemed to know quite what to do with X Squadron, now fully equipped with number, 617, badge showing a breached dam, and motto: *'Après moi le deluge'*, adapted from something Louis XV's mistress Madame de Pomadour said. They settled down to keep their corporate hand in with training.

At the end of May, McCarthy did alternate high and low formation flying on four consecutive days in Q-Queenie, her leaks repaired, and on right through June with cross-countries and more of the same, and on and on, halfway through July. New squadron, one op, what next?

Normal service for 9 Squadron had resumed with raid after raid on the Ruhr, after a nine-day stand-down. Bob Van Note and the rest were slated for Dortmund, 23 May, a huge raid with over 800 bombers, which devastated the city and dismantled the steelworks entirely. Then it was Düsseldorf, Essen, and Wuppertal, or at least the Barmen half of Wuppertal, which was about 1,250 acres of houses and factories lying in a narrow valley overlooked by wooded hills. It was a Saturday night. Many of the chief civic officials were out of town, as they were every weekend. Well, Wuppertal had never been raided before.

Van Note reported: *Large concentration of fires appeared to be in the closely built-up city area of Barmen and extending into the narrow belt.* The town's firefighters were not prepared for a raid of this magnitude, over 700 aircraft, and their senior officers were enjoying an evening elsewhere. In the narrow byways of the old centre, accurately hit by concentrated bombing, the fires caught and set off a raging tempest. As with Lübeck just over a year earlier, this raid demonstrated what could be achieved with incendiaries and conventional explosives: the firestorm. Something like 1,000 acres, 80 per cent of Barmen, was gone.

Ops were briefed than cancelled on 2, 5, 6, 7, and 9 June, and Van Note only wanted three for his collection. Düsseldorf and Bochum followed, 11 and 12 June, big raids destroying hundreds of acres, thousands of buildings and killing thousands of people. Düsseldorf, efficiently as one might expect, listed 42 factories making goods for the war effort having to cease production, while 35 more could function only partly.

Oberhausen, 14 June, and for Van Note it was all over. He'd done it, he'd survived a tour, flying 20 out of the 30 in his faithful Lancaster ED493 WS/A-Apple. He could transfer to the USAAF as a captain, serve on attachment with the Air Ministry on strategic planning, be awarded his DFC in the August, and marry Miss Marjory Sullivan of Lincoln.

Winning of awards, announcement thereof in the *London Gazette* and the actual presentation were often long separated by wartime priorities. One day in October 1944 the happy couple, she in a fur coat, he in his USAAF uniform with wings and Bronze Star, would set off from their London apartment for Buckingham Palace. There, Captain Van Note would become the first American officer to receive his DFC from King George VI.

Jonah Reeves didn't go to Oberhausen; he was navigating on a special cross-country exercise, and next night it was *intensive high-level bombing practice*, and the next: *The five special crews continued their training.* On the afternoon of 20 June the target was revealed: tonight the five special crews would go in bright moonlight as part of a group of 60, to the old Zeppelin sheds at Friedrichshafen, shores of Lake Constance, the Bodensee, where the enemy was making Würzburg radar sets, the devices used by nightfighter ground controllers.

It would be the first ever shuttle raid: go, bomb, do not return through the flocks of waiting fighters but fly on, land far away, recover, and hit somewhere else on the way back. In this case, far away was the north African base at Blida, on the coastal strip near Algiers, and the somewhere else would be the Italian naval base at La Spezia. It was also a technical first, using an aiming method called offset marking, and a technical second, following Gibson and the dam busters by having a raid manager, a master bomber who would decide the detailed conduct of the raid on the spot.

Offset marking was a development made necessary by the bombers' increasing success. When target indicators were accurately bombed, smoke could obscure them and make further marking very difficult. The notion in 5 Group was another step up in skill, to mark somewhere a specified distance and direction away from the target and do a timed run from there. The raid manager would judge if the marking was right, or adjust the bombing runs accordingly.

All such innovations ignored, or regarded as given, the inconveniences of opposition. On this night they found the defences extremely fierce in the moonlight. The manager moved the bombing height up by 5,000ft. It was not a big target, although beside it were other valuable objectives including the Maybach tank-engine works and an aircraft research establishment where, unbeknown to the Allies, the Germans were working on an entirely new kind of fighter-bomber.

The Dornier Do335 had two engines, not in the wings but nose and tail of the fuselage, one pulling, one pushing, and it was designed to fly at well over 400mph. One day it would do almost 500mph, the fastest piston-engined aircraft ever, but too late to fight for Germany. Also at this site, again not known to Allied intelligence, was a subsidiary branch of the Peenemünde programme to develop the secret rocket weapon later known as the V2.

Reeves's pilot, Red Wakeford, reported: *Bombs aimed by indirect method, time and distance run from predetermined point. We thought we got a hangar. Good fires seen.* One in ten of the bombs dropped hit the radar factory and smashed about half of it and its equipment. Some of the others hit the tank-engine works and the secret factories. The Germans had long-term plans for V2 production there; the plans now had to be torn up.

No. 9 Squadron had taken off around 21:45, bombed at about 02:45 and were landing in Algeria around 07:45 looking forward to a couple of days off in the sunshine. The dam busters also had been having days off, too many days off, but in the middle of the boredom of training flights, snooker and crosswords came a most unusual trip. They were going up to London to see the Queen, and the King, the 33 of them who had been decorated. Guy Gibson had been awarded the Victoria Cross and there were five Distinguished Service Orders, the highest honour for serving airmen apart from the VC, including Joe McCarthy. They had a boozy time of it on the train and partied most of the night, waking up in the Savoy Hotel in time to comb their hair and set off for Buckingham Palace where Queen Elizabeth, a small and elegant lady, took quite an interest in Big Joe and so she should have. He was unquestionably the first ex-Coney Island lifeguard to be awarded the British DSO.

From Algeria, 9 Squadron headed for home, hitting La Spezia on the way. Flying on, they saw the Alps mostly covered in silver cloud except for the highest peaks, Mont Blanc for instance, poking up in the fairytale moonlight to remind even the most battle-hardened soul that there was still beauty in the world.

Aileen Walker was a WAAF waitress in the officers' mess:

We were all waiting for them to come back and when Red Wakeford and Jonah Reeves and their boys came in, they were all carrying bunches of bananas except my young man, Harold Hawkridge.* Nobody had seen a banana for years. They were like treasure. Anyway, I said to him, well, if you can't be bothered to bring me some bananas back, I can't be bothered to see you any more. He said, I've sent you something a lot better than bananas but you'll have to wait for it. Just a couple of weeks.

That was 24 June. Wakeford, Reeves, Harry Hawkridge and co. had work to do the next night, to Gelsenkirchen, when they came home early with a turret u/s, and on 28 June at Cologne. It was cloudy. The pathfinders were late and dropped skymarkers. Only half of the

* Wakeford's bomb aimer.

Oboe Mosquito contingent got there to drop target indicators. Wakeford reported: *Primary attacked 0145, 18,500 feet. Bombed on ETA. Flares subsequently seen to drop in same position. Bombing results not seen apart from dispersed glow of fires below cloud.*

Bombing results were extraordinary. The dispersed glow of fires represented 600 aircraft inflicting the greatest reverse for Germany of the whole Battle of the Ruhr: 6,500 buildings destroyed, another 15,000 damaged, 4,377 people killed, 10,000 injured and 230,000 made homeless. A government led by a conventionally sane statesman might have begun sueing for peace after such a blow. Now it was plain what Bomber Command could do, and the increasingly effective daylight attacks of the 8th United States Army Air Force meant unrelenting bombardment for the Fatherland.

Cologne again, 3 July, and as always there were fighters on the way. Unusually, there were also fighters over the target, the first example of the German *Wilde Sau* (wild boar) stratagem. Rather than relying on radar and control from the ground to pick off his Tommy in the bomber stream, a wild boar lurked above the city being bombed, hoping that the flak gunners would stick to an agreement not to fire above a certain height. In the glare of searchlights, flares and the glow of fires below, the wild boars would pick out targets of opportunity. On this night they claimed they'd had 12 victims but the local flak gunners made the same claim, and of the 33 bombers lost to enemy action that night, at least 20 fell to fighters patrolling the coastal regions. Only one was definitely shot down by a fighter at the target but there is no doubt that the wild boars mounted plenty of attacks. So unused were bomber crews to it that several misreported being shot at by their own.

Who shot Jonah Reeves we shall never know, but he went down on his fifteenth op, with all his friends in Lancaster ED689 WS/K, on the way in to the bombing run in the early hours of Sunday 4 July. His mother, remarried and back in Oneida, living on Grove Street as Mrs Holden, received the telegram on the Tuesday.

The aircraft ended up in the River Rhine but they never found Jonah or Red Wakeford, or Harry Hawkridge. Their names are engraved at Runnymede. Jonah's name also appears on the honour rolls of Durhamville and Oneida.

Aileen did receive the something that seemed better than bananas, a letter from her sweetheart proposing marriage. For an instant she thought it must mean that Harry was missing but alive. Then she saw the date it was written. It had been posted from Algiers.

Noting that loss was Sgt William Wrigley Watts Turnbull, pilot, of San Antonio, Texas, and known, naturally enough, as Tex. His father, Elliott Bay Turnbull, had been born in Pueblo, Mexico, of English parents in 1880. The family moved to Texas when Elliott was 10 and, by the time William Wrigley was that age, dad was a sales manager in the oil business and they were living at 530 Geneseo Road. Mother Annie, born in Texas, also had English parents, so there were strong connections with the old country for the lad, youngest of three brothers.

He and his crew could have allowed themselves the odd cold butterfly when they saw their first op on the battle order: Cologne, 8 July. This was the third raid in a week. Thousands of buildings were rubble and half the population was homeless.

Bomber Command's 619 Squadron was formed at Woodhall Spa in April 1943, first operated 11 June to Düsseldorf and towards the end of that month received its first American in the bulky shape of Nick Knilans, there to learn about the opulent and eccentric life that was the lot of operational bomber aircrew:

> Breakfast in the sergeants' mess was tea, which I was getting used to, and either scrambled powdered eggs or fried bread and tomatoes, or sausages which were supposed to be 40 per cent meat although we doubted it was that much. I would walk then to the pilots' room of B Flight to see my flight commander, Sqn Ldr Jerry Scorer. He kept two machine-gun bullets at the front of his desk. If they were laid horizontal, there were no ops that night. If they were upright, the war was on.

The war was about to start in earnest for Sgt Knilans, the farmer's boy from Wisconsin. Over the next few months the name of Knilans would become synonymous with scraping through horrors. Comparative statistics do not exist but it would be a fair wager that Knilans's percentage of ops coming home on three or two engines was higher than any other pilot's with the possible exception of Joe McCarthy, but first he had to have his L-driver trips.

As a useful induction, second dickies depended largely on the attitude of the senior pilot. Sometimes the student would be told to keep out of the way of everybody, as was Knilans with Sqn Ldr Scorer on that same Cologne trip Tex Turnbull was on. Knilans: 'I could see the surf line as we crossed the French coast. I knew that the German radar was plotting our height and course, and the information would be passed to their flak batteries and nightfighters. I became fully aware that we were being hunted. They meant to kill us if they could.'

Knilans spent most of the time sitting on the emergency bed, plugged into the oxygen and the intercom:

The sky over Cologne was as bright as a cloudy day, and we were leaving this lit-up area when the rear gunner shouted 'Dive port' and fired his guns. Scorer responded instantly and we dropped like a stone to our left. 'Corkscrew,' yelled the mid upper, and Scorer put the aircraft through a series of violent climbs and turns. The fighter didn't attack and the gunners didn't fire again, the tail gunner complaining that he couldn't because the corkscrew had been so brutal that he'd been pinned in his seat.

It had been a Bf109, a wild boar, and it had followed them part-way through the corkscrew before they lost it.

News would soon reach Nick Knilans that his mate, Ken McLean, the inventor of the Highland Torpedo, had gone down on that Cologne trip, his first, all crew killed. Flt Sgt Kenneth Hector Wally McLean, of Vulcan, Alberta, was 20 years old.

Three nights later, Knilans was seconded to a more kindly dicky, Flt Lt Stanley Jones, but his abilities as a magnet for jeopardy were confirmed:

We were for Turin and the skipper let me stand behind his seat and observe there. We flew in cloud across France and into clear air near the Alps, when yellow streaks of cannon shells flashed over our port wing. 'Dive starboard,' one of the gunners shouted. 'What the hell,' said the pilot as he complied. Both gunners were firing and shouting, then it stopped. They said they'd got the bandit. He'd exploded. The skipper thought he must have been following us in the cloud for quite a while. The gunners said he must have been a new boy to attack us like that in full view. Usually they came at us from below, where they couldn't be seen.

At Turin, Knilans's opinion was that the searchlights and flak were disorganised compared with Cologne. The target indicators went down a few minutes either side of 02:00 and Jones bombed then, as did most of 9 Squadron, the exception being Tex Turnbull who was half an hour late and so had only the fires to aim at. As dawn broke, Knilans stood and watched as they flew up the Bay of Biscay at wave-hopping height and landed back at base at 09:18, after a journey of 10 hours and 50 minutes. 'I was a bit upset to be served only grease-fried bread for breakfast.'

After two second dickies, the new pilot was generally considered ready to take command of his own ship and crew, the members of which had not had any second dickies. For those six boys and men, the first op was for real when they would, of course, be very glad that their skipper was so experienced.

There had been talk about disbanding 617 Squadron but it was decided to keep it, get it back up to strength and give it special jobs to do. Guy Gibson VC, DSO and Bar, DFC and Bar was told that 75 operations was enough. He was grounded and relieved of his command, to be replaced by Sqn Ldr George Holden DSO, DFC and Bar who took over Gibson's crew for their first op since the dams, to electricity transformer stations in Italy. Rebellion was fomenting against Mussolini, the Italians' enthusiasm for the war was dissipating, and the Germans were frantically reinforcing in the south to try to hold the invading Allies in Sicily. Any reduction in the power supplies to the railways would have a correspondingly beneficial effect on the invasion.

In total 12 Lancasters of 617 would go, 15 July, with 12 more from other 5 Group squadrons, including 3 from No. 9. There were three targets, all in the north: San Polo d'Enza, which was where McCarthy was going, Aquata Scriva, and Reggio nell' Emilia, which was 9 Squadron's target. The raid was a failure. The targets were hidden by mist, two Lancasters collided and fell, another crash-landed at Blida, and no damage was suffered by the transformers. As Joe McCarthy put it, 'If we'd had some flares with us we might have been able to see what we were doing.'

All three of our current Americans were in the air on 24 July. McCarthy and 617 were dropping bombs on the Tuscan port and naval base of Livorno, on their delayed way back from Algeria. They had little effect, as once again they were aiming blind through mist.

Turnbull on his third and Knilans on his first were off to Hamburg. This was the beginning of Operation Gomorrah, a six-raid attack including two daylights by the 8th USAAF, which would virtually annihilate Germany's second city. It was also the first use of a new RCM (Radar Counter Measure) called Window. Sheets of strong black paper were glued to thin aluminium foil and cut into strips, 27cm (almost 11in) long and 2cm wide. Floating down through the air, these lowest-tech devices utterly overwhelmed the enemy radar with false signals. The Würzburg ground control sets, linked to the fighters and the flak guns, and the airborne Lichtenstein sets carried by the fighters for close work, were rendered useless.

Nick Knilans:

We were carrying bundles of aluminum strips, black on one side, silvery on the other. Joe [Tate, bomb aimer] was to push them down a tube into our slipstream which burst the bundles into drifting clouds of strips. Over Hamburg, the searchlights whirled in circles instead of in steady motions. The flak barrage was widely scattered and exploding at many levels.

Another eyewitness, from 9 Squadron, described the same sight:

There was a marked absence of fighters and the ground defences seemed to be in serious disarray, with searchlights waving aimlessly about the sky and the flak bursting in confused patterns well below the main concentration. We saw two aircraft shot down but from the lower echelons of Wellingtons and Stirlings, which must have meant the flak batteries were having to rely on visual sightings because of the effect Window was having on their equipment.

Tex Turnbull bombed as per briefing with the city well ablaze, and saw a pall of black smoke up to 15,000ft. Other 9 Squadron crews reported the smoke at 18,000ft and fires still visible from 175 miles away. The Lancasters bombed from 20,000ft; like many, Knilans's photograph showed little more than smoke. His excitement was due when he reached home.

Aerodromes had a simple, practical arrangement of angled lights called the flight-path indicator. A pilot coming in to land too high would see a yellow, too low a red, and on the correct approach he'd see a green. Knilans, undercart and flaps down and slowed to landing speed, couldn't see any colours at all, his vision obscured by a thin layer of cloud at 1,000ft. At least, that's what the altimeter said.

Knilans recounted the moment: 'Joe was in his bomb aimer's compartment at the front of the aircraft, looking down through his Perspex, and all of a sudden he shouted "There's the ground." I slammed the four throttle levers full forward with my right hand, hauled back on the control column with my left, and yelled "Wheels up" at Ken [Ryall, flight engineer, 18 years old].'

There was a gravel pit near the end of the runway used as the base swimming pool, and beyond that the ground-crew barracks, hidden among trees. In the dim dawn light, Knilans recognised the familiar outlines of the gravel pit. Only thing was, they were in it, doing 100mph:

> The port wing struck a sandbar between two of the ponds we swam in on our days off, but we staggered upwards barely above stalling speed, slashing through the tops of a grove of trees with a thunderous roar of straining engines. Airmen came hurtling out of the barracks built beneath as we stripped branches off the trees and the trees stripped bits off our aircraft. My crew said nothing.

Something was wrong with both port engines and Ken Ryall had to stop them, so Knilans landed by eye on the two starboard ones, ignoring his altimeter which, as they came to a halt on the runway with only one brake working of two, registered 960ft. 'The groundcrew called me over to look at the port wing. The propellors had three blades, and all six had their tips bent back. It was after half past four in the morning. By 09:00 we were in the flight room being told we were on ops again that night.'

Joe Tate: 'Nick told me that I'd saved all their lives. All I'd done was see the ground. He saved our lives after that. Of course, we didn't know what we'd been saved for.'

That night was Essen, an attempt at the most important industrial target while Window was still working at maximum surprise effect. It was a big raid, over 700 aircraft, and a successful one. Perhaps Herr Doktor Gustav Krupp would have had a stroke anyway, or maybe it was the massive damage done to his factories that brought it on. Nick Knilans's damage was caused by several flak hits on his starboard wing, which lost them petrol and the use of one engine. It would have been death for them all had a heavy flak shell exploded in the main petrol tank rather than passing through.

The RAF was generally sympathetic enough to bomber crews not to send them to Germany three nights running but 26 July was a night off anyway, the only activity being six photoreconnaissance Mosquitos checking Hamburg. Knilans and crew did what most of them did when not required to fly for their lives:

We spent the afternoon resting in our Quonset hut [actually the less well-insulated British Nissen hut] looking forward to an evening at the pub. We could have caught a bus into Boston or Lincoln and gone to a dance but it was easier and more flexible to cycle to the Tollgate Inn, our local pub, handily situated near the Waafery. Next morning, the squadron leader's bullets were upright and we were off to Hamburg again.

The flak and searchlights were the usual nuisance and Knilans escaped from a fighter by hiding in the smoke rising from the ruined city. Tex Turnbull reported no special incidents and another American, Brig-Gen Fred Anderson, commander of the 8th USAAF, also watched from a Lancaster. He did not see a typical night. Losses over the two raids were light, averaging less than 2 per cent, showing the beneficial influence of Window.

The plan had been to remove Hamburg from the face of the earth. After those two raids, with the firestorm caused by the second one, there was still some of it left. Bomber Command went twice more, 29 July and 2 August, although the 8th USAAF had given it up as a bad job because they couldn't see their daylight targets through all the smoke.

The August raid was a failure, largely due to the filthy weather. Knilans: 'We were briefed by the met officer that we might encounter some severe thunderheads but he expected the target to be clear. We took off in a heavy, gusty rainstorm. It was like flying into a bottle of ink. All I could see were the luminous needles on the instrument panel.'

They managed to climb above the rain and were rewarded with the sight of huge columns of thunderclouds towering above them. As they approached Hamburg, they were dismayed to find dense, mountainous black anvils of cumulonimbus covering the city. If they were to bomb the target they'd have to do it from inside a thunderstorm. Knilans:

We had barely entered the storm cloud when the aircraft was caught in a strong down-draught. I pulled back on the stick but we were still descending. Blue streaks of static, St Elmo's Fire, flowed over the windshield and wings. Rime ice was forming on the wings and props only to break off and bang against the fuselage like flak. I struggled with the stick and rudder pedals while watching the altimeter unwind.

They had dropped 5,000ft in seconds and the Lanc would not obey commands. Something had to be done. 'I said "Drop the bombs and let's get the hell out of here", and the 12,500lb of bombs fell away at the same moment as we hit the updraught on the other side of the thunderhead.'

The Lancaster shot upwards as if it were no more substantial than a ping-pong ball on a fairground fountain. Knilans tried to control his rocket-like ascent with the stick hard forward against the instrument panel and full-right rudder. 'We popped out of the cloud at 21,000 feet standing on our starboard wing tip. The crew sat in stunned silence. I hadn't had time to be scared.'

Somehow in the middle of all that, a flak shell had passed through the tailplane no more than 2ft from the rear gunner. Nobody noticed, but flying home south of Bremen they did see some flares go up. These were signals from the ground to the radar-less wild-boar nightfighters. The Tommies were here. Knilans:

Joe shouted 'Bandit, ten o'clock low' and both gunners swivelled and saw the Bf109. Roy [Learmonth, Australian mid-upper gunner] got off a short burst, Gerry [Jackson, Scots rear gunner] a much longer one. Ken saw a lot of the bullets strike home as we dipped into a cloud and lost our attacker. Thankfully, that was the end of the excitement for the night.

The bombing had been widely scattered, with many crews choosing to go for alternative targets or dropping on whatever looked likely. It hardly mattered in objective terms. Hamburg, the greatest port in Europe, was finished. More than two-thirds of its population had fled.

A German nightfighter pilot, Wilhelm Johnen, among those totally bemused by Window over Hamburg, had this to say: '40,000 people were killed, a further 40,000 wounded and 900,000 were homeless or missing. This devastating raid on Hamburg had the effect of a red light on all the big German cities and on the whole German people. Everyone felt it was now high time to capitulate before any further damage was done, but the High Command insisted that the Total War should proceed.'

That 40,000 was an accurate figure for the second night, the firestorm, when many, many people were suffocated or poisoned by carbon monoxide as the fire sucked all the oxygen out of shelters and basements. Such a death rate was most exceptional; fatalities were usually in the hundreds. The first, third and fourth Hamburg raids were nearer the norm, with 2,000 killed altogether.

Every senior officer of the Luftwaffe wanted all aircraft production and all efforts of every sort directed to defence against the bombers, night and day, but the man in charge of Germany still dreamed of victory. 'The British will only be halted when their cities are destroyed. I can only win the war by dealing out more destruction to the enemy than he does to us,' said Hitler.

The second problem was that the Luftwaffe had no means for carrying out his wishes. Hitler believed he could win with his secret weapons programme, rumours of which had been reaching the Allies for months, but it was far from readiness and tangled in all sorts of problems. Earlier in the war they might indeed have destroyed cities, when the RAF nightfighter force hardly existed. If they had gone back to Coventry, say, and hit it three more times, instead of just the once, and repeated the medicine on other provincial centres instead of trying to obliterate London, what effect might that have had on British morale and industrial production? Flying from France, they would have had no trouble finding Birmingham, Leeds–Bradford, Manchester, Liverpool, Newcastle, Bristol. All of these places and more, where British war production was concentrated, could have been given the Hamburg treatment but, by now, the *Angriffsführer England* was almost powerless. After a series of meetings with his most senior aides, Göring issued the order. Defence was to be everything, whatever Hitler might say. They had to stop the bombers or lose the war.

Until the spring of 1939, the Handley Page Heyford biplane was standard issue in Bomber Command. These are 9 Squadron B Flight pilots in front of a Heyford in 1938.

At the outbreak of war, a mere seven active service squadrons were equipped with the RAF's only modern bomber, the Vickers Wellington. These are 9 Squadron's first Wellingtons; squadron letters KA were changed to WS as hostilities began. L4275 KA/H, flying centre beyond B, was lost in Britain's first modern air battle, 4 September 1939, Brunsbüttel, all crew killed.

This wartime advertisement was produced by the Royds agency, which employed Sedgwick Whiteley Webster of Litchfield County, Connecticut. RAF fighter pilots were known as the Brylcreem Boys.

OPERATIONS RECORD BOOK.

Appendix   R.A.F. Form 541.

DETAIL OF WORK CARRIED OUT.

Date 27/28th November 1941. (Cont.) By 9 Squadron

Aircraft Type and No.	Crew.	Duty.	Time Up.	Time Down.	Details of Sortie or Flight.	References.
WELLINGTON Mk.III 5397	SGT. RAMEY, SGT. ARMSTRONG, SGT. AMPHLETT, SGT. STEVENS, SGT. RUTHERFORD, SGT. BILSBOROUGH	Attack DUSSELDORF 'B'	1713	?	Bombed target area, and bursts seen. Starboard engine caught fire after crossing Dutch Coast and crew baled out over HERNE BAY. Two of crew being drowned and the rest safe.	I 227
3985	SGT. WILMOT, SGT. HARRIS, SGT. WELSH, SGT. SHEPHERD, SGT. CASSIDY, SGT. HAWKINS	do.	1715	2108	Bombed target area, and bursts seen.	
3390	SGT. TELLING, SGT. SAMPSON, P/O. SAUL, SGT. BANKS, SGT. EVANS, SGT. AITCHESON	do.	1721	2106	Bombs dropped about ¼ mile South of aiming point in built up area. Bursts seen, and incendiaries started fires	
3397	SGT. TAYLOR, SGT. PATRICK, SGT. JASPER, SGT. HENRY, SGT. SANDERS, SGT. WATSON	do.	1724	2126	Bombed target area, bursts seen one of which was very bright.	
3305	SGT. BULFORD, SGT. CLARKE, SGT. POLLARD, SGT. CALVER, SGT. RUSHTON	do.	1731	2150	Bombs dropped in believed DUISBURG and bursts seen. Landed at MOUNT FARM, HARWELL	
3283	SGT. SHAW, SGT. VIGGERS, P/O. INSOH, SGT. SWIDERSKI, SGT. STUFFIN, SGT. LOVIS.	Attack Docks & Shipping at OSTEND	1741	1936	Owing to Navigational error attacked DUNKIRK, bombs being dropped on Docks 6,7, and 8.	

128

Sgt Warren Ramey was from Whitefish Bay, Wisconsin. The official report of his ditching reads: 'Crew baled out over Herne Bay. Two of crew being drowned and the rest safe.' This is how RAF understatement summarised the horrors of war. Despite the honest assessments of the other crews, only one or possibly two of the 86 bomber crews on duty that night actually hit the target town, and nobody hit the railyard target.

Sgt Ramey signs for his crew's property to be released from custody by Herne Bay police. Warren Ramey, aged 17, was featured in his high-school magazine 'The Tower', 1936 edition. His caption read: Never works, never worries, never flunks, never hurries.

Kent County Constabulary,
St. Augustine Division,
Herne Bay Station,
24th November, 1941.

Sir,

OCCURRENCE.

Kent County Constabulary,
St.Augustine Division.
Herne Bay Station.
29th November,1941.

d from Inspector C.W.Setterfield, Herne Bay Police
the undermentioned property :-

Property of Sergeant RUTHERFORD.

est.
er wool-lined sleeveless coat.
g helmet.
leather gloves.
 skull cap.
glove.
hute and harness.

Property of Sergeant Pilot RAMEY.

g helmet and attachments.

Property of Sergeant STEVENS.

est.
hute and harness.
er wool-lined sleeveles coat (damaged and wet)
        Property of Sergeant AMPHLETT.
lest.

Miscellaneous.

of wool lined boots damaged (recovered from plane)
ined boot   (::::::::::::::::::::)
g helmet (Name inside Sergeant WALTON. R.A. No.1177185
         (Found on Coastal Road, Chestfield.)

Received

Sgt. W. T. Ramey

Date.

Nov. 29, 1941

Witness.

With America in the war after Pearl Harbor, Bomber Command could drop messages from Franklin D. Roosevelt as well as from Winston Churchill.

Aircraftman Storey, in early days of training with the RCAF, was photographed by his beloved sister Susan at the Storeys' holiday house on Great Cranberry Island.

This photograph of Anderson Storey, of Jamaica Plain, Massachusetts, Wellington and Lancaster pilot killed on the last of his tour of 30 operations, was found in the Roll of Honour file at his old school, Deerfield Park Academy.

The Storey family home, 220 Perkins Street, overlooks the famous pond in Jamaica Plain.

New, purpose-built home for No. 9 Squadron: Bardney aerodrome, Lincolnshire. The dots on the dispersals are Lancasters. This photograph is said to have been taken on a German reconnaissance flight.

A contemporary picture of St James, Long Island, where Joe McCarthy was born.

Big Joe was always good for a laugh, such as putting a flare down the Wing Commander's chimney.

In ED877 AJ/A, 'Dinghy' Young and all his crew perished in the sea after being hit by flak on the way home from the dams. In total, 8 out of 19 Lancasters were lost on this raid.

YEAR 1943	AIRCRAFT		PILOT, OR 1ST PILOT	2ND PILOT, PUPIL OR PASSENGER	DUTY (INCLUDING RESULTS AND REMARKS)
MONTH / DATE	Type	No.			
—	—	—	—	—	—— TOTALS BROUGHT FORWARD
MAY	LANCASTER				
13	" "	Q ED 915/6	SELF	CREW	BOMBING — TACTICAL RUN'S
13	" "	Q ED 415/6	SELF	CREW	BOMBING — SPOTLIGHT RUN'S
14	" "	Q ED 915/6	SELF	CREW	X COUNTRY — SPECIAL EXERCISE
17	" "	T	SELF	CREW	OPERATION'S MOHNE — SORPE DAM MAY-22- D.S.O.
29	" "	Q ED 915/6	SELF	CREW	HIGH LEVEL FORMATION
30	" "	Q ED 915/6	SELF	CREW	LOW LEVEL FORMATION
31	" "	Q ED 915/6	SELF	CREW	LOW LEVEL FORMATION " " BOMBING
31	" "	Q ED 915/6	SELF	CREW	HIGH LEVEL FORMATION
	Martin SH.O.1 O.C. B-FLIGHT		Summary	MAY 1943	
			UNIT	617 Squadron	LANCASTER
	Gibson WING Comm		Date	31-5-43	
	O.C. 617 Squadron		Signature	Joseph C. McCarthy	

GRAND TOTAL [Cols. (1) to (10)] 715 Hrs 10 Mins.   TOTALS CARRIED FORWARD

A historic document: the page from McCarthy's log book listing his flight to the Sorpe dam.

Joe McCarthy (left) with men from other 617 crews, in London to meet the King and Queen after the dams raid.

Top row, left to right: Colwell, Strong, Stenback, Sukeforth, Silcott, Ruhl, Taney, Mock, E. A. de Schweinitz
Fourth row: Campbell, G. de Schweinitz, O'Brien, Lovern, Rappe, Gelwick, Youngblut, Mendenhall, Barber, Varner
Third row: Ickis, Vosmer, Bartley, Morrison, Bacon, Sneddon, Meyer, Blood, Polzin, Highfill
Second row: Reed, Gosch, Griffith, Cummings, Krueger, Beaver, Partridge, Bereman, MacLeod, Van Note
Bottom row: Brink, Chapman, Gordon, Church, Ainsley, Aldred, Nossaman, Theobald, Pfannenschmid

Robert Van Note, first on the right, second row from the front, at the University of Colorado, 1940. He was from Boulder.

Bob Van Note, on the left, reading the papers in the early summer sunshine outside the officers' mess, RAF Bardney. His companion, New Zealander Sq/Ldr Murray Hobbs DFC, would be killed on 25 June 1943, shortly after this photograph was taken.

Capt and Mrs Van Note with his DFC outside Buckingham Palace, 1944.

Van Note, between college and air force, having learned to fly at the Spartan School of Aeronautics in Tulsa, Oklahoma.

Crews of 9 Squadron at the general briefing before the first ever 'shuttle' raid, 20 June 1943: daylight to Friedrichshaven, fly on to Algeria; hit an Italian target – La Spezia – on the way home, 23 June. American navigator Flg Off Jonah Reeves, from Madison County, New York State, is standing, third from right, wearing a Mae West life-jacket, looking over skipper Red Wakeford's shoulder.

Next stop: Blida aerodrome, Algeria, via Friedrichshaven. Flg Off Reeves is at the top of the ladder as the Wakeford crew board 'their' Lancaster ED689 WS/K. After two more trips to Germany, they were shot down in this same Lanc at Cologne, 3 July, all killed.

Nick Knilans from Walworth County, Wisconsin, and crew. Standing, from left: Gerry Jackson, rear gunner (would be killed 4 October 1943), Ken Ryall, flight engineer, Roy Learmonth, mid-upper gunner; seated: Harry Geller, navigator, Nick Knilans, pilot, Joe Tate, bomb aimer, Les Knell, wireless operator.

At about the time Knilans and Tex Turnbull were joining the war, 9 Squadron's honours board was already showing quite a lot of experience. The unofficial motto 'There's always bloody something' was the favourite utterance of an irascible medical officer, surveying queues of the halt and the unserviceable in earlier days.

Keep smiling through, just like we always do: WAAFs at Bardney. How else could they keep going?

"I think it's wonderful how the little ones manage to keep up with the big ones."
Punch cartoon, 3 September 1943.

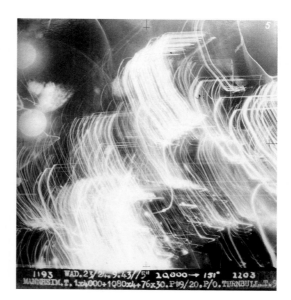

Plt Off William Wrigley Watts Turnbull of San Antonio, Texas, found the light flak rather spoiled his photograph of Mannheim at night, September 1943.

Pilots of 9 Squadron, autumn 1944. From the left: McDonnel, Stowell, Keeley and Laws. All were survivors.

RAF Woodhall Spa, home of 617 Squadron from January 1944.

The Gnome & Rhône engineering works at Limoges, before 617 Squadron bombed it, and afterwards, in February 1944.

A raid's worth of the giant Tallboy bomb, here seen at Bardney but first used by 617 flying from Woodhall Spa to the railway tunnel at Saumur, June 1944.

The Stabilised Automatic Bomb Sight, Sabs, used by 617, was a tricky and temperamental piece of kit which rewarded high skill with great accuracy.

Sgt J.E. Stowell of Detroit, Michigan, nicknamed Jesse, in training and ready to find a crew.

Brest, 14 August 1944, Ed Stowell's fourth operation, looking to sink old warships about to be used to block the harbour.

Tallboy photograph posed for a newspaper at Bardney. Armourers would never have stood beneath one otherwise. Note chain release mechanism.

The mighty *Tirpitz* lies at anchor in Kaafjord, an offshoot of Altenfjord in the very north of Norway. Note the anti-submarine nets.

Tallboy about to be loaded at 9 Squadron. Armaments officer Plt Off 'Mick' Maguire (right) looks on.

Maguire auditions for a part in *Dr Strangelove*. Perhaps this was the Tallboy that hit the *Tirpitz*.

Cliff Newton (right) from Detroit, Michigan, 9 Squadron pilot, explains the third *Tirpitz* raid for the benefit of a *Daily Express* photographer in the briefing room at 617's HQ, Woodhall Spa.

Next stop for Newton and the rest of the No. 9 *Tirpitz* raiders, the officers' mess party.

Ed Stowell with Lancaster PB289
WS/B, which he took to Bordeaux,
Givors, the Sorpe dam and Nürnberg.
The aircraft was transferred to 189
Squadron and lost without trace over
Politz, 22 December 1944.

After the war, the bomber
squadrons took important and
interested officials over
Germany to see what had been
achieved. This was what was
left of Essen, powerhouse of
the German war machine,
home of Krupp.

Bremen from 2,000ft, May 1945.

Chapter 8

WHAT SHALL WE DO WITH A DAM BUSTER?

The dam busters were still feeling like spare tools. Since their ineffective Italian bombing trip they'd been again, to Bologna to drop some leaflets, a job that McCarthy likened to selling newspapers on a street corner, but men in the highest places had a very different kind of employment in mind.

Despite the difficulties, it was decided that the transport system between the industrial Ruhr and the rest of Germany should be disrupted now, rather than waiting for the invasion. Air Vice-Marshal Cochrane, AOC 5 Group, wrote a letter to Harris, 22 June 1943, who had asked him to investigate the possibilities of using Upkeep, the dam busters' bouncing bomb, against the Rothensee shiplift. In his letter Cochrane said he'd met Barnes Wallis that afternoon, and the latter had been quite clear that Upkeep would be no use against the shiplift and neither would any conventional bombing.

On the subject of railways, Wallis had raised the possibility of an Upkeep bowled down a slope to hit a viaduct pillar. Cochrane wondered if a conventional but very big package, a 12,000-pounder, might do to breach canal banks. The conversation had turned to viaducts again and the pair of them, bomber and scientist, had gone to look at a remarkable feat by the Luftwaffe. A fighter pilot in a Focke-Wulf 190 had attacked a slender railway viaduct in Brighton. He'd hit a pillar with a single small bomb and the whole arch had come down. The two could only admire for the moment but Wallis was expected to come up with something that would knock down the rather more substantial, more important and infinitely better defended viaducts in Germany. Next day Cochrane, in creative mood, wrote to the inventor at his Vickers-Armstrongs office.

Dear Wallis,
I had a thought in my bath this morning which I pass on to you for criticism. When I was young I seem to remember reading that the

natives of some obscure part of the globe bring down their prey by throwing two balls tied together by a piece of string. Do you think we might apply this ancient principle to the problem we were examining yesterday at Brighton?

We could either tie together two 2,000lb bombs or arrange for a big and little brother consisting of an 8,000 pounder tied to a one or two thousand pounder. All our bombs are fitted with fairly strong eye bolts and I thought that 50 feet of good strong wire cable joining them might do the trick.

The two bombs and the wire would be released simultaneously from a height of say 200 feet and at a distance [from the target] of two to three hundred yards. They would leap and slide towards the target, arguing hotly which side they would pass and, being unable to make up their minds in time, one would go for each side with the result that they would both be brought up with a jerk and find themselves lying close to a concrete pier. In this position they would both explode.

Such were my early thoughts and it now only remains for you to prove that mass times velocity produces a total of energy which could not be restrained by any wire which could be carried in an aeroplane. Should there be any doubt about the mathematics, let us do a practical trial. One never knows.

Cochrane, a much-admired man of great integrity and loyalty and the architect of 5 Group's pre-eminence in Bomber Command, had perhaps strayed out of his own field into a stranger's. His version of the Mexican *bolas* never went further than the Cochrane family bathtub and Wallis turned his mind to a big, big bomb that was aerodynamic enough to hit, more often than not from 20,000ft, a target the size of two football pitches. It would penetrate 100ft below the surface before exploding and would thus destroy the Air Ministry's holy grail, the Rothensee shiplift.

If such a bomb were to be produced, another problem would become apparent straight away. The bomb might be aerodynamically perfect but it would still be dropped from a moving Lancaster, very high up, very likely under attack at the time. Where were the crews that could promise that sort of accuracy, to make the most of the bomb?

Using new equipment called Sabs, the Stabilised Automatic Bomb Sight Mk 2A, Harris instructed that 617 Squadron, the dam busters, were to train 'for the precision bombing of selected targets'. The sight had a gyroscope that allowed it to compensate for some of the minor aircraft movements that were inevitable on a bombing run, making the bomb aimer's job that much easier. The Mk 2 of this bombsight had already been in service as far back as February but Harris had withdrawn it. Bomb aimers needed too much practice with it to keep up a high standard; operational and other training commitments made this impossible. Sabs also had a couple of technical problems which were cracked in the 2A, but it remained a complicated and therefore temperamental piece of kit.

From the crew's point of view, its main drawback was the amount of straight and level flying you had to do on your bombing run. To be sure that the best was obtained from the equipment, the aircraft had to maintain position for around 12 miles, 5 minutes, which gave the enemy many more chances of a better shot.

To breach the canals, ordinary sticks of bombs, thousand- and two-thousand-pounders, would not fill the bill but there had been a trial at Shoeburyness of another 12,000lb bomb, a much less sophisticated article than Wallis's project. On its first drop it had broken up in flight but had looked promising. Further experiments showed that it would be suitable for breaching canals if it hit within 40ft.

This bomb, the 12,000lb HC (High Capacity), in effect a triple cookie with a tailfin bolted on, had all the aerodynamic qualities of a giant oil drum, which is exactly what it looked like, so only low-level runs in excellent visibility could show any kind of accuracy. It was said to be liable to blow up if the aircraft crashed on take-off because of the inadequate safety margin in its detonator. There were additional factors for bomb aimers, too. Joe Tate explained:

It was a great big thing with a TV, terminal velocity, quite different from the normal bomb. Also it all went at once, as it were. The armourers would normally set a mixed load, of incendiaries, say, and a cookie and some one thousand pounders, to drop in a certain order, taking account of the TVs so they all arrived at once and the effect on the aircraft was more gradual. But when the 12,000-pounder went, you felt like you were jumping off a trampoline.

Still, there wasn't much else until Wallis got ready his special earthquake bomb, codenamed Tallboy, which might be months yet and the canals were seen as essential targets. They were carotid artery and jugular vein combined. Compared to them, British canals were mere ditches. The Dortmund–Ems, for instance, could take ships up to 800 tons, being 100ft wide, 12ft deep and 170 miles long. It had been built as a trade route from the Ruhr to the North Sea. Westphalian coal went north, Scandinavian iron ore came south. Now along the Dortmund– Ems floated great cargoes for military industry. It was still the main way into the Ruhr for the iron ore but the swap was not for coal any more. Now, it was the only practical way out for prefabricated U-boats, from the factories to the assembly yards by the sea.

The canal had its vulnerable points, lengths that were highly embanked so that the water was carried well above the surrounding countryside. Smash open an embankment, drain that stretch of canal and an important part of the German war effort would be set back by months, said those in favour.

The Germans realised all this quite as well as the British and everywhere that there was vulnerability, in canal bank, aqueduct or railway viaduct, it was matched by heavy defence. Also, embanked stretches of the canals mostly had safety gates; if there was a breach, only the water between the safety gates would drain away.

Even so, if the 12,000lb HC could be dropped near enough on target, the plan for the severance of transport between the Ruhr and the rest of Germany could be implemented. This was the plan, outlined at a conference, 20 July:

OBJECT. To destroy the three railway viaducts at Bielefeld, Altenbeken and Neuenbecken, which will close all rail traffic going north and east to and from the Ruhr, with the exception of the quite inadequate Münster–Osnabrück line; also to breach certain points on the Dortmund–Ems canal south of the junction with the Mittelland canal, which will close all inland water traffic with the Ruhr.

FORCE REQUIRED. A force of modified 'Upkeep' aircraft of No. 617 Squadron to carry out the attack on the three viaducts. [They were still thinking about games of bowls for the gods, rolling a bouncing bomb along the ground.] A force of Lancaster II aircraft carrying 12,000lb bombs for attacking the canals.

TACTICS. It was suggested that these two attacks should take place on the same night, carried out from low level under moonlight conditions.

A footnote to the conference memo described the prescient contribution of the man at the sharp end, Acting Wg Cdr Holden: 'OC No 617 Squadron was keen that the main bombing force should operate on the same night to provide cover. He also suggested that long range night fighters should take part in the low level attacks to neutralise the enemy ground defences.'

Trials and discussions went on for weeks. Harris sent a message to Cochrane:

With the ever increasing need to strike hard at the enemy, the importance of maintaining the maximum offensive against his large industrial towns and cities needs no emphasis. It is not considered expedient to detach even a small force from this primary task and all suitable targets of importance that require special forms of attack, necessitating special equipment and training, must be the sole responsibility of 617 Squadron which was formed for this purpose.

Another lengthy paragraph, politely phrased between gentlemen but unambiguous, told Cochrane to take his pick from the Ministry targets and get on with it. Cochrane picked the canals. They could be attacked with the 12,000lb HC with modified Lancs during the September moon, provided bombing trials worked out. Operation Garlic, without the railway viaducts, without the shiplift, was on its way. A diversionary raid, Operation Triplet was promised, as was fighter cover.

Air Marshal Saundby, Harris's deputy, added a little handwritten note to a circulating memo, 4 September: 'Is it wise to lay on Operation Triplet in the moon period?' He might have asked, since it was Bomber Command practice generally to avoid the full moon, if it was wise for 617 Squadron to lay on Operation Garlic in the moon period, but he didn't.

Without knowing what the target would be, for most of August McCarthy and all the crews of 617 Squadron Lancasters had been training in low-level formation flying and had had good results in bombing practice with the giant oil drum. It was time to do it for real on 11 September, or the nearest suitable day after. Despite the earlier plea by Holden for a mainforce raid on the same night, the case was quite the opposite. Nothing at all was scheduled for 8 to 14 September, neither Operation Triplet nor anything else.

McCarthy had been practice bombing at Wainfleet, 13 September, dropping from 300ft and 500ft, getting an average 45yd error. At 21:55, 14 September, the order came from 5 Group HQ. *Most secret. Execute Garlic zero hour 0040 hours BST.* The only Lancasters flying that bright, moonlit night over Germany would be the eight of 617. McCarthy and the two other remaining dam-buster captains were, luckily for them as it turned out, not on the list.

The attempt was abortive. All eight took off but were recalled because of a change in the weather. Clouds came to obscure the moon. The Recorder of Operations, in the sparse language typical of these official stories of life and death, summarised thus: *Owing to weather conditions, the formations were recalled at 0030 hrs. Shortly after receiving the recall, the majority of a/c observed a terrific explosion on the sea. This is presumed to have been Sqn Ldr Maltby who failed to return. The remainder returned safely to base.*

Sqn Ldr David Maltby DSO, DFC, 23 years old, was the first of the surviving dam-buster pilots to be lost. In turning low over the sea, he dipped his wing in and crashed, killing himself and all his crew. Possibly the inadequate fuses in the 12,000lb HC had been at fault. Possibly the aircraft blew up anyway.

There was more practice for McCarthy as news of Maltby's loss sunk in. He dropped his bomb from 200ft, with a 13yd error, but at 18:50 hours, 15 September, when the secret cypher message Y34 arrived, he still wasn't on the battle order: *Execute Garlic night 15–16 Sept. Zero hour 0114 hours BST.* It would be almost exactly four months since the dams raid. The only other focus of attention for enemy defences would be a raid of 40 Lancasters attacking Montluçon, a Bourbonnais town in central France, which would not be much of a diversion being 500 miles away from Greven, the canal target.

Eight aircraft under the command of Sqn Ldr Holden took off again to attack the Dortmund–Ems Canal. The visibility over the target was very bad, a thick haze preventing accurate locating of the target. On the inward journey Sqn Ldr Holden's aircraft was seen to be hit by light flak and to crash.

George Walton Holden DSO, DFC and Bar was a 30-year-old officer with long experience. He'd done his bit. He could have had a staff job. He could have been at an OTU, telling the boys how easy they had it these days. Instead he chose active service – again – and, on his first operation with the squadron he had taken over from Gibson, he was shot down 20 miles short of the target. Four of his much-decorated crew were in their mid-twenties, first tour of ops completed long ago, and had been members of the crew who led the dams raid, Guy Gibson's.

The raiders had lost Maltby and seen Holden go down. They were going to make the job pay, and soon Holden's deputy had gone too. *No contact could be made with Flt Lt Allsebrook so Flt Lt Martin took over command of the remaining aircraft.* Other aircraft ranged far and wide, flying low over more light flak emplacements in their attempts to spot the right stretch of canal with the road bridge they had as their marker.

They had to fly low – 150ft – or they couldn't see it, and when they did see it they were on top of it so there was no chance of a proper run.

Flt Lt Knight called up on R/T and stated that his two port engines were stopped. He asked for permission to jettison and return to base. Permission was granted but nothing further was heard from this aircraft. Flt Lt Wilson asked for permission to attack. Permission was given but nothing further was heard from him, as was the case with Plt Off Divall. Plt Off Rice could not identify the canal owing to poor visibility so he came back over the coast and jettisoned. Flt Lt Shannon dropped his bomb which was seen to explode on the tow path on the East bank.

Of nine crews, each with an extra man as front gunner, three crews came home. Of 72 men, 7 parachuted into Holland and the rest died.

Cochrane met Micky Martin more or less as he landed from the raid, promoted him to Squadron Leader and put him in temporary charge of the shattered 617 Squadron. The very next night they were to provide crews for a joint effort with No. 619 against the Antheor viaduct in the far south of France, near Cannes, which was a weak point in a main railway route into Italy for German supplies. After bombing, they would fly on to the base at Blida in Algeria. McCarthy would be going on this one.

Like all viaducts, tall, thin and usually in an awkward place, Antheor was a difficult target. The small inlet of the Mediterranean that it crossed was one in a series of lookalike inlets and bays; at night, it would be easy to get the wrong bay. The idea was to fly down the valley and dive bomb it with thousand-pounders, hoping to stick darts in the spindly supports rather than through the wide open spaces of the arches. They found the right inlet but missed the viaduct. Joe McCarthy bombed from 300ft, but bombs exploding on the ground caused damage no more threatening to the stonework than the initials and hearts already carved there.

The spectacular losses on 617, with only 6 original crews left out of the 21 that trained for the dams, made it hard to recruit replacements, yet it could have been argued that 617, far from being a suicide squadron, was actually quite a soft option. Take any 21 crews in any mainforce squadron in May 1943 and see how many were left by mid-September. Very likely it wouldn't be as many as six, and meantime they'd have flown a whole tour of ops while 617 had flown four.

One of the crews volunteering for 617 was from 207, led by Warrant Officer (WO) Gordon Weeden, a Canadian who had two more RCAF men in his crew, double-trained navigator and bomb aimer WO Edward Walters, from Oakmont, Pennsylvania, and gunner WO2 Robert Cummings, also from PA, possibly Punxsutawney. All the way through September, October and November, McCarthy and the rest would fly practice flights, some with the bouncing dams bomb from greater heights, but no missions would come their way.

Meanwhile, 617 had some sharp comments directed at them in pubs and hotel bars by men who flew ops three times a week. Tex Turnbull was out there 9, 12 and 14 August, for example. He would fly three consecutive Berlins, 18, 22 and 23 November. Nick Knilans attacked Hannover, Mannheim and Hannover again over five nights.

Tex and Nick both missed one of the most famous raids, on the experimental weapon establishment at Peenemünde, an isolated 2-mile peninsula on the Baltic coast, east of Greifswald and almost into Poland. Information was coming to British Intelligence from some of the slave labourers there who were seeing things that were inexplicable in ordinary aeronautical terms.

It appeared that the enemy was preparing some sort of pilotless, automatically guided weapon which could hit London from 200 miles away. There was even information suggesting a rocket that could reach New York. Some senior figures including Lord Cherwell, Paymaster General in the British government and personal scientific adviser to Churchill, argued that such a project could not be because, according to known science, it was impossible. Others said that perhaps the Germans knew some different science.

In fact, Peenemünde was where Wernher von Braun was trying to make a successful rocket, the one that Londoners would eventually get to know as the V2, which the Germans called the A4. In August 1943 the V2 was a long way from being viable and, anyway, was a hugely expensive way of delivering a small payload of explosive. It never would play much of a role in the war and possibly von Braun wasn't really thinking about that. His real interest was outer space and, when the war was over, von Braun would contribute in very large measure to the American post-war missile programme. He would design the first US satellite, Explorer 1, and the Saturn rocket that would take Americans to the moon, and all that so nearly didn't happen.

A total of eight Mosquitos of 139 Squadron flew high over Denmark dropping vast amounts of Window. That, coupled with the foreknowledge from spies that a big raid was on for northern Germany, plus the radar signals showing a large force of bombers massing over the North Sea, convinced the Germans that Berlin was in for a Hamburg experience. When the Mosquitos reached Berlin and began dropping their pathfinder flares on the city, millions ran for the shelters and every available Luftwaffe fighter was sent to the capital.

Meanwhile, 600 RAF bombers began their work 100 miles away, 3 waves of 200 each bombing in 10 minutes, crushing 100 buildings including laboratories and workshops and forcing the troubled project to pack up and relocate, setting it back by crucial months. Because of marking errors, bombs missed the houses where the scientists lived and instead hit the slave labourers' quarters. They also missed the workshop where Wernher von Braun was sheltering. The man who almost single-handedly invented that intellectual benchmark, rocket science, escaped with his life and his design drawings.

As the last bombers over Peenemünde turned for home, the fighters arrived from Berlin. It was havoc. Lancs and Halifaxes were picked off with ease, flying low, doubly visible by flame and moonlight. At least 15 bombers went down a few miles from the target, in a short and sharp turkey shoot. As the rest flew back over Denmark, the fighters scored again. A German force of about 30 aircraft shot down more than their own number of Lancs and Halifaxes. The total score was 38 heavy bombers lost directly to enemy action during or after the raid, including 29 aircraft of the third wave. In addition, three more crashed or had been brought down on the way there and another two crashed at home. And 5 Bf110s from a *Staffel* of *Jagdgeschwader 1* shot down 12 bombers between them. Had the whole 200 fighters that had been waiting over Berlin, instead waited over Peenemünde, and had they shot down a similar share of bombers, the RAF would have lost an unbearable number, perhaps half the force. Those eight Mosquitos and their Window had saved Bomber Command from utter disaster – or, to look at it another way, allowed an attack, a moonlight attack, which could not otherwise have been contemplated. Among the many dead was bomb aimer Sgt Robert Carson Jordan RCAF, 434 Squadron, age 27 of Glen Rose, Texas.

Harris, having done what was asked of him, returned to his proper job, the perfection of area bombing, and a new target. On op number seven, Tex and crew went to Leverkusen, 22 August, and knew they'd got there because they identified nearby Bonn and Cologne by the flak barrages. Turnbull's first Berlin, 23 August, was yet another milestone night for Bomber Command: the most aircraft down in one raid. The defences were fearsome and 63 bombers were lost altogether; 5 of them were in accidents not due to enemy action but the Germans still had an 8 per cent success rate.

The bombing was mixed, with many meadows, woods and villages to the south of the city being hit, yet some loads falling in the city centre. Tex came home happy: *More impressive than Hamburg. Rear gunner saw fires from 150 miles on homeward journey.* Most unhappy was Herr Doktor Goebbels who was Gauleiter of the capital as well as Hitler's propaganda maestro. There were strict orders about air-raid shelters and who had to go to which one. Many people didn't follow orders and more than 850 of them were killed, which was a lot considering how inaccurate the bombing had been.

September 1943 turned out to be American Month at 9 Squadron. Tex Turnbull was already there; 1-Lt Eric Roberts, USAAF, came on the 5th and Raymond Baroni, a mid-upper gunner from Glendale, California, would turn up later. Roberts was a US citizen from Merchantville, Camden County, New Jersey, although born in Liverpool, UK. He and his brother Norman had applied to fly with the USAAF after Pearl Harbor. Norman got in, Eric was turned down. Determinedly, he applied again but through the RCAF and won his wings as a sergeant pilot. In the final stages of training he transferred into the USAAF on what was called detached service, staying with the RAF to fly as trained. Apart from the smart London-tailored uniform, the usual reason for the transfer was the pay, far more than RAF pay, and the $10,000 insurance paid to next of kin if killed. The RAF paid nothing on insurance and paid their flying officers, a rank equivalent to a USAAF first lieutenant, at a rate of 18*s* 6*d* a day, about £30 in today's money.

Turnbull was now a pilot officer but on Canadian rates, considerably higher than RAF but not as high as USAAF. He would have met Roberts in the mess and told him what Berlin had been like, 3 September, and wished him luck on his second dicky to Munich, 6 September. The whole squadron was stood down for training for a fortnight, during which Tex had news from home. His father had died, 9 September, aged 64 after a long illness. Tex, on active duty and far away, could not go to his dad's funeral.

Roberts didn't fly his first op as skipper until Hannover, 22 September, and in the force of over 600 were 5 USAAF Fortresses on their first op in the night-time. All the American virgins came home, also an experienced Yank in Canadian clothing, Nick Knilans, now pilot officer:

I'd been off to London for a new uniform. I always stayed at the Regent Palace Hotel, just off Piccadilly Circus, in the middle of a circuit of pubs and clubs that meant I was never short of somewhere to go. I also liked the tea dance in the afternoons, somewhere in Covent Garden, where it was usually not too strenuous an effort to find attractive and generous hearted young ladies.

Back at Woodhall Spa, my crew gave me elaborate salutes as I packed my things in the hut for my move to the officers' mess, which was in the Petwood Hotel. We had central heating, spacious grounds, tea in bed and waitress service at mealtimes. If you're going to a war from a foxhole, this was the sort of foxhole to be in.

[After Hannover] Joe told me our photograph was poor because the aircraft was not level at the time of exposure. Too true, because I hadn't wanted to hang around after the bombing run. We'd seen several bandits engaging other bombers and I'd made a speedy turn out of the glare. Besides, nobody ever got a medal for a pretty picture. I'd got to bed at 01:00 and was in the flight room by 09:00. We were on again.

Eric Roberts, Tex Turnbull and Nick Knilans were all on again, to Mannheim. Route marking and target indicating were spot on from the pathfinders and, despite some creep back later in the raid, around 1,000 buildings were destroyed.

Knilans was at Hannover again, 27 September:

Joe said 'Bombs away, steady for the photo', at the same moment that Roy in the mid-upper turret shouted 'Bandit, twelve o'clock high.' I looked up to see an aircraft diving straight for us. I hauled the Lanc around and down to port, and Gerry at the back said 'It's a Halifax. I could have reached out and touched it.' The Halifax had been badly hit and we watched it burning fiercely on its way down.

Seeing such a thing, knowing that but for the grace of God it was you in there, dying, burning, it was only natural for the mind to slip briefly into a sympathetic, philosophical pause in its otherwise continuous tasks of battle.

I was startled by the crump of an anti-aircraft shell exploding near us, the bits of flak rattling against the fuselage and windows. I asked around for damage reports and we had petrol leaks. Ken and Harry worked out that we only had enough fuel to reach the nearest point of England, somewhere about the mouth of the Thames. I made a Darky call, and another, and another. We were running on empty. A sweet feminine voice suddenly came on, saying 'I have you, T-Tommy. Steer 095 degrees', and we ended up on a tiny grass fighter airfield near Gravesend, landing by the dim light of gooseneck flares.

These flares were a primitive kind of paraffin lamp, like a watering can with a wick in an extended spout, hence the name.

Roberts's next was to Bochum, home of the massive Bochumer Verein steelworks, producing 160,000 tons a month of raw material, and this was gunner Sergeant Ray Baroni's first op. Hagen was next for both, an iron and steel town also making U-boat batteries, perfectly situated in the middle of Happy Valley. Knilans was there. He bombed at 21:06 from 18,500ft, Roberts at 21:08 from 18,590ft, Baroni's crew at 21:08 from 17,500ft, and there were 240 other Lancasters doing much the same. This raid was a triumph of Oboe sky marking in ten-tenths cloud. In round numbers, 50 industrial firms were destroyed and another 160 damaged. Knilans saw 'a large blue explosion lasting about eight seconds' and others saw it too. This may have been the battery factory being wrecked which, according to Albert Speer, slowed down U-boat output considerably.

As Knilans turned for home, he had to switch off the starboard inner engine. He was flying on three yet again, and there was trouble ahead:

> The met officer had briefed us about a series of squall lines across our homeward track. I was able to hold us up at 18,000 as we passed over the first one but my plan was to dive to 500 feet and go under the next. It was very tiring and at times a nerve-tingling experience. Very heavy rain and strong winds battered the aircraft, while lightning and ice added to our problems. It was a struggle to keep us airborne.

Joe Tate: 'Next morning, when the groundcrew were working on our engine, they found an unexploded flak shell in it. If that had exploded, we'd have been goners.'

Only two Lancs were goners, one to the Germans and one, from Knilans's squadron, to the weather. 'One of ours became disoriented under these conditions [Flg Off Derek Joss aged 20, and crew] and flew across south-west England. They ditched in the Bristol Channel, all killed.'

Chapter 9

TO BE OR NOT TO BE

When these American boys volunteered to fight against Nazi Germany, they expected danger, possibly fatal, and physical and mental challenge. Even so, there were some things they could not have foreseen.

Tex Turnbull was on leave, Eric Roberts and Ray Baroni were on nights off, Joe McCarthy was on training flights in preparation for special ops, so only one of our Americans was due for Kassel, 3 October, and that was Nick Knilans. In the afternoon the squadron boss, Wg Cdr Abercrombie, called Knilans into his office to discuss a matter which, considering the job they did, came up surprisingly rarely.

Night after night these young men climbed into their aircraft and flew in the darkness to Germany, where waited highly skilled fighter pilots and anti-aircraft gunners who would do their level best to kill Tommy. Night after night Tommy would see his fellows going down in flames, and morning after morning there would be empty chairs in the mess. Crews finishing a tour of operations were such a rarity that every member of aircrew knew that death was a far more likely end to a flying career in a bomber squadron. And yet, and yet, they did climb into their aircraft and they did go to it. Joe Tate:

> You had to believe it would be the other chap who went down. In everyday bombing life, your main fear was showing your fear. Standing around, waiting to get on the aircraft, everybody felt the nerves. Some would try to lighten it with wisecracks, but it was one of the worst times. Once you were on the plane you were busy, then you had the build-up to take-off, and the actual take-off, struggling into the air with a huge load of bombs. We all felt a lot better once we'd got to 500 feet.

Only occasionally did someone get the screaming habdabs and have to be taken away. It was known for a pilot, going on his second dicky in among the flak and the mayhem, to realise quietly that he wasn't up to the task. Sometimes, a member of a crew would get halfway through his tour then find that his courage and his confidence had collapsed and he couldn't go on. In the First World War, such a man would have been shot for cowardice. In the RAF in 1943, he would be classified as LMF, Lacking Moral Fibre, busted down to the ranks, and given menial work around an aerodrome. He would be forced to wear his aircrew badge so that everyone seeing him would know that Aircraftman Second Class Smith used to be at least Sgt Smith and a flight engineer, or a wireless operator or, in Nick Knilans's case, a gunner.

Rear gunner, tail-end Charlie, was widely believed to be the most dangerous position in a bomber. It was certainly true that if anyone was killed without the whole lot of them going down, it was probably going to be one of the gunners. The rear gunner was also lonely, cut off from the rest of the crew, and he was exposed more than the others to temperatures well below zero. He was given special heated gear to wear but that didn't always work, and if it did he could still be very cold indeed.

He was trained to manipulate and fire a hydraulically powered arrangement of four machine-guns, but if you asked him what his job was he wouldn't say that it was firing guns. He'd say it was watching. He had the best view of all, and he spent all his time, hours and hours of it, staring into the black night in a state of constant nervous readiness, prepared to take instant command of the aircraft when he saw a fighter coming in. He had to decide in a fraction of a second on the best evasive action, he had to issue the order, preferably before the fighter started shooting, and he had to hope that his captain would react with no delay whatever. Only then did he try to work out where in the sky the fighter would be while his skipper was throwing the bomber about, and train his guns on that piece of blank space.

Gunner training was the shortest at six months. As the minimum age for entry to aircrew training was 17½, all these responsibilities, including instant temporary command of a Lancaster bomber under fire, could be held by a boy of 18 and often were.

Knilans's rear gunner, Gordon Hunter Jackson known as Gerry, was older than that, 22, and married. His wife Phoebe had just sent him a telegram announcing their first-born, a son. That, Wingco Abercrombie told Knilans, must have been the straw that broke the camel's back or, in this instance, that broke the gunner's spirit. He had asked to be taken off flying duties. He would be reclassified, from Sgt Air Gunner to AC2 LMF.

The Wingco had been most unwilling to accede to Jackson's request and had pointed out that after tonight's raid there would be nine days' leave. If he flew on the raid, tomorrow Jackson could go home, see his baby, talk to his wife and parents, and come back to the squadron in perhaps a different frame of mind.

'Plt Off Knilans,' said Abercrombie, 'Sgt Jackson agreed to this, but you have to agree too. Are you willing to fly on ops with a rear gunner who may not be entirely up to scratch? It's your crew. You must say yes or no.'

This was a challenge nobody expected, to have to take a life-and-death decision on behalf of others, based on nothing but gut feeling. Logically, Knilans knew, Gerry Jackson should be ditched and replaced.

'I'd better not mention this to anyone, then, had I, sir?' said Knilans.

'Thank you, Nick. Well done,' said the Wingco.

At dispersal, while they had the traditional cigarette and chat after doing their checks, the crew talked about their leave plans and congratulated Gerry on his new family. Gerry was a chain smoker anyway, so nobody noticed anything different about him. Nick, watching closely, thought his man seemed nervous but cheery enough, and away they flew.

'We were airborne at 18:48. Our course would take us across the North Sea into Holland, then into Germany between Münster and Hamm before turning south towards Kassel, at 19,000 feet. At around 21:20, I heard "Monica calling", from Les [Knell, wireless operator]. "How far?" said I. "Mmm, about 300 yards," replied Les.'

Monica was a form of radar meant to pick up enemy fighters. She could not discriminate between RAF and Luftwaffe – all aircraft were the same to her – nor could she tell from which direction they were approaching. She could only give their distance. Joe Tate: 'The closer together the beeps, the nearer was the aircraft, so a steady pip, pip, pip, that was probably another bomber in stream, but if it speeded up you knew there was an aircraft coming towards you, probably a fighter.'

It was as well that Les, Nick and the others didn't know that Monica had recently developed into a very attractive lady, a femme fatale, in fact. The Germans had devised an instrument called Flensburg, which picked up Monica's radar signals and used them to home in on the transmitting aircraft from as much as 45 miles away. Knilans:

I rolled the aircraft so the gunners could see below. 'There's a Lanc down there,' said Gerry. 'Five o'clock down, three or four hundred yards.' We all thought that must be what Monica was detecting but, as I brought our own Lanc level again, a stream of tracer, both cannon and machine gun, went straight through our port wing about a yard from my head. I could hear, feel and smell other shells thudding into the aircraft. Instinctively I threw her into a fierce turning dive to starboard, yelling 'Where is he?' to anyone who was listening.

Some of the shells had shattered the mid-upper turret's Perspex. Tiny fragments filled Roy's eyes. 'I can't see,' he cried. 'I'm blinded.' 'What about you, Gerry? Can you see him?' There was no reply from the rear turret.

Knilans was doing a very enthusiastic corkscrew when the flight engineer said he would have to feather the port inner engine. Knilans said he would have to corkscrew on three, then. He was also doing it with a great many holes in wings and tail, a factor that made the aircraft less responsive, heavier to lug about the sky, but Nick was a big strong chap. They had to lose the fighter. Another attack like that would surely finish them.

In the cavalry, troopers charging to attack do not stop to help a fallen comrade. The equivalent in Bomber Command was phrased thus: 'Press on, regardless'. Pilots who embodied this spirit more than the average were known as press-on types. Knilans agreed with the 'press on' part but not entirely with the 'regardless'. Nevertheless, they were near the target, so they might as well press on, drop their load and stay with the bomber stream, rather than turning back and risking being on their own with one and possibly two gun turrets u/s.

After we bombed, Roy spoke up and said he'd seen cannon shells hitting the rear turret, but before he could spot where they were coming from he'd had one in his own turret, which passed through without exploding, hence the Perspex fragments. He still couldn't see. I told him to come down and get on the rest bed. No point in sitting up there with his head sticking out. I descended to 12,000 feet, where we wouldn't need oxygen, and told Ken to get the fire axe and go and see what had happened to Gerry, who'd still not said anything.

Ken reported that the intercom wires were cut. No wonder Gerry was quiet. Then Ken spoke again. 'Oh, Christ Almighty, skip. He's tipped forward over his guns. He's not moving. I can't get to him. The turret's on the beam.' 'Can you see any more damage?' I asked. 'What, through the holes, you mean?' said Ken. 'Yes, I can see plenty. You've got just about enough fins and tailplane to get us home.' I thought this was an undisciplined and unprofessional way to report but it wasn't the time to say so.

The turret being on the beam, that is swivelled right over to one side, meant that the door to it from inside the aircraft was inaccessible. If Gerry was alive they couldn't help him and, with both turrets out of action, Knilans could not take shortcuts. He would have to stay on the route as briefed. He let down the undercarriage to see if the port-side damage to wing and engine extended to their landing gear. By torchlight, Ken reported a flat tyre.

I asked him to go and take another look at Gerry. No change. He had to be dead. So our only injured man was Roy who said he was all right apart from being blind, so I thought that, rather than try landing on the emergency grass field at Manston with a flat, we'd carry on home to friendly tarmac. When we got there we were cleared to land immediately. I let down as far to the right as I could on our runway but the port wheel-rim dug in and pulled us left. I gunned the port outer to try and counteract it, which at least stopped us spinning although we ended up off the runway on the port side with our wingtip slightly underground.

Les had radioed ahead for ambulance and fire truck. While Knilans told his crew they didn't have to stay to watch, the ambulance headlights were trained on the turret. Gerry was illuminated. Roy stayed but the others went, while firemen and Knilans struggled to get the turret open. At last, Knilans could reach in and pull his friend free.

I lowered his stiff body to the ground and took off his goggles, oxygen mask and flying helmet. His still features were unmarked. I brushed his hair back out of his eyes and his forehead was like ice. He'd been hit in the middle of his body and there was a lot of blood. One of the ambulance people turned away to be sick. The driver and I put Gerry on a stretcher and into the ambulance with Roy. After all that, I guess I needed a few minutes to myself, so I walked slowly back to the briefing room for interrogation. The MO came in and said Gerry had died instantly, cut in half by cannon shells, and gave me two sleeping pills.

135

The WAAF who was to drive me back to the Petwood turned out to be a pal of Gerry's. He'd asked her to gather up his personal effects if he didn't come back and send them to his folks in Dumfries. She couldn't drive for the grief and the tears. I gave her my two sleeping pills and another WAAF said she'd drive.

Knilans and crew had a 48 added to their nine days' leave. When they came back, they found a new gunner, Robbie Robinson on his second tour, to replace Gerry, a fully repaired Lancaster, and an op on the battle order. They put Robbie in the mid-upper turret and moved Roy Learmonth to the rear. Target: Kassel.

Among the 409 bombers going to Frankfurt, 4 October, were three B-17s, the last time the USAAF joined the RAF on a night raid, and Lancaster JA690 WS/M-Mother, captained by the Merchantville 1-Lt, Eric Roberts. It was a successful raid in clear weather, with accurate marking. The docks on the river and the eastern half of the city took a thorough pasting. Roberts saw the target, some good fires and *a very big orange explosion*.

Next was Stuttgart, night of 7 October, the first time a device called ABC was used, by the specialised squadron No. 101. ABC stood for codewords Airborne Cigar and it was a massive piece of kit with four VHF radio sets. One scanned up and down the airwaves, seeking transmissions from German radio. When a blip showed on his cathode ray tube, a German-speaking, extra wireless operator tuned one of the other sets to that frequency and listened. If it was a nightfighter ground controller, the w/op transmitted a warble so the fighter pilot couldn't hear his instructions. That it worked was amply demonstrated by the lengths to which the Germans went, to try and fool the system. They even tried having lady sopranos singing the instructions so the listening RAF might think it was a civilian station.

With that and a diversionary raid by a small force of Mosquitos on Munich, hardly any nightfighters arrived in time for the night's main attraction and only 4 out of 358 Lancasters went down, 2 of them from 9 Squadron. One was ED836 C-Charlie, a 42-op veteran old lady skippered by a pilot with a month's experience. They'd been well on the way home, 90 miles back from the target when they were spotted. As the nightfighter raked the Lanc with cannon fire, the bomb aimer managed to jump through his hatch. The rest were killed, including that keen boy from Camden County, son of Frederick and Annie, kid brother of Norman, 1-Lt Eric George Roberts of the USAAF and 9 Squadron RAF, aged 23.

In the morning, after hearing about Roberts, Tex Turnbull and Ray Baroni saw they were flying together that night. Tex's usual mid-upper was out of commission and Ray was spare. If the Germans got them over Hannover, that would be the entire 9 Squadron US contingent wiped out in 24 hours. No, it couldn't happen. Tex was a lucky pilot in a lucky aircraft. He would do half a tour in this Lanc, LM361 WS/T, and good old T would go on to almost 50.

Eric Roberts missed a fellow USAAF airman's arrival by four days. Technical Sergeant James Hannon was a bomb aimer from the Bronx, crewed up with Plt Off Bill Chambers. They arrived 11 October and flew their first, 20 October to Leipzig, where they saw nothing on a night of appalling weather. Ray Baroni went too, and a long way it was with 16 Lancs lost and about 90 more getting lost, or not reaching Leipzig anyway.

Tex went to Kassel in the same night sky as Knilans. Photoreconnaissance the next day showed a shattered city. The Germans reported over 60 per cent of housing unusable and 155 industrial buildings destroyed or seriously damaged, including all 3 Henschel aircraft factories. This was better news than the Allies realised. Henschel had been building the pilotless secret weapon, the V1 flying bomb.

Total effort for that night was 645 aircraft attacking, 45 lost, 7 per cent, but Tex and Ray came home all right. Even Nick was okay, despite being coned over the target, being hit by flak which wounded the new gunner, and having to return yet again on three and make another lop-sided landing. The groundcrew complained about all the extra work and the station commander, Grp Capt Johnson, asked the Yank if he couldn't take better care of the King's property.

Next up was Modane in southern France, where German troop trains were assembling in the marshalling yards and the railway for Italy went into a tunnel. In Baroni's aircraft they saw *a high portion of the attack (falling) on the yards and the tunnel entrance*, and in Hannon's *several explosions . . . in the valley*. Knilans: 'We passed south of Mont Blanc, gleaming starkly in the moonlight. Swiss village lights twinkled in the valleys. The German troop trains were clearly visible as we made our bombing run. Joe said he could see the men running for shelter, but there was not much shelter to be had and there was no opposition at the target.' This was a remarkable raid, a bombing success and not one aircraft lost.

Just as Göring's and Hitler's preoccupation with London had cost them advantage early in the war, so Harris's with Berlin. The Big City was formidably well defended and it was widely spread out, its streets not suitably arranged for a Hamburg firestorm. It was a long way and, no matter how the routes were varied, the Germans would not have too much trouble guessing the destination of the bomber stream. The use of Window had made the old cell system obsolete, so new and better tactics were developed for the nightfighters. On these longer journeys the slower and lower flying Stirlings and early marques of Halifax suffered terrible losses. Squadrons flying these aircraft had to be withdrawn before they ceased to exist.

The Battle of Berlin is said to run from 18 November to 31 March 1944, when Harris was forced to desist by the need to soften up targets closer to home, ready for the D-Day invasion. The main struggle was up to the end of January, by which time the nightfighters were having a wonderful run and Bomber Command, out of range for Oboe target marking, was in danger of spiritual fragmentation. Aircrew could see their bombing was poor. If the marking was scattered, so was the attack. In fact, they were inflicting more damage than it looked from 22,000ft but the big fires and high smoke and vivid explosions did not seem to compensate for the many, many flaming torches falling to earth.

These were four and a half months largely wasted in strategic terms. At the end of the time, contrary to Harris's original belief, Hitler was no more likely to surrender than he had been before.

Tex Turnbull and Ray Baroni were 9 Squadron's first American representatives in the new battle for the capital, on the first night, 18/19 November. They were in the air for 6¾ hours and bombed from 24,000ft. *Every sign of scattered bombing. Pathfinder flares widely dispersed. Few glows of fires seen through clouds.*

Poor weather also meant fewer fighters about. Next time, 22 November, it was the same and, with Ray and Tex flying with their usual crews and John Hannon on his third, 9 Squadron could be proud of their own record total of three volunteer Americans in German airspace at once. The difference with this raid was the effectiveness.

At 764 aircraft it was the biggest hit on Berlin so far, and it caused the most damage there of the whole war, not that the crews could tell much from it. Turnbull: *Nothing seen through cloud*.

They went again the next night and a dozen big fires were still blazing from their previous efforts. Turnbull: *Carpet of fire estimated 12 miles long by three miles wide. Glow seen for 100 miles. Great improvement on last night, in fact no comparison. Best of the five attacks we have taken part in.* Five Berlins. That had to be more than enough for any man, surely. Baroni was in the middle of a sequence of five Berlins on the trot.

On 26 November they noted *defences active*. Too true, Nick Knilans would have agreed:

There was a raid on Frankfurt which would attract the fighters, which then wouldn't have enough fuel to get to Berlin. We were at 20,000 feet, on our way to the Big City, when Robbie piped up. 'My turret's u/s,' he said. 'Monica calling,' said Les, 'about 600 yards.' I just had time to ask Roy in the back if he could see anything when a bright stream of tracer shells zipped across the port wing and Roy shouted 'Corkscrew port'. I could hear his guns chattering as I tried some gymnastics with a kite full of bombs and petrol. 'It's a Junkers 88,' said Robbie. 'Feathering the port inner,' said Ken. Marvellous, I thought, levelling out after losing a lot of height, and in the corner of my eye I spotted the Junkers. 'Nine o'clock high,' I called. No reply from anyone. 'Can't you . . .' I didn't finish the sentence because his wing dipped as he turned to come in. I sideslipped hard to port as he flew right over us, all guns blazing. 'I hope you bleeders saw him that time,' said I.

Standard tactics would be for the Junkers to make a wide circle and expect to find us again, still on our course. 'Roy, watch for him behind you. I'm going to turn all the way around.' 'Right ho, skip,' said the Aussie. I did the tightest turn I could and must have got inside the bandit's circle. I heard Roy's guns. 'You got him,' yelled Robbie, and I looked down and saw him falling straight down in flames.

Another standard tactic was for the fighters to work in pairs. One would attack and draw fire. The other would hang back and see from our gun flashes exactly where we were. 'Watch out on the dark side,' I said, meaning the other side from the shining moon, but the second fighter wasn't orthodox. A dark shape hurtled towards us from directly in front. I put the kite in a dive and shouted 'Fire straight up.' 'Bf110,' said the excited voice of Robby. 'He flew right through the bullets.' 'Course for Berlin, Harry, please,' I asked our jolly navigator, knowing his pencils and stuff would be all over the floor.

The Junkers had shot away large pieces of elevator as well as disabling the port inner. Knilans was wrestling with a joystick that wanted to leap forward to smash into the instrument panel alternately with cracking back into his seat. All they could do was hold steady for a gentle descent over the 250 miles to Berlin. They bombed at 13,000ft in a brightly lit hell of searchlights, flak, aircraft falling all around and a tumbling cascade of 4,000lb cookies from the higher Lancs threatening to knock their wings off. Straining to keep up with the stream in their continuous slow descent, they crossed the Dutch coast at 2,000ft. Flight Control at a fog-bound Woodhall Spa recommended a diversion to Scotland. Knilans demurred, on the grounds that he'd never get there, so they were sent to Spilsby, a new aerodrome near Skegness.

It was just as foggy at Spilsby. I couldn't see the runway lights above 100 feet so I did my circuit hoping there were no church steeples. I slept on a snooker table in the mess while a van came for us from Woodhall, and we went home at walking pace with a WAAF in front holding a torch.

Ray Baroni's fourth take-off for Berlin, 2 December, was another bad, bad night for Bomber Command. Of the 43 bombers lost only 1 was not due to enemy action, a rate of 9 per cent.

SECRET No 9 Squadron Combat Report
Date: 2 December 1943. Time: 2013 hrs. Pos: 52.30N 13.20E.
Ht: 20,500 ft. Target: Berlin. Lancaster 'X'. Captain: Plt Off Bayldon.
On getting a warning indication on special apparatus the pilot told the gunners and started to corkscrew to starboard. Some few seconds later both gunners saw a T/E A/C approaching from astern at about 800 yards. MU [Baroni] told pilot who continued corkscrewing and both gunners opened fire. The E/A fired one burst from cannon and machine guns, the trace of which was seen to pass above the bomber. Also the E/A is believed to have fired a 'Rocket Shell' which is reported to have burned out and disappeared before reaching the bomber. E/A disappeared on port quarter and was not seen again.
MU gunner Sgt Baroni 30 rounds.
Rear gunner Sgt Richardson 50 rounds.

Turnbull went to Leipzig the following night with over 500 bombers causing a lot of damage a long, long way from home and suffering not too badly until, on the way back, a large part of the bomber stream strayed over Frankfurt. A dozen went down there and, for a while, that was it. Bomber Command stood down for 12 days apart from some minor incursions, then it was back to the Big City. If the capital was destroyed, Germany had to fall – that was the belief, and any sacrifice was worth the prize. There were more records on 16 December: the most bombers going and the most not returning, a night to be remembered as Black Thursday. Of the 54 bombers lost, 2 were 9 Squadron's. DV293 WS/Y fell 25 miles from Berlin. The mid-upper gunner, Californian Sgt Raymond John Baroni RCAF had chased off German fighters on several occasions, twice in one night at Kassel, so he could have said he'd done his bit, helped them get this far but now, like 20-year-old Capt Bayldon and the rest of them, he was of no further use to the cause. This was their fifth Berlin in a row which, as already observed, was more than enough.

American newspapers reported the raid next day. The *Los Angeles Times*: '[Berlin radio announced] British bombers tonight again attacked the capital of the Reich. The attack was described in Berlin as a terror attack on a considerable scale. Well-informed circles point out that it was carried out in poor visibility. Residential quarters in the capital were hit.' The *New York Times*: 'Immediately after the attack Berlin broadcast a talk for overseas listeners, saying: "The enemy will never destroy the Berlin population's will to win. Factories in Germany are working full blast to produce weapons of retaliation, which will come."'

Tex Turnbull, like all the other flyers, knew nothing yet of secret German weapons of retaliation. His job was to wreck Berlin, a senior man now, taking second dickies regularly. It had been cloudy that night. They saw nothing unusual, just a lot of other bombers spiralling from the sky in flames. For Turnbull and crew there would be three more Berlins, eight altogether.

Tex was remarkably skeletal, from a tall, thin family. The motherly young WAAFs worried about him. Aileen Walker remembered:

That man, Turnbull, I did look after him. He was so, so thin and spoke so, so slowly. I'd go to him [in the officers' mess] and ask him if he'd like some second helpings and he'd say no, he'd had quite sufficient, so we could never feed him up. One night I came off duty and there he was, leaning on my bike. I said, what are you doing? He said 'I'm holding your bike for you. I'm going to walk you home.' Well, he walked me home, he was blind drunk, and when he stumbled and fell I took my tie-pin off and held it ready in my hand. He had a certain reputation, did Tex Turnbull.

After the Black Thursday Berlin, Nick Knilans and gunner Roy Learmonth were called into the new CO's office. They hadn't really got to know him yet, Wg Cdr Jeudwine. Judging by his attitude, Knilans's recent transfer to the USAAF, with accompanying new uniform and pay rate higher than an RAF wingco's, had made no difference to disciplinary status.

'The Group Captain wants to see you two. You really are in the shit this time. Come on.' As the two old pals followed their bristling CO, they whispered their concerns.

'What have you been up to, Roy? Put some WAAF up the stick, have you?'

'Not me, Nicky. Must be you.'

The Wingco drove them over to HQ at Coningsby and stood them to attention in the august presence of the base commander. 'Ah, Lt Knilans. Telegram for you.' Nick unfolded it with slightly shaky hands and read it: 'Congratulations on being given the immediate award of the Distinguished Service Order. Signed, Air Chief Marshal Harris.' Roy's telegram congratulated him on his Distinguished Flying Medal.

Officers got the DFC, the Cross, while other ranks got the Medal. Although the great majority of bomber aircrew were sergeants and flight sergeants and, until late 1944, many pilots were too, only one DFM was awarded for every nine DFCs. Knilans's DSO, equivalent to the American DSC, was second only to the Victoria Cross, Britain's highest award. Everyone was rather pleased. It was the squadron's first.

Over at McCarthy's squadron, 617, they'd also been given a new CO, a legend among legends, Wg Cdr Geoffrey Leonard Cheshire DSO and Two Bars, DFC, the same Cheshire who had started the war wave-hopping with Dinghy Young. He had been first-tour complete by January 1941, volunteered for another and spent yet more months being shot up over the Ruhr. He was briefly an instructor but badgered his superiors to put him back on ops so they made him a wingco, gave him a squadron, and he was happy again until March 1943 when, with three tours finished, he was put behind a desk and promoted to group captain, at 25 the youngest and probably the most World-War-Two-decorated in the RAF. He hated it and persuaded the brass that he could be demoted, back to operational rank of wingco, and off he set on his fourth tour.

Cheshire could hardly have been less heroic as a person. He was tall, posh, austere and gaunt enough to be starving. He may have looked like a librarian in the Ancient History department of the British Museum but he was an exceptionally brave and skilful flyer, an enthusiastic advocate of low-level target marking, and of practice, practice and more practice.

A telephone call from RAF Tempsford looked like an offer of a change from practising. Could 617 kindly lend three Lancasters and crews to SOE? Tempsford was the aerodrome in Bedfordshire from which the secret drops of weapons, supplies and personnel were made to the various resistance movements – Czech, Danish, Norwegian, Polish, French – organised by the Special Operations Executive. There was to be an especially large firearms drop in northern France involving very low flying, which is what 617 had been practising all these months. Cheshire detailed three of the recent recruits for the job, Clayton, Bull and Weeden. Clayton and crew had been to the Antheor viaduct; it would be a first op with 617 for Bull, and Weeden with his two Americans.

They were headed for somewhere in northern France, in Picardie, where the Somme *département* joins the Pas de Calais, near St Pol, not far from Amiens. Somewhere there would be a hastily lit bonfire or set of flaming torches, in a field, near a village, somewhere. They were flying very low, looking for a spark in a haystack, an easy target for flak guns they had not been led to expect. Luckily for them, Clayton and crew couldn't find it and went home.

Bull went down at Terramesnil, two killed, the rest parachuting, and Weeden went down a little further inland, all killed, including bomb aimer WO Edward Joseph Walters, 26, son of Anna Walters of Oakmont, Pennsylvania, and rear gunner WO2 Robert Cummings, son of Thomas and Mary Cummings, nephew of John Glynn of Punxsutawney, Jefferson County, Pennsylvania (of Groundhog Day fame).

Elsewhere, arguments were still fierce among the politicians and high commanders about the threat of German secret weapons. Hitler had been openly boasting about how such weapons were going to win the war so the assumption had to be that there were some. Empty promises would have been very bad for the public spirit. The question remained: what were they? It was believed that there was some sort of rocket, a ballistic missile. Probably there was some sort of pilotless aircraft-cum-bomb, but how far down the line were the Germans with either or both and what sort of threats did they pose? Bomber Command had wrecked part of a research station at Peenemünde in the August but how big a setback had that been? Had Peenemünde been the base for all such projects, or were there others?

In the autumn of 1943, the French Resistance had reported strange and urgent building works in country districts not far from the northern coast, with land being requisitioned and large numbers of workers forcibly recruited. One agent, a builder, sent a signal about six rather peculiar constructions near Abbeville in the Somme, that his firm was helping to put up. Aerial reconnaissance on 3 November showed that all these sites were identical, with the same set of buildings, and they all had what looked like a launching ramp aimed at London. A particularly distinctive type of building at each site had the shape of a ski laid on its side, which was estimated to be a storage hangar for the weapons, with a bend at the end to deflect bomb blast. By 8 November, 19 of these 'ski sites' had been spotted. Next day, the total was up to 26, and by 22 November, 95.

Clearly these establishments were not for launching rocket ships, therefore they had to be platforms for the rumoured radio-controlled flying bomb. This demonstrable truth was largely taken to mean that there were no rockets after all.

On 28 November, a Mosquito came back with pictures of revitalised works at Peenemünde showing long ramps pointing out to sea, the same kind of ramps as were at the ski sites. Also on one of the pictures was a small aircraft with very short wings, implying high speed, and no cockpit. Maybe it was a 2-ton flying bomb. If all the known ski sites and some unknown ones each launched ten 2-ton bombs a day, London could experience a Hamburg firestorm.

The range of opinion among ministers and senior officers was about as wide as it could be. Some advocated the immediate evacuation of London. Lord Cherwell, who did not believe in the possibility of a rocket, forecast that the little pilotless aircraft would carry a bomb less than 1 ton, that the Germans would not be able to launch them in numbers and that many of them would fall before reaching their target, which they were liable to miss by miles in any case. He said that if London took one hit an hour from the flying bomb that would be as much as they could expect and that wouldn't be until March or April.

Lord Cherwell's prophecies proved to be quite accurate except for the timing. The first V1, the doodlebug or buzz bomb, would hit a railway bridge in Bethnal Green, 13 June. The Germans were experiencing huge problems with supplies of the V1, mainly because the success of bombing raids on Kassel had crippled the means of production. The weapon was not yet sufficiently developed for reliable operational use, and it was indeed only a 1-ton bomb. Nobody among the Allies at the time knew this or would take any notice of Cherwell who seemed far too sanguine about the whole secret-weapon business. These ski sites had to be destroyed and the job was given mainly to the 8th USAAF.

There were a couple of forays by 617 too, and RAF Stirling squadrons. The bombing was very accurate but the Oboe marking was off so nothing was achieved. Joe McCarthy was on a ski-site raid, but cloud obscured the markers. They stayed an extra quarter of an hour and still couldn't see anything so they went home.

By 24 December, the USAAF had dropped 1,700 tons of bombs, equivalent to about 320 Lancaster-loads, and destroyed 3 ski sites. No. 617 Squadron's and McCarthy's last raid of 1943, 30 December, was no better.

The New Year didn't show an improvement either, not for aircrew anyway. It was Berlin, 1 January, and Tex and Nick were at it again. Tex had to come home after 2 hours' flying with a petrol leak, a turret u/s, another gun u/s and the electrics playing up. Nick got there, bombed through ten-tenths cloud and listened to an unusual radio programme on the way home. 'Les played his reception over the intercom. There seemed to be a terrible row going on between German pilots and German WAAFs. We enjoyed quite a few minutes of it.'

This was a ground-based version of Airborne Cigar, featuring real conversation rather than warbled jamming and was a kind of counter-counter measure. Defeated to an extent by Window and other scientific tricks, the Germans had developed *Zahme Sau*, Tame Boar. The essence of it was Junkers 88s as night scouts, flying alongside the bomber stream but not attacking, their crews feeding information to the ground controllers who would co-ordinate and analyse the data and transmit a running commentary on the whereabouts and likely movements of the bombers to more fighters, some of which would also not attack but drop flares to illuminate the Tommies. Joe Tate: 'That was murder, if you were near one of those flares. They lit you up like daylight. It was a terrible feeling.'

In England, RAF operators would interrupt the commentary, pretending to be nightfighter controllers and issuing what the RAF would call 'duff gen', false information. Initially the poor German accents of the RAF spoofers rather gave them away, also their lack of nightfighter slang, for instance the bomber stream was *dicker Hund*, fat dog. The English actors got better at it and the Germans got better at countering it, so it was quite common for arguments to break out with genuine and spoofing ground controllers each insisting he or she was the right one. In a famous exchange, the real German became frustrated and started using bad language. 'Der Engländer schimpft,' ('The Englishman is cursing') said the actor. 'Der Engländer schimpft nicht,' said the German. 'Ich bin es, der schimpft.' ('The Englishman is not cursing. It is I who am cursing.')

This night was also Nick Knilans's first acquaintance with FIDO: Fog, Instant Dispersal Of. It was a device that would have had modern health and safety people collapsing with heart attacks. An arrangement of metal pipes, drilled with small holes and filled with paraffin, was lit as the aircraft approached through the fog. The fierce heat dried the air to a certain extent. 'I aimed at the glow while enveloped in thick fog with wheels and flaps down. We broke into clear air at 100 feet. The flames were shooting up 50 feet as we touched down between two walls of fire.'

Losses on 1 January were 29 out of 421 Lancasters, 6.9 per cent, with 2 more crashing at home in the fog. The skymarking had been poor, so the return on investment was 1 industrial building, 21 houses, 1 canal lock, and a great many trees in the Grunewald.

Another bombardier, Sgt John Enoch Wilkes known as Pappy, came from Barrington, Rhode Island, via the RCAF and had an extremely hairy first op, Berlin, 2 January 1944. They'd been first in line for take-off, not an easy thing for sprog Aussie skipper Flt Sgt Colin Peak with the rest of the squadron waiting behind. Also waiting were the fighters at the target, having had 40 minutes' warning from their night watchmen.

Berlin was always the worst. Pappy Wilkes, lying flat on his mat in his Perspex bomb-aimer's compartment, must have seen some of the 27 Lancasters go down in flames. When the gunners cried 'Corkscrew' and the pilot threw the aircraft around the sky, and the gunners shouted that their guns had jammed, and a Bf109 came in to help the Ju 88 that was attacking them, Wilkes may well have wished he'd stayed in his wooded, riverside, peaceful, small home town of Barrington.

Back at base, concern increased. Flying Control had heard nothing from Plt Off Geoff Ward, a skipper with 19 ops including 5 Berlins, and where was the new boy, Peak? Ward never did come back but Peak, Pappy Wilkes and the boys landed at 07:34 after 8 hours in the air, first up and last down. If ops were all like that, what chance had they?

Wilkes and Hannon were back on duty, 5 January, and their crews and Knilans's were bound for Szczecin. In Hannon's aircraft, *Streets could be seen outlined by incendiaries*. In Wilkes's, they thought the *bombing well concentrated and good fires resulted*. They were right, with 1,750 houses destroyed or seriously damaged, 50 industrial buildings and 8 ships sunk in the harbour. Knilans had an argument with jolly Harry Geller when, coming home over the sea, he saw a distress flare. Despite protestations, he flew low to find a dinghy with men in it and circled while the w/op sent a signal to Air-Sea Rescue. This was a dangerous thing to do. While the rescue aircraft was homing on their radio, the nightfighters could also be doing so. A seaplane showed up as dawn was breaking and all were grateful as Nick turned for home. The men in the dinghy were seven of 626 Squadron, about 100 miles off Withernsea. Their Lanc had run out of petrol. All were saved.

Brunswick, capital of an agricultural region of northern Germany known for its asparagus, beer, sausages and jam, was also a metal-working centre and had not been seriously attacked yet. Hannon and Turnbull were there, night of 14/15 January, and the general opinion was of a good, concentrated attack through heavy cloud. Secret listeners in England had heard the German running commentary start when the bombers were still some way off the Dutch coast. They feared the worst. Nightfighters joined the stream near Bremen and stayed in among it all the way to the target and back to the coast again, shooting down almost all of the 40 Lancasters lost on the raid, 8 per cent of the force. The Brunswick city report noted the destruction of 10 houses and the deaths of 14 people.

Recently transferred to the USAAF, it could be tour expired after the American standard of 25 ops. With only two more to go, Lt W.W.W. Turnbull had been even luckier than his compatriot Van Note. All his reports had been technical, about the flares, the marking, the accuracy of the bombing, and never a mention of fighters, flak hits, alarms and panics. If ever an exception could prove a rule, Turnbull was it. His reputation, stated in his DFC citation, also included 'high skill, fortitude and devotion to duty', but would Turnbull be an American like Van Note, tested to the last but delivered of his trials, or an American like Storey, victim of the best joke the Fates could devise, dead on his last trip? *Some undershooting and overshooting. Pathfinders rather early in the attack. Concentration improved later*, said his Interrogation report on his last op, Magdeburg, 21/22 January. Not written down but doubtless mentioned was his encounter with a nightfighter. They were attacked coming back and for 15 minutes the two aircraft pirouetted about the sky, the old-faithful gunners Sgts Michael and Bolt firing for all their lives while German cannon and machine-guns tore holes in LM361. Both protagonist crews would claim damage to the other but not destruction, so William Wrigley Watts Turnbull could write to his mother to tell her he was fine, just fine.

Pappy Wilkes was on that one, and he did two more Berlins before Leipzig, 19 February. Anyone who came back from that op had to be a deeply affected man. The Germans took little notice of the diversion at Keil and fighters got among the bombers from the Dutch coast onwards. As if that were not enough, winds were not as forecast and some squadrons got there early and had to mill about waiting for the pathfinders, to the delight of the home defences. Wilkes and the rest of No. 9 arrived as the pathfinders were dropping their TIs and Wanganui skymarkers and lost only 1 Lanc out of the 20 that took off, almost certainly to a nightfighter. Elsewhere in this large bomber force, 823 aircraft, it was much worse. There were 79 Lancasters and Halifaxes shot down, the majority by fighters, and 3 more crashed without direct interference from the enemy. One in ten bombers, just about, was lost, for a cloud-covered target with scattered results.

The Luftwaffe saw this period of the air war as a victory. Leipzig was one of three key moments which, at the time, seemed to signal defeat and withdrawal for Bomber Command. The other two were to come: Berlin, 24 March, and Nürnberg, 30 March. Pappy Wilkes would be there.

John Hannon flew his last to Stuttgart, 20 February. Bombing was scattered again but caused plenty of damage; the Bosch factory took several very effective hits. Losses were light, due to a large diversionary exercise over the North Sea by training flights and a feint attack on Munich. Alas for Hannon, the 1.5 per cent included ED654 WS/W. They fell near Welzheim, about 20 miles south-east of the target. It was John Hannon's seventh.

Wilkes was at Stuttgart too, and he went to Schweinfurt, Stuttgart once more, Frankfurt, and then that last big Berlin when exceptionally strong northerly winds blew many of the bombers off track. The flak had at least as many as the fighters because so many strayed over defended areas they were meant to avoid. Of the 74 bombers lost, only 1 was not due to enemy action, and matters were about to get worse.

On the night of 30/31 March, a friendly weather forecast encouraged the planners of a major raid on Nürnberg, even though it was the moon period. The forecast was reversed, the raid went ahead and Pappy Wilkes, now 2-Lt USAAF, thought he'd hit the target in which case he was one of very few. Most bombs did nothing more than plough fields and uproot trees.

Against that small credit had to be balanced an enormous debit. The nightfighter controllers, ignoring all diversions, had set their traps. They and the flak shot down more than 80 bombers on the way to and at the target, and more on the way home. Including crashes due to errors and failures not enemy induced, Bomber Command lost 105 Halifaxes and Lancasters that night, over 13 per cent. 1-Lt Helmut Schulte got four, Lt Doktor Wilhelm Seuss also, and 1-Lt Martin Becker shot down six Halifaxes on their way in, landed, refuelled, and felled another on their way home.

Losses of this magnitude were unsustainable, of course, but the raid on Essen a few nights before had had excellent results for losses of only 1.3 per cent. The *Luftwaffe War Diaries* claim that their Nürnberg success forced the RAF to admit defeat: 'It was the biggest night air battle of World War II and the total loss of 12 per cent of the operating force was too high even for British Command. The night air offensive was suspended, its failure being plain. But if the German nightfighters had won their greatest victory of the war, it was also their last.'

There was certainly more than a grain of truth in this, but a consideration at least equal to nightfighter success was the need to prepare the ground for the coming invasion of France by the Allies. Wilkes's squadron had already been to two French railway targets before Nürnberg, and that was now to be the way of it.

Chapter 10

SPECIAL JOBS FOR
SPECIAL MEN

RAF Coningsby had been the home of No. 617 Squadron until January 1944, when they swapped with 619 and moved to Woodhall Spa, a small, single-squadron station thought suitable for the secret activities of the special-purpose boys. This was a considerable improvement for them, not least in the officers' mess, the Petwood Hotel, equipped with swimming pool, tennis courts and golf course. Regrets were equal and opposite from the officers of 619 and one pilot wanted to stay.

Joe Tate: 'He [Knilans] didn't bother telling us anything about it. All we knew about 617 was that they were some sort of specialist squadron and they'd done two raids, the dams and the canal, and lost a lot of men.' Any objections were met with Knilans's impeccable logic. Hardly anyone on 619 had yet survived long enough to complete a tour, so 617 could not be any worse.

Wingco Cheshire wanted to experiment with low-level target-marking techniques. The results so far on the ski sites had shown accurate bombing of markers that had been dropped in the wrong place. At first, support for low flying from the high command was not universal. It was felt that a Lancaster flying a complex marking op at 200ft in the dark would probably crash and, if not, would be easy target practice for flak and machine-guns. The compromise, as compromises so often will, gave 617 the worst of all worlds. Their marker crews were to fly low-ish but no lower than 2,500ft, which meant that the bombsight wouldn't work properly, the marking would not reach the required standard, and the aircraft would still be an easy target for ground fire, although very little flak was expected around the ski sites.

They tried the method at Domart-en-Ponthieu, 21 January 1944, after letting three Oboe Mosquitos go first. Cheshire went in to inspect. Ignoring the 2,500ft restriction, he flew as low as he felt like and dropped

151

some markers of his own, not the green target indicators of the Mosquitos but the red spot fires, which burst at 3,000ft and burned on the ground for 10 minutes. Flying over again he reported to his squadron the position of the markers relative to the target and they, including Joe McCarthy, aimed accordingly. They hit two skis, one other building and a launching ramp. At Freval four nights later, with McCarthy and Knilans on his first with 617, Micky Martin did the marking with red spot fires and got one within 50yd of the target. Accurate the markers may have been but they were small and difficult to see in the bombsight. Joe Tate thought he'd got a direct hit on their second run. He and the rest didn't hit the spots but did crater the site extensively and dug up two approach roads.

Using heavy bombers at night and adapting Oboe for a new purpose was proving only a partial success. Stirlings and 617 Lancs had dropped almost 2,000 tons of bombs for little reward, although they hadn't lost anybody, plus they'd earned some negative PR from the French farmers around the ski sites who'd had buildings wrecked and livestock killed. Worst were the civilian casualties; there had been quite a few. One good result of the raids had been the demotivation of the local labour force, and delayed action bombs reinforced their unwillingness to work on construction. The Germans had to bring in slave labour.

Bomber Command passed the ski-site job back to the 8th USAAF and the 2nd Tactical Air Force. Their daylight raids throughout the spring seriously disrupted the V1 programme and caused the wholesale abandonment of surrounding countryside by the local French who, if they needed any further excuse, hated the Germans even more for it.

Air Vice-Marshal Cochrane, AOC 5 Group and a 617 enthusiast, encouraged Cheshire with his low-level marking. Cochrane was always looking to improve bombing techniques and this idea seemed to him worth his full backing. If it worked, 617 could be switched to those kinds of target requiring a degree of accuracy previously considered impossible. The doubters, which included the officers commanding the pathfinder squadrons, considered the idea too dangerous. Cheshire believed the risks were not so great and were well worth taking. Besides, it would give 617 a role in life, one they had failed to find after the dams.

The first official trial would be in the February moon. Part of the great Gnome & Rhône engineering works at Limoges was making engines for Messerschmitts but the factory was in the suburbs. No attempt had been made on it because, by conventional methods, large numbers of civilian deaths were inevitable. Knilans, quite taken by the informality of the briefing for his ski-site trip, was impressed again. Rather than the standard classroom-style lecture, concluding with a patriotic exhortation from the CO telling the boys how this was the most important raid they'd ever been on, at 617 the pilots gathered around a table, looked at a map and discussed the best way of doing it. The other trades met together too, bomb aimers with bomb aimers, navigators with navigators and so on.

There would be 12 Lancs on the mission, 5 with the 12,000lb HC bomb, the light case super-blockbuster. Dropping a single-decker bus was about the nearest equivalent, in weight and potential for accuracy. A further 6 Lancs would carry 14 1,000lb HE (High Explosive) standard bombs, and 1, Cheshire's, would carry a load of incendiaries.

The target was clearly visible and identifiable and Cheshire began by diving down to chimney height. Knilans: 'He flew over the factory roof three times to give the workers, mostly French girls, plenty of time to scatter. He dropped a load of yellow incendiaries on his fourth run and ordered the squadron in to bomb his markers which were dead centre.'

The bombing was almost all dead centre too. 'I saw one 12,000-pounder fall in the river short of the target, and one stick of 1,000-pounders also missed. All the rest of the bombs fell in the factory compound. Later photographs showed we had reduced 24 of the factory's bays to rubble and left only the shells of the remaining 24.'

The Limoges factory had been defended by two machine-guns. What would happen to the low-flying markers and the higher flying bombers on their 5-minute Sabs bombing run, if there were flak guns and fighters about? Even so, those in high places had to give credit for the accuracy and the amount of damage so few bombers could cause. No French had been killed nor any aircrew injured. It was a surgical strike, a new kind of bombing.

The Antheor railway viaduct had increased in importance as the Allies landed in Italy and began to try to fight their way up from Anzio. Each day thousands of tons of supplies were transported across the viaduct on their way to fuel the Wehrmacht. The Germans realised that a raid was bound to come and so increased the defences. On the night of 12 February, in poor weather, 617 went to test those defences to the full. Cheshire and Martin couldn't see to mark the target above 3,000ft and so repeatedly had to fly down the twisting valley which, at its end, formed the little sea inlet the viaduct crossed. Every time, the searchlights found them and the gunners shot them up.

Martin, with yet another daring low-level run inside the steep-sided ravine, almost succeeded while Cheshire was drawing the enemy fire at 4,000ft. At the last moment the gunners on the viaduct saw Martin and turned on him. Cannon shells smashed into the aircraft's nose as the bomb aimer was pressing the button. Flt Lt Bob Hay DFC and Bar, squadron bombing leader, dams and canal veteran, was killed instantly.

Martin, pulling up and clearing the viaduct by the finest of margins then dropping again to wave-top height, found that his flight engineer was wounded and the throttles and pitch controls were badly knocked about. In effect, they were on two engines at zero feet. The bombs were still there and they couldn't get rid of them because of shell damage, and they had no hope of getting home.

Cheshire saw all this and marked the target as well as he could, telling his men the flares were 100yd overshot. Knilans: 'We dropped down to 3,000 feet too, and my gunners opened up on the searchlights. They all went out. I climbed back to 10,000 feet and Joe called our bomb run, the viaduct silhouetted against the surf along the beach, then went down again for a low-level fast flight across France.' The squadron managed one 12,000-pounder within 15yd and several within 80yd, but the viaduct stood where it was.

In an epic journey where every new danger and mechanical failure was met with inspired improvisation, Martin at first aimed for an advance Allied fighter base on Corsica. Radio messages told him there were no medical facilities or doctor, so he struggled another 150 miles to get them to an American airfield at Cagliari in newly liberated Sardinia, where they buried Bob Hay.

For this superb effort Micky Martin was awarded a Bar to his DSO and posted to headquarters. Now only Dave Shannon, Ken Brown, Les Munro and Joe McCarthy remained of the dam-buster pilots.

The Antheor experience had finally and firmly convinced Cheshire that low-level marking was essential if small targets were to be hit precisely, but also that low-level marking in a Lancaster against a well-defended target was too dangerous by far. If the technique was to be developed and proved, and expanded for use by larger forces than 617 alone, some targets had to be found that were important to the Germans' war effort but where interference would be minimal.

Such criteria narrowed the field to one type of target only: factories in France making war supplies. They were lightly defended, partly because the fatherland came first when defence matériel was allocated and partly because such factories tended to be surrounded by French workers' houses.

A French historian gave a view from the ground of the raid on the Caudron-Renault factory at Albert in Picardie, 2 March, where they were building BMW engines for the Focke-Wulf 190:

> The squadron flew over Albert and surrounding districts for 20 minutes, voluntarily. The time of the raid had been chosen to be after the workers had gone home but before the populace had gone to bed, to give them the opportunity of reaching the shelters. The first red light on a parachute fell in the market square, 1,500 metres from the factory, then more red lights illuminated the objective. At 21:15, after the fall of a red-fire marking bomb, the attack began. The aircraft circled above the town before coming to release their bombs in turn on the factory, each detaching from the circle at the moment it passed over a farm beside the Albert–Arras railway then coming in to attack following the line. All the bombs, except one which hung up and fell in open countryside, hit the bullseye. The metal frameworks and walls of the various workshops were thrown down. Six months' stock of engines, a quarter of the entire German requirement from French factories, was destroyed.

Nick Knilans viewed the same events from the air:

> Camouflage nets had been placed above the factory, painted to resemble roads and small buildings. We bombers dropped flares that lit up the local landmarks, by which the markers located the target. Cheshire's bombsight was u/s so it was Munro who dropped two red spot fires on the roof. There were 13 of us [including McCarthy] with 12,000lb blockbusters and only one fell outside the compound. We dropped ours from 10,200 feet and Joe claimed a direct hit as usual. The lack of searchlights, flak and bandits made a most pleasant change and we were back home four hours after taking off.

The raid caused six deaths: three Belgian workers on fire duty, trying to remove the incendiaries, and three citizens outside the factory who had heart attacks as a result of the blast.

Possibly the most difficult of these French targets was the Nadella needle-bearing works at La Ricamarie, near St Etienne, Lyons. About

10,000 bearings a month were being made there for aero engines. On either side of the little valley in which the town sat, were Ben Nevis-sized mountains. The target itself covered about the same area as half a football pitch and was right in the middle of a residential quarter. On the first attempt, contrary to predictions, the cloud base was below the tops of the hills so they had to abandon, but not before a recce. Knilans: 'I flew below the clouds and across the city at 2,000 feet. We could see the factory, but if we'd bombed from that height we'd have gone up with it as well. Cheshire called off the attack so we returned to base and made a most careful landing with all our bombs aboard.' Next time, things turned out better, as Knilans recounted: 'We took off for St Etienne, 10 March, and circled the city while the leaders tried to mark. Cheshire made six runs over the factory. His markers bounced off the roof and into the town. Munro undershot with his incendiary markers.' McCarthy dropped his incendiaries from 160ft but they were not satisfactory either.

> We kept circling at 8,000ft. An Australian, Arthur Kell placed his markers onto the factory roof. Joe claimed our first two 1,000lb bombs hit the red flares and the rest of them caused a large explosion. It was nearly midnight. We landed two minutes short of eight hours in a flight. I had not been out of my seat. Photographs taken the next day showed that only the factory walls remained. Twelve crews had placed their bomb loads inside a factory compound 40 yards by 70 yards.

Kell, described in a French report as 'un grand flandrin', a great lanky fellow, indeed placed his incendiaries at the very heart of the factory. The official French report said: 'A very precise bombardment; the dimensions of the rectangle in which bombs fell was not more than 350m by 100m. But it was a useless, pointless act of vandalism which must be judged harshly.'

Astonished by the success of the raiders in finding such a difficult target tucked away in a residential district, the local Vichy commissar wanted to know 'if these English bombers didn't have some secret helpers on the ground'. One side effect of these attacks was much better co-operation by factory owners with the French Resistance in the matter of sabotaging their war production. If the owners didn't co-operate, well, a wireless message might be sent to 617 Squadron.

Cheshire had made Joe McCarthy a flight commander with accompanying promotion to squadron leader. On these high-precision raids to French targets, McCarthy was a deputy leader, marking from very low down. On the night of 16/17 March they attacked the Michelin tyre factory at Clermont-Ferrand, with six Lancs of 106 there to drop parachute flares. By the light of these, McCarthy dropped his incendiaries from 100ft, flying through surprisingly intense opposing fire from machine-guns and other automatic weapons. The main workshops were wrecked.

Next on the list were two explosives factories, once the French state gunpowder makers. At Bergerac they bombed from 8,000ft, which Knilans thought might not have been quite high enough. 'We received a severe jolt when another crew hit an ammunition dump. The armourers had arranged for their 1,000lb bomb to hit first, setting off their 12,000lb just before it landed, creating a larger blast area. It worked to perfection.' It certainly did. The explosion lasted 15 seconds. The following night they were at Angoulême, destroying the Pouderie Nationale. McCarthy dropped four green TIs and one 8,000lb double cookie.

The Sigma aero-engine factory at Vénissieux in the Rhône Valley, south of Lyons, was to prove more difficult. The first attempt used delayed action bombs with low flying forbidden. Flares did not light the way well, marking was therefore imperfect and they were ordered back two nights later. The flares were better this time. Cheshire, flying low over the river as permitted at own discretion, was trying to find the ideal place for his markers when McCarthy came in from the opposite direction and dropped his incendiaries on a row of saw-tooth factory roofs as seen in a photograph at the briefing. Cheshire followed and placed his own markers on the same bit of roof, then realised it was the wrong one by 400yd. Calling McCarthy on VHF, he gave direction and distance from their mistaken drop and McCarthy made another run, scoring a direct hit with two red spot fires on the main manufacturing hall. By now, the bombers had been circling for 20 minutes overhead. Cheshire called them in to bomb McCarthy's reds but they aimed for the other ones and kept doing so, despite Cheshire's anguished cries into the radio. 'Regret limited damage only', was his other message, when they got home.

That op was Sqn Ldr Joe McCarthy's fifty-second; he was 24 years old. Cheshire wrote in his log book: 'Sqn Ldr McCarthy has completed an exceptional and very distinguished second operational tour of duty.' The citation for the Bar to his DFC said: 'This officer has completed numerous sorties as captain of aircraft in which he has taken part in difficult and hazardous operations at low level. Sqn Ldr McCarthy has displayed exemplary skill and courage which, combined with his unfailing devotion to duty, have contributed much to the success achieved.' And he wasn't finished yet, except for having a fortnight's leave.

They went back to Vénissieux, night of 29/30 March, and there was no confusion. Knilans: 'My regular bomb aimer Joe Tate was off getting his commission and a new uniform so I was honoured to have Sqn Ldr Richardson in his place. He talked about bombing accuracy so much that he was nicknamed "Talking Bomb". He must have been over 40 years of age.'

Richardson, tutor to 617 in the use of the Sabs, well deserved his nickname. He was rather elderly for ops – he had been an RFC pilot – but he loved his gyroscopic Sabs more than anything in life and managed to fiddle himself quite a few trips with it. Knilans:

> We were carrying an 8,000lb blockbuster and two thousand pounders. Old Talking Bomb was quite excited as we had been circling over the target queueing up to bomb. Once on the run he was cool, though. He hit the centre of the factory from 8,600 feet. All of the bombs were reported to have fallen inside the walls. The Wingco flew around the compound directing the last bombers as to which end of the plant they should aim at.

The Vichy report stated that, while the factory's machines were in large part undamaged, the factory itself *est à reconstruire entièrement*. There were no civilian casualties, the population having been evacuated after the first raid.

That was the end of Nick Knilans's first tour. He and his crew had various options, such as a posting to Training Command where the relaxed atmosphere of 617 would be replaced by routine and tight discipline. Nick might well have been sent back to the US, while the crew would be split up and at some point could expect individual recalls to second tours, almost certainly with fresh-faced sprog skippers.

Another option was to volunteer for a second tour starting now. Lt Knilans, USAAF on detached service, could not get promotion if he stayed, there being no higher USAAF rank on the squadron for him to step into, but that didn't worry him much. Another 20 ops didn't sound too bad and lately they'd been over France rather than Berlin. All the crew had been made officers, so they could all live in the Petwood Hotel, and they had good friends locally. Yes. Why not? Of Nick's originals, only Joe Tate demurred, as he had every right to do. He was a teacher by profession and training bomb aimers appealed.

Chapter 11

FATE, TIME, OCCASION, CHANCE, AND CHANGE

C-in-C Harris, perhaps underestimating Hitler's total and delusional grip on Germany's war, had failed to make Germany capitulate by bombing alone. An invasion would be necessary after all, and Bomber Command was to do everything it could to prepare for that fateful enterprise. This meant cutting off the German forces in northern France from the possibility of reinforcement and resupply, which in turn meant destroying factories in France and disrupting the transport system, without exposing the location planned for the invasion. Harris knew his bombers could do this but warned of unacceptable numbers of French casualties. The target marking was just not good enough, but the success of 617 in surgical strikes on small targets hinted at a way forward.

The problems with markers skidding and so overshooting, because they were dropped at such low level, had been overcome by dropping them in a dive. Low-level dive bombing in a Lancaster had hardly been the first thought in the aircraft designer's mind and, even though it worked, Cheshire thought that a different aircraft would be better and began badgering for a Mosquito. By the end of March his wish had been granted. He had also promised to fulfil Air Chief Marshal Harris's condition: the Mosquito was on loan, with more promised, only if the arrangement led to a raid on Munich.

If 617 Squadron was to keep Mosquitos for its own use, it had to prove itself able to mark Munich properly, where there were 400 guns and where a truly successful op had still to take place. Cheshire was happy to assure Harris that Munich could be marked but first the technique had to be tried against something a little less well defended. The raid was set up where the entire Cheshire philosophy, Mosquito and all, would be put to the test. Nick Knilans heard about it in the saloon bar of a Lincoln hotel, the White Hart, when an Australian navigator he knew came in. After congratulating each other on still being alive, the Aussie said he'd heard that 617 Squadron was going to lead 5 Group from then on, instead of the pathfinders.

This was news to Knilans and very disturbing the next day for Cheshire, since only he, McCarthy and the other two flight commanders were supposed to know about it. Such leaks were not as rare as they should have been, throughout the war. Also of concern was a message received from the Resistance to say that a large cash reward had been offered for anyone able to produce a member of 617 Squadron. They'd have to shoot one down first.

Cheshire's method, which would become 5 Group's method, was employed for the first time, 5 April, at Toulouse. It showed the advantages and a potential disadvantage. No. 617 and others of 5 Group circled as Lancasters dropped flares to light up a big aircraft-repair works on the outskirts of the town, so that Cheshire could see to mark. He went in twice through heavy shelling but was not sufficiently satisfied to drop his markers. Knilans: 'Cheshire made two low-level passes over the factory roofs. I could see his Mosquito zooming about through a shower of light flak shells and searchlights. He dropped his red spot fires on the third pass.' They were in the middle of the factory complex. He called in the bombers but shortage of fuel meant he couldn't stay until the end. It didn't matter.

McCarthy, starting a third tour, and Munro dropped more red spot fires absolutely on the button, on top of Cheshire's, and the Lancs of 9 Squadron and other 5 Group units bombed almost perfectly. Next day, reconnaissance pictures showed a devastated site with only a few near-misses, which proved the advantage of the system. The disadvantages for the time being remained as potential only. Flak had hit just one Lanc while they were milling about, circling, waiting for the marking to be pronounced good, and there had been no enemy aircraft. On some later raids, the fighters would have a great time.

Cheshire's repeated circuits had meant that most of the local Toulousians had had time to reach a shelter or to run into the country. Even so, there was a civilian price: 22 dead, 45 wounded, 100 houses down.

Woodhall Spa was fog-bound so the squadron was diverted coming home from this raid, to an American bomber base in Norfolk, at Westcott. There, Knilans met a friend, a Halifax pilot. They'd trained together. They worked out that the 2 of them were the only ones left alive out of the 30 who had been on their twin-engine trainer course at Burton upon Trent.

Knilans continued to stay alive, in one of 17 Lancs of 617 that went to Saint Cyr-l'École, not far from Paris, at the bottom of the garden of the palace of Versailles, where there was an important signals station and depot. This was a 617-only raid, begun by Cheshire diving down in his Mosquito and placing his markers off-centre. Munro tried to back up but his reds were off too. Instructions were given to compensate in the bombing but the first stick hit the spot, so Cheshire told the rest to bomb on that.

Knilans's w/op was monitoring transmissions from a radar station on the English side of the Channel coast, which had the range to detect any bandits near where they were.

Les chirped up as Munro was marking. 'Skip,' he said, 'that radar fellow says there's bandits about.' He switched me through so I could hear. A calm voice in my headphones said 'Seven bandits have taken off and are ten miles from your position.' I told Joe to get ready to bomb. He replied that we hadn't been ordered in yet. I said to get on anyway. Cheshire came over the radio to say we were to bomb 150 yards short of Munro's markers.

The radar voice spoke again. 'Bandits closing fast at five miles.' 'Steady, steady,' said Joe. 'Bandits at three miles and your altitude,' said Mr Radar. 'Bombs gone,' said Joe. 'Oh, bloody good show, everyone bomb on that,' said Cheshire on the VHF. 'It's a direct hit, right in the middle of the target.' He sounded excited and delighted. 'All seven bandits one mile,' said Mr Radar. 'Home, chaps,' said I, and nobody saw any bandits.

Also on that date, 10 April, there were raids on five sets of railway yards, at Ghent, Aulnoye, Laon, Tergnier, and at Tours, which was where 9 Squadron went as part of a force of 180 Lancasters, all of 5 Group. Pappy Wilkes hadn't flown since Nürnberg. In the meantime he'd been granted a new rank, Flight Officer, invented by the USAAF to correspond more closely with the RAF's pilot officer, thought to be somewhere between 2nd and 1st lieutenant. Only one Lanc went down on this raid and that was DV198 WS/U-Uncle, a long-lived veteran of 52 ops. Flt Off John Enoch Wilkes of Barrington, Rhode Island, was on his fifteenth, halfway through his tour, when the flak found the Uncle over the target and she fell into a Tours suburb called St-Pierre-des-Corps. The seven bodies were buried at Nantes. Wilkes's was later removed to the USAAF Cemetery at St-Laurent-sur-Mer, Calvados.

Cheshire's Mosquito marking was such a breakthrough that Cochrane told him to set up three more crews of two, pilot and navigator. The pilots were dam-buster Australian David Shannon, plus new recruits Kearns and Fawke. They were to do nothing from then on except fly Mosquitos. The first op they flew together was marking for 5 Group, including 617, at the marshalling yards of Juvisy on the southern edge of Paris, 18 April. There were 202 Lancs altogether, and the 9 Squadron pilots' reports all compliment the marking as accurate, with one, two or three red spot fires visible depending on the smoke, and a great success it was for only two Lancs down.

Knilans wasn't there for an exceptional reason. From the end of December 1943, meetings and conferences had been held and memos and reports had flown about, to try and define what use Mr Barnes Wallis's new bomb, codenamed Tallboy, would be. Could it jam the Rothensee shiplift? Could it penetrate a U-boat pen? Could it demolish the Sorpe dam? When, O when, were we going to find out?

The original idea of Tallboy had been as a delayed action earthquake or 'Earth displacement' bomb. Barnes Wallis had put forward the notion as early as 1940 that, as modern warfare was dependent on industry and industry was dependent on power, the destruction of the sources of power – hydroelectric dams, generating stations, oil refineries – was the most direct route to victory. Instead of relying on direct hits with small bombs to do this, a 10-ton bomb should be developed, plus an aircraft capable of carrying same to 40,000ft and dropping it accurately from there. Such a bomb would set up a pressure wave as it exploded under the ground, and destroy the target from beneath.

No such aircraft had been contemplated and so the idea, although sound in theory, was forgotten, until the wartime requirements surfacing in 1943 brought it back onto the agenda. There was still no aircraft capable of lifting a 10-ton bomb but a modified Lancaster could carry a 6-tonner up to 18,000ft. Tallboy Medium was born. From that height it would not have time to reach its terminal velocity, estimated at 2,590mph, later measured in trials at 1,930mph but eventually found to be 2,727mph. Such a height would, however, allow it to break the sound barrier which, as every schoolboy used to know, occurs at around 760mph. At that speed, it was hoped it would burrow underground to 70 or 80ft. Surely, at that speed, it would also go through a U-boat-pen roof?

There were all sorts of production problems in war-stretched British industry. The few firms that had the know-how and the equipment were already at full tilt on other projects, but room would be found somehow and the Americans agreed to help out and make some, as soon as the Limeys knew what it was they were supposed to be making.

Tallboy Medium was shaped like a fat rocket ship with a very sharp nose. Compared to the other 12,000lb bomb, the HC, the flying oil drum/single-decker bus that 617 Squadron had dropped on the Dortmund–Ems canal, Tallboy was a thing of beauty, an enormously menacing and businesslike weapon which looked as if it could destroy anything. At least, this is how it looked to Nick Knilans and Joe Tate as they watched it being fitted inside Lancaster ME561 AJ/R-Roger.

Knilans had flown in AJ/R ever since he'd been with 617 Squadron and she had always been a bit of a beast. The crew's complaints about shaky landings, and the pilot's complaints about having to haul her physically into the air, had been answered when engineers from Avro found that certain essential components on the tail had been swapped port/starboard and fitted upside down.

The Tallboy had a novel tail construction too. Shock waves caused by it breaking the sound barrier would move the bomb from its course and so the tail fins were offset to impart spin to the bomb as it fell, keeping it straight as rifling does for a bullet.

Knilans flew to Boscombe Down, 22 April, and took off with his Tallboy at 19:00 two days later, to drop it on the Ashley Walk bombing range in the New Forest. The scientists wanted to record the descent of the bomb from the worm's eye view and so they had the brilliant notion of putting an upward facing cine-camera in the safest place, close to the target.

Joe Tate: 'They'd experimented before with this bomb, of course, but they wanted an operational crew to try it out and they chose us. Our normal practice targets were large triangles laid out on the beach at Wainfleet. This was a cube, like a hut, and at 18,000 feet it didn't look very big.'

It was a raised concrete platform, 10ft by 10ft and 8ft thick. A standard bomb wouldn't have done much to it if hit directly, and nothing at all falling a distance away. What effect a Tallboy would have was the question of the day.

It was Joe Tate's final flight. He wasn't going to carry on with ops but he was going to have one last hurrah at an aiming point. They missed it by 100yd, which was extremely good when nothing at all was known about the way the bomb would perform. The worm's eye may have recorded how his safe haven became a crater 80ft across, but the camera was never found. Two more bombs were dropped that day and three more the next, by which time the 617 crews had got the aiming error down to 83yd, with the earth tremors being felt over a mile away. It looked like a very promising new weapon.

Munich was scheduled for 24 April. Before that, 617's low-level marking would be tried out at Brunswick, but results were not good. Red spot fires were placed accurately by 617's Mosquitos. Joe McCarthy's Lanc had a mixed load of markers, to keep the spot fires burning, and 1,000lb bombs which he dropped on target, but cloud and radio confusion led to most of the force bombing the reserve TIs, which were several miles out. They would have to sort out their problems for Munich in two nights' time.

Munich was vital, with the marshalling yards the central feature. Another raid, twice as big, was mounted the same night to Karlsruhe, and a force of six Lancs dropped Window simulating a raid heading for Milan. German fighters were called to these other invasions leaving Munich mostly to its flak, which was quite intense enough. Of the 244 Lancs taking part, 9 went down, including 1 of 9 Squadron and 1 of 617 but the Mosquitos flew through it. McCarthy on this op had a bomb load new to him, six red spot fires and the rest J bombs. The J was a novelty, an incendiary inside a tube of methane which acted like a giant flamethrower at 1500°C. They'd been taken to Brunswick by 9 Squadron for the first time and now 617 had them.

The general opinion among returning crews was that Munich had been a success. Later reports bore this out: 2,500 buildings destroyed or badly damaged and the railways a mess, many times more wreckage than all the previous attempts put together.

It was a busy time at 9 Squadron with 13 ops in the month of May and many replacement crews coming in, including one with navigator

Flt Sgt James Morton Stevenson whose parents had emigrated to the USA from Scotland. While they decided that the family would move into one of the newly built apartments in Parkchester, Bronx, New York City, their young son had made his own decision and instead hurried off to Canada to join the RCAF. His first op was a D-Day feint to Cherbourg, night of 28 May, more precisely to the German guns at St Martin-de-Varreville. There were attacks on five batteries that night all along the coast. No clue could be given about the real destination for the invasion.

It was hardly a difficult job for a navigator, even on his first trip, to find a spot on the French coast but when they got there things were less straightforward. They saw the markers go down but were ordered on the wireless, by Morse code not voice, to orbit until called in. Nobody liked orbiting over German gunners and it was a relief when word, or rather dots and dashes, came to tell them to bomb. They flew home safe and sound, perhaps wondering when and where the invasion would be, not knowing what their role would be in it or, indeed, if they'd live to see the day.

The battle order WAAF at 9 Squadron still had Stevenson's skipper, Cliff King, down as a flight sergeant although his promotion to pilot officer had come through, 5 June, noted in the Operations Record Book in standard but quaint fashion since he was already there, as *Plt Off C.R. King posted to 9 Squadron on appointment to commission*. Whatever, King, Stevenson and crew perused the typed list and saw they were on ops.

They didn't know it but they would be part of an historic event, a massive attack on German positions on the Normandy coast by 1,000 bombers, dropping 5,000 tons of bombs, more than ever before on a single night. Including diversions and various small-scale activities meant to complicate and confuse, there would be over 1,200 aircraft of Bomber Command in the air, a new record, and only 9 would be lost to enemy action, plus 3 to mechanical failure.

The small-scale, confusing activity with the greatest responsibility of all was the task of two squadrons, 617 and 218. Since Knilans had dropped the first Tallboy, the rest of the squadron had had no chance to train with it because, throughout the month of May, they had been training for Operation Taxable, a task as secret and as important as any bombing mission could be, except that Operation Taxable was nothing to do with bombing. Almost every day, 617 Squadron had gone on what they called navigation training exercises over the North Sea, off the Yorkshire coast.

Sir Robert Cockburn, a physicist who had led the development of VHF radio in military aircraft, and of radar countermeasures including Window, now had a scheme for the dam busters. Trials against a radar station at Bempton, between Filey and Bridlington, had shown that by having a good number of aircraft flying fairly low over the sea in elongated, overlapping circuits parallel to the coast, gradually closing in towards the shore and gradually increasing the amounts of a new type of Window dropped at precisely timed intervals, the illusion could be created on radar screens that a mass of shipping was approaching. All aircraft had to keep strictly accurate distances from each other as well as from the coast. It would be extremely hard to do but, if done properly, the Germans would be fooled and would be forced to keep large resources away from the real invasion in Normandy.

Knilans was at the 617 Squadron briefing:

This Dr Cockburn guy came and said he wanted us to simulate a convoy 14 miles wide, crossing the Channel at seven knots. Eight double crews [normal crew plus extra pilot, navigator and three Window chuckers] would fly for four hours, then to be relieved by another eight crews. Each plane would fly 35 seconds on course, then a reverse course for 32 seconds. Then a slow turn back on the first course, meanwhile throwing out a load of Window. We could not vary our height or our speed by more than the smallest fractions [3,000ft, 160mph]. I had to do this for two hours, after which Jimmy Castagnola [recently arrived pilot] would take over. Joe McCarthy was with his close pal Dave Shannon. They did everything together, including dropping a flare down the Wingco's chimney which got them on the night duty rota for quite a while.

We practised precision flying by day and night, with the navigators timing us on stop watches. We were allowed no leave, but that wasn't so bad at the Petwood, and there were some very nice WAAFs and lasses from the village. We were confined to camp 4 June and told the next day we were on.

It worked. Overlord headed for Normandy while 617's illusory Window invaders headed for the Pas de Calais. The Germans didn't pay it much attention at first. They had already convinced themselves that the genuine article was another spoof fleet, the one headed for Boulogne.

A particularly battle-scarred and experienced squadron, No. 218 of 3 Group, had been selected to experiment with a new blind-bombing aid called GH, which was a system based on signals from the aircraft being reflected by ground stations. It required great technical accuracy from the aircraft crews but could produce excellent results. Being the only front-line squadron equipped with and trained to use GH, they were the obvious last-minute choice for the emergency idea of a second D-Day spoof, Operation Glimmer, at Boulogne.

There was a sudden rush of training flights, noted in log books as 'special local cross-country' or similar, and they were ready for take-off late on the night of 5 June. Like 617, they took extraordinary crews. All of them realised that the lives of many Allied soldiers depended on them.

After hours of flying precisely in the required orbits, edging towards the coast at the supposed speed of an invasion fleet, the crews of 218 were rewarded with the flashes of German heavy batteries opening up against the fictitious formation of vessels. E-boats were sent out to attack the invisible invaders and, of course, could find nothing.

When the Germans realised they'd been had at Boulogne, they reconvinced themselves for a time that the real invasion must be the other one, 617 Squadron heading for the Pas de Calais, while elsewhere on this hectic night of deception and double bluff, Stirlings were dropping dummy parachutists and more Window – Operation Titanic – and more Stirlings and American Fortresses were jamming all the enemy coastal radar in the Channel region with a Mandrel curtain. Mandrel was a device that reduced the enemy radar's range and thus cut the amount of time the Germans had to launch a counter-attack against incoming air or seaborne forces.

That part of the incoming air force which was 9 Squadron, including Jimmy Stevenson the American Scottish Canadian navigator, had to find Pointe-du-Hoc, near the quiet little Normandy town of St Pierre-du-Mont, marked on the Operation Overlord map as gun batteries threatening the forces due to land at Omaha Beach. Tomorrow, the US Rangers would be wading through waves and bullets, struggling up Omaha and trying to take that same Pointe-du-Hoc promontory. It was the bombers' task to make sure that they would at least get as far as the beach. Doing the same for all the other units coming ashore, strung along miles and miles of hellish golden sand, RAF bombers also attacked the guns at Fontenay, Houlgate, La Pernelle, Longues, Maisey, Merville, Mont Fleury, Ouistreham and St Martin-de-Varreville. As 9 Squadron flew home that early morning, they saw the armada below, thousands of ships and boats, thousands of white wakes. The first gallants of the Allied armies were already ashore.

No one can doubt the savagery and horror that met the invaders of the Normandy landings, nor the determination and heroism that inspired them to victory. The bomber crews could only look down from the relative safety of their aircraft and hope that what they'd done, to fool the Germans and to reduce their fighting capacity, had made the thing possible, rather than impossible.

James Stevenson had not been with the squadron long enough for anybody to get on much more than nodding terms. He'd been going in the sergeants' mess for a couple of weeks during busy and exciting times, keeping with the chaps he knew as new crews tended to do, and it was ops again on D-Day plus one, an attack on German Army positions at Evel, near Argentan, a small town in the département of Orne, Normandy. This was another thousand-bomber night, largely hitting railways and other infrastructure, helping to clear the way for the Allies' push into France.

Most of the 9 Squadron crews met little opposition. They all attacked the target at around 01:15 from between 5,000ft and 6,000ft. There were some hits and some misses, a lot of smoke and not much seen in the way of results. For 9 Squadron, business had been as usual as they could have hoped it to be. They turned for home.

The raiders were expected back between 03:00 and 03:45. At 03:05 the first one was down and by 03:50, of the 20 aircraft flying from Bardney, 19 had come back. A-Able was late. Nothing had been heard. The crew wasn't familiar around the station, there hadn't been time, so the anxiety had a different quality. After all, it wasn't the wingco who was missing, or someone on his thirtieth like Andy Storey had been. These boys were only on their third. The girls on Flying Control didn't know that two of the boys were married, or that the young navigator, only 20 years old, had come over from New York.

They also didn't know that shortly before 02:30, a few miles away at Waddington base station, the D/F (direction finding) unit had picked up a very weak signal from A-Able, asking for the way home. This was not at all unusual. Even with the Gee box, aircraft often got lost. That was why Waddington D/F was there, and they'd tried to get a fix to help but no acknowledgement came and no further contact could be made. Nobody could have guessed where WS/A might have been when her call was transmitted.

At Bardney, the tired flyers of 9 Squadron were interrogated and went to bed. The WAAFs waited, and the officers in command, until there was no point in waiting any longer. If A-Able hadn't gone down or landed somewhere by now, she'd be out of petrol. The conclusion had to be reached. One of their aircraft was missing.

It was only 20 miles away. Plt Off King had had no time to enjoy his new rank nor draw his increased wage packet. He was lying dead in the burned out wreckage of his aircraft near Belvoir Castle, by Grantham. The promotion of Flt Sgt James Morton Stevenson to pilot officer was on its way but he, too, was lying dead in the wreckage.

By the River Loire, 100 miles from the coast, was the town of Saumur, between Tours and Angers. Saumur was a main railway junction and it had a tunnel through which would pass German reinforcements from south-west France to the invasion combat region. It also had a railway bridge, crossing a road and the Loire. Two raids with conventional bombs had failed to make an impression and now there was news of a Panzer division to be expected imminently, using the Germans' favoured mode of transport, rail. Despite having been forced to neglect Tallboy and Sabs practice, 617 Squadron was ordered to prepare an operation in haste: the first use of the new Tallboy bomb in anger. The objective of the raid was to block the entrance to the tunnel at one end and knock down the bridge at the other.

On 8 June, 3 Mosquito markers, piloted by Shannon, Fawke and Cheshire, set off with 25 Lancasters of 617, 19 of them with Tallboys for the tunnel, including McCarthy on his sixtieth op and Knilans on his thirty-fifth, 6 with thousand-pounders for the bridge. In addition, 83 Squadron provided four Lancs, with H2S sets and variously loaded with flares and more 1,000lb bombs.

Shannon had to come home with engine trouble. The four Lancs of 83 Squadron found that H2S didn't help much when the target was a piece of level ground so their sticks of flares, supposed to provide light for Cheshire, were not very accurate. Nevertheless, they, with the moonlight, were enough for Cheshire to see what he was doing as he dived and placed his spot fires from 500ft, he estimated about 40yd short of the tunnel entrance.

As the first few bombs hit, the crews felt a little deflated. Instead of the massive flash they had with the 12,000lb HC, these earth-piercing bombs showed only a blink of red light as they went in. Exploding under the soil, they put up a lot of muck and smoke which obscured the flares, so the rest of the Tallboy force had to go around several times before getting a good view on their runs. From heights up to 10,500ft, two of them got their bomb in the cutting leading to the tunnel and one, missing the marker by less than 20yd, landed on the tunnel roof and went right through it, bringing down enough debris to block the tunnel for months. The Germans would just about have it clear when the Allies reached it in August.

The 1,000lb bombs didn't bring the bridge down but it hardly mattered. That part of the reinforcement threat had been removed. Now of immediate concern were German E-boats in the Channel. The very fast – 35 knots – agile and heavily armed German motor torpedo boats, much bigger and more formidable than their British and American counterparts, were harassing the cross-Channel shipping which brought men and supplies for the Allied invaders. Royal Navy destroyers were finding it very hard to catch these hit-and-run speedboats before they slipped back into their impregnable docks – impregnable, that was, until Tallboy.

There were two ways it was thought the Tallboy might work. One, it could penetrate the very substantial and cleverly constructed pen roofs; two, it could cause a tidal wave in the harbour and smash the boats up against the quayside. In response to the invasion traffic, many more E-boats and other light attack craft were gathering in the harbours of Le Havre and Boulogne than could be accommodated in the pens.

These were among the most heavily defended targets in France and first up was Le Havre, 14 June, and it was to be a daylight raid, something Bomber Command hadn't done for over a year. Another novelty would be fighter escort by Spitfires, a comfort that would continue for the short-range French targets that would be 617's lot for a while. As well as RAF and RCAF Spitfire squadrons there would be Free French, Norwegians, Poles, Belgians, all anxious to help in the great task of liberation.

At Le Havre, 617 crews took an extra man, a volunteer who could act as front gunner to shoot up the flak positions. Sqn Ldr McCarthy was there, flight commander, and Knilans: '22 Lancs of 617 followed Wingco Cheshire in his Mosquito. He dove down from 3,000ft to 700ft before releasing his red target markers. He was completely encased in hundreds of rounds of light flak shells. He escaped one more time.' The 617 Squadron ORB described the same incident thus: *The Squadron Commander dropped four red spot fires to act as a guide to the approaching bombers which were attacking in three waves.* 'Taffy, our new bomb aimer [Sgt G.G. Rogers], said most of the Tallboys landed in the harbour although some seemed to go through the bomb-proof roof of the pen.'

Two did penetrate and explode, making big holes and displacing walls beneath. A third made a crater but didn't go right through, possibly because the bomb didn't work properly. It was believed that other pens at other bases had even thicker and more ingenious roofs. Still, the Tallboy was all they had, and almost all of the E-boats at Le Havre had been sunk.

Knilans's aircraft was holed by flak and his mid-upper, Sgt Alf 'Bing' Crosby, with him since the Albert trip, was wounded in the leg. 'He said it would be all right to wait until we returned to base to have it treated.'

So successful was the raid and, in the terms applied at the time, so free of incident, that the squadron was ordered to Boulogne the next day. There was a line of cloud all along the French coast and prospects did not look very good for high-level bombing by the 22 Lancs of 617. Cheshire found the sky clear below 10,000ft and the leading aircraft dived to that level to bomb, following the markers put down by pathfinders for the 130 Lancasters that were bombing the harbour and shipping conventionally. Conditions were really too poor for visual bombing with the Tallboy monster and Cheshire decided to recall after all, but not until some had been through the flak maelstrom: 8 of the 11 that did bomb were hit by flak.

There were more problems, too, ones they weren't used to. Joe McCarthy, knocked off course by the flak, returned to his run to find that his Tallboy had gone without his permission. Another crew had the opposite experience, a Tallboy that refused to go. In the daylight, Knilans saw something he would never have known about at night.

He'd taken Plt Off James Castagnola, his D-Day Taxable pilot partner, along for the ride to Le Havre and he came to Boulogne too. He preferred the excitement to waiting back at the mess and, in his capacity as extra observer, saved the lot of them. Knilans:

Our crew had a bit of a fright as we finished our bomb run among the flak shells whistling past us. 'Look up, Nicky,' yelled Jimmy Castagnola. I did, and saw a dozen thousand pounder bombs coming at us. Another squadron's Lancaster had dumped their bombs through the clouds. I made a very steep, diving turn to port. Roy in the rear turret claimed he could have patted one of the bombs as it fell past.

The raids on Le Havre and Boulogne removed the E-boat as a threat to Channel shipping. One report counted 130 of them sunk. Those left had to retreat to Ijmuiden on the Dutch coast. On the way back from Boulogne, some aircrew reported seeing fighters, or what they assumed were fighters, small, very fast, with their tails on fire. These were V1s, flying bombs, a few days into their campaign, heralding a new emphasis for 617: Tallboy versus Hitler's secret weapons.

Chapter 12

SECRETS ONE, TWO, AND THREE

Still some weeks away from the battle front but a long way from his mechanic's job in 1939, an American pilot was completing the second to last phase of his training. Before moving on to Lancasters, he and his crew were converting from two engines to four via the Short Stirling, the bomber originally meant for war but withdrawn to safety. That is to say, it was safe from the Germans, if not from its learner pilots and its own design faults.

The Stirling was notoriously difficult at take-off and landing and these always provided nervous moments for aircrew. The captain on this occasion was one Sgt John Edward Stowell, AKA Jesse, of Royal Oak, Detroit, Michigan. They were coming home from a night cross-country and the Stirling they were flying had had a long and bruising career in the hands of novices. If an aircraft could be weary, arthritic and resentful, this was it.

As they made their approach, the only sound was of the skipper asking the flight engineer to lower the undercart. Stirling undercart legs were notorious for collapsing. All sat in hopeful, fingers-crossed silence while Sgt Stowell concentrated his mind on softness. The wheels touched, skidded a little, and they were rolling along the runway, smooth as you like. Stick back, tail down, fine for a short while, then there came a terrible juddering and shaking, and an awful grinding noise so loud it could be heard above the engines. Crew members started shouting. Skipper yelled for quiet as he brought the big bomber to a stop.

He opened up the starboard outer to turn to port onto the perimeter track, but nothing happened. 'I can't get the bloody thing to move,' he said over the intercom. 'I'm not surprised,' said the rear gunner. 'We left our tail wheels about half a mile back and I'm sitting here with a flaming great hole in my turret, which is half flaming full of lumps of tarmac. I've got my legs over my guns to prevent damage to either.'

'Well,' said the skipper, 'get your flaming feet off your flaming guns, stick them through the flaming hole and walk us off the runway or we'll be here all night.'

Throughout the winter and spring months, while the Stowell crew were converting to heavies, the Allies had been bombing the ski sites and a power struggle among the German High Command had been moving to a kind of resolution. The A4 (V2) rocket project was Wehrmacht property. The Fi103 (V1) flying bomb project, new codename *Maikäfer* (cockchafer), was Luftwaffe. A special-purpose army unit, 65 Korps, had been formed to operate all secret weapons.

Hitler wanted his revenge rockets and flying bombs immediately. The campaign must start before the expected invasion could be mounted. The manufacturers of the Fi103, Volkswagen, had nothing like the numbers of skilled engineering staff they needed to meet their production targets and the V2 was some distance away from being ready.

The whole thing was a mess, as well as a race to see which weapon could become effective first, and a matter of politics, influence and double-dealing to obtain resources to help win the race. The simple and cheap Volkswagen V1 – each cost £125 to make, about £4,000 in today's money – was technically less glamorous but it did look like working. Many of the ski sites had been wrecked by Allied bombing but that didn't seem to matter, British Intelligence noted. The enemy wasn't bothering to repair them any more and was instead building a different, much less complicated kind of arrangement which, with numbers well dispersed and camouflaged, was also harder to hit. Another curious thing was that these 'modified' sites – 61 at the latest count – didn't look finished. They had no ramps or rails for launching.

Intelligence decided that such vital components must be prefabricated. When they were put up, the attack on London would begin. The Air Staff, three days after D-Day, 9 June, thought that it would be at least two more weeks before pilotless aircraft would be over London. Bad weather on 12 June had allowed aerial photography of only nine modified sites but there was activity at six of them. Wg Cdr Kendall, directing the photoreconnaissance operation, thought the bombardment 'could be expected to begin at any moment'. While the Air Ministry disagreed and filed his report, Hitler ordered the mass offensive to begin that night.

Orders from the Führer were one thing; practical supplies and a functioning operational method were another. Zero hour was postponed and postponed. In the end, by 04:00 on the morning of 13 June, the exhausted troops of 65 Korps, with everything going wrong that could, had managed to launch 10 V1s towards Tower Bridge from the 55 sites which were trying. Of the 10, 4 crashed on take-off and 2 did not reach England. Even so the results, compounded by heavy artillery shelling of Folkestone and Maidstone, were enough to cause alarm.

The first ever buzz bomb, doodlebug, V1, fell at Gravesend, 20 miles short of Tower Bridge. Cuckfield, Bethnal Green and Sevenoaks were the other accidental recipients. The Bethnal Green one killed six people and destroyed a bridge, but not The Bridge. Ministry men and staff officers all thought this odd but could not agree on the character of oddness. Some said it was a pathetic damp squib, illustrating the inability of the Germans to do the job properly. The V1 was all gong and no dinner. There was no need, after all, to send 3,000 American bomber sorties against the modified sites. Some took a different view, saying it was a false start, a temporary setback, and the real thing was imminent.

Intelligence also suggested, sometimes to deaf ears, that the V2 supersonic rocket was nearing operational readiness. There was also the possibility that the Germans might launch the V2 with atomic or bacterial warheads, the argument being that the estimated small payload would not justify the weapon's obvious expense if it were only ordinary explosives. Hahn and Strassman of the Kaiser Wilhelm Institute in Berlin had found the evidence for nuclear fission in 1938, six years earlier. Hahn saw the potential of the process for generating electricity. Someone else in Germany might have seen the potential for the atom bomb, as had the British and the Americans.

Two days after the Boulogne raid, a directive from Wg Cdr Carey-Foster, HQ Bomber Command, reached 5 Group HQ, listing targets that 617 Squadron were to take on 'at the first opportunity' with their own miracle bomb, the Tallboy:

- U-boat pens at Brest
- Four rocket sites in the Pas de Calais
- Keil canal – lock gates etc.
- Dortmund–Ems canal aqueducts
- E-boat pens at Boulogne.

On the night and morning of 15–16 June, 244 V1s were launched from 55 sites, of which 45 crashed straight away destroying 9 of their own launching sites and a French village, and 73 reached the London conurbation. One bug doodled all the way into deepest Suffolk before dropping harmlessly into a field. The Germans had surprise assistance at first from the London anti-aircraft gunners who fired enthusiastically at these alien craft and brought down quite a number. After a couple of nights it was pointed out that some of the buzz bombs might miss if they weren't shot down, so the guns fell silent.

Hitler came to northern France to see for himself and was immensely proud of the German nation that was able to fight with weapons so advanced. He assigned top priority to V1 production and, to allow for an increase well above the current rate of 3,000 a month, a cutback in the V2 programme. The feeling among V1 field commanders was that 100 a day were nowhere near enough to force a victory for Germany. The Allies would simply retaliate with new ferocity.

On 18 June, the weary but admirable 65 Korps launched their five-hundredth doodlebug. On the same day Gen Eisenhower, Allied Supreme Commander, ordered that V-bomb targets for his air forces had to rank above everything else except the most urgent needs in the developing fight for France. Hundreds of sorties were being flown against V1 sites, with few losses since Hitler's promised ack-ack guns and fighter squadrons had yet to arrive, but the threat of the V2 had not been altogether forgotten and there was something obviously serious going on with these gigantic concrete pill boxes, the *blockhausen*. The Allies suspected much and didn't know enough. Until the *blockhausen* could be overrun by ground forces, the only option would be to bomb them.

A V2 assembly and launching site had been partly constructed in woodland on the edge of the village of Éperleques, near Watten, north of St Omer. Its early stages had been wrecked by an American bombing force the previous autumn but work was going on again and 5 Group was ordered up to put a stop to what was thought to be reactivation. The Éperleques *blockhaus* was now one of the least vulnerable buildings of the war, a truly bombproof concrete mass, a great, dull, implacable, lumpish slab of a place meant to house the means for preparing and firing V2s but which was never tooled up. At this time its plant for making liquid oxygen was a resource for the much more important V2 site a few miles down the road at Wizernes.

Wingco Cheshire and Sqn Ldr Dave Shannon led 617 to the first of these blockhouses at Watten, 19 June. Knilans:

Cheshire dropped his smoke bombs from a steep dive down to 2,000ft. His markers failed to ignite. Shannon dove down into the flak coming up from 70 guns in the bright sunshine. His bombs began sending up their smoke about 50 yards from the target. We were ordered to let our Tallboys go from 18,000ft. Taffy gave me the go-ahead for our bombing run through the box* of exploding shells before us.

I kept the needle of the bombsight on my instrument panel right on the centre mark. 'Bomb gone,' yelled Taffy, as the red light went out on his bombsight. There was no surge upwards. The Tallboy was hung up. 'All switches on safe,' cried Taffy, rather distraught. 'OK, Taffy,' I said. 'We'll take the damned thing home.' Before I could close the bomb doors, the Tallboy dropped away some 20 seconds late. Photographs later showed that my Tallboy had made a huge crater 2½ miles south of the target. The other 17 Tallboys landed within 100 yards of the buildings. A 40-yard miss would do more damage to the walls than a direct hit on a 20ft-thick roof.

In fact, no weapon of the period, not even the Tallboy could do more than knock a few flakes off Éperleques and that was all they managed. One bomb did near-miss by 40yd, McCarthy's, after he'd circled for 50 minutes over the target. It produced an enormous crater but no earthquake.

Knilans: 'The next day we were briefed to bomb the construction works at Wizernes in the Pas de Calais. My Lancaster seemed suspended in space as I flew along at 18,000 feet. The patchwork of fields and villages in southern England rolled by below me as if on a treadmill. The sun kept the cockpit warm.'

Les Knell, the w/op, passed on the message that they had been recalled to his skipper:

I had mixed emotions of disappointment and relief – disappointment because we were all psyched up to carry out our assigned task, relief personally at not having to fly through another hail of exploding

---

* Box barrage – three-dimensional stretch of sky on the estimated bombing run, filled with heavy flak.

shells. My take-off weight had been 60,000lbs. I would have to make a very careful touch-down. A hard landing might collapse the undercart legs, or the Tallboy might break loose.

The thought of a loose Tallboy concentrated the mind wonderfully and all 19 pilots made very careful touch-downs. Knilans:

My crew were sent off on leave. I went to London and the Regent Palace Hotel again. The prospect of good times was more than enough to overcome the fear of the buzz bombs that were coming down day and night. If you were in a pub you could hear the steady droning noise of one approaching. All talk would stop. Someone would say 'Come on you little bugger, come on.' You would be safe if the buzz bomb flew overhead before its engine cut out, and you could stay in the pub.

The buzz bombs exploded on impact and did considerable blast damage. In a movie theatre they would flash a notice on the screen, air raid alert, and a few people out of the audience would get up and go to the shelters. The all clear notice would appear on the screen a few minutes later, and the procedure would repeat several times before the film was over.

Nick Knilans's attitude to good times versus doodlebugs was severely tested one evening. He'd been interviewed by Ed Murrow of CBS for his *This is London* radio programme, a daily broadcast back to the USA, and returned to the Regent Palace to freshen up before venturing forth for more fun and games.

I crossed the lobby and entered the elevator, asking the girl operator for the sixth floor. She and I were alone as we began our upward trip and we were almost there when we were severely jolted by something like an explosion without sound. The elevator dropped like a stone for 40 feet before the emergency brakes stopped it. The operator and I said nothing. She just took me back up to my floor and opened the door to the hallway where a thick cloud of dust enveloped us. Every door had been blown off its hinges and was lying across the hallway carpet. Broken glass and rags were heaped around. In my room, the floor and the furniture were covered with bits of wood and glass from the blown-in window. The V1 had hit the top floor and killed some of the staff while I was in the elevator.

McCarthy was without his beloved Lancaster LM492 Q-Queenie, flown from new since December, away being repaired after flak had holed the petrol tanks in the starboard wing at Boulogne, so he was in Y-Yorker in a raid of 16 plus 2 Mosquitos again for Wizernes, 24 June. All they would see would be concrete but beneath it was a futuristic structure of mind-boggling ingenuity which looked forward 50 years to the scenes of grand dénouement in all those James Bond films, with instrument panels in a vast cavern, railway lines, complex machinery, men in white coats (and German uniforms) and, central to the piece, rockets aimed at world domination. At Wizernes, instead of an impossible hero averting Armageddon by virtue of cinematic special effects, there was 617 Squadron with Tallboys.

Wizernes was one of the great civil engineering feats of the war and was a tribute to the genius of Fritz Todt, the man who built the *Reichsautobahnen* and the Siegfried Line and who had been the Nazi minister for armaments and, later, fuel and power. Killed in an air crash, he didn't live to see the 'Führer's dream', the rocket-launching bunker at Watten, planned in early 1942, but his Todt Organisation, a kind of Nazi science and engineering company with limitless slave labour, almost made possible a wonder at Wizernes.

Hitler had agreed in September 1943 to a design by the Todt Organisation's chief engineer, Xavier Dorsch, for the second V2 bunker at Wizernes, and to the release from prison camps of the necessary personnel. Dorsch's plan followed the *Verbunkerung* strategy, which was to build the roof first, a concrete roof invulnerable to air attack, then dig out the accommodation beneath it. This method was already in use at the V1 sites at Siracourt and other places. For Wizernes, instead of the usual concrete slab, Dorsch proposed a dome made of a million tons of concrete.

On the edge of a quarry near the Boulogne–Lille railway line, they built the dome, about 75yd across and 20ft thick, then they excavated the rocket-launching base underneath it to take control apparatus, transport, fuelling and servicing points and, beyond the dome, a vast network of underground storage silos, barracks, hospital, workshops, stores and so on. The rockets, upright, would go through the preparation zone beneath the dome on wheeled bogies and emerge at the other side through steel doors 5ft thick and 5ft tall, into the open, ready to be fired.

The weather was fair and Cheshire dived in, again through thick and furious flak. His markers hung up so Fawke went in and placed his smoke bombs on the side of the dome despite being hit a number of times. The bombing was well concentrated, with smoke and dust forcing several of the crews into multiple runs before getting a clear shot. As a result, four Lancs took flak damage, one fatally, 617 Squadron's first loss since Munich. In the daylight, they all saw him go and they all knew who it was. Flt Lt John Andrew Edward DFC was one of the seven skippers who had taken an extra man as front gunner. The watchers saw four parachutes come out before the aircraft exploded in mid-air.

Still, business had to be done. Joe McCarthy led the attack. Down went the Tallboys, piercing the earth, arrowing into the silo roof and, crucially, burrowing beneath the dome. One pilot described it as being like darts going in around a dartboard, every one a double. After the 11 seconds' delay on the fuses, the bombs exploded far beneath the surface. It was, indeed, an earthquake. No quarry had ever seen an explosion like it. The dome was dislodged and the railway tunnel blocked. Although 'the construction itself has not been hit by the new 6-ton bombs . . . the whole area around has been so churned up that it is unapproachable and the bunker is jeopardised from underneath', said a contemporary German report. They would try to carry on at Wizernes, a huge investment, but it would eventually have to be abandoned in favour of mobile launching sites.

After Éperleques and Wizernes, there were two more so-called 'large' sites where German activity had been monitored, at Siracourt and Mimoyecques. These made up Wg Cdr Carey-Foster's 'four rocket sites in the Pas de Calais' on 617's list. The exact nature of the large sites was not known but it was assumed they were all for launching V2s. Siracourt was actually a V1 *blockhaus*, designed along Verbunkerung lines with a touch of Henry Ford: components in at one end, flying bombs out at the other to be launched at 50 a day. Mimoyecques was the almost-finished home of a weapon unknown to Allied Intelligence, the 'high-pressure pump' or London Gun, the V3.

Cheshire, still not satisfied with his marking, had already said he wanted to try it in a smaller, nimbler aircraft. The North American P-51, the Mustang, seemed ideal. It was an out-and-out fighter/pursuit aircraft with a top speed of almost 440mph but it had a much longer range than most – twice that of a Spitfire, for instance – and it could carry two 1,000lb bombs under its wings. The Mustang had started life as a request from the British to North American for a high-altitude, long-range fighter and the first ones went into RAF service in 1942. Cheshire put in a requisition for a Mk III and it duly arrived at Woodhall Spa, after modifications by Lockheed engineers. Stories circulated that Cheshire had been given the machine privately by admiring American generals, that an American pilot had flown one over and left Cheshire knowing nothing more about it than a brief tour of the cockpit could give him, and that he'd had no chance to test-fly it before taking off for Siracourt. The latter story is true. Cheshire sat in the cockpit reading the instruction book, not so much worried that the first time he took off in a Mustang would be on ops, but that it would be the first time he'd had no navigator to help him find his way home again.

He put his markers down almost perfectly on the Siracourt concrete slab on the evening of Sunday, 25 June. McCarthy and the rest went in with their Tallboys and the site appeared to cave in entirely, with 12 Tallboys observed close to the aiming point and four very close. It was a spectacular success. Siracourt had disappeared, they thought as they went home.

When the dust settled, one direct hit on the roof showed up as a crater and a hole, and one very near miss had caused some damage. The site was still under construction, the earth beneath not yet fully excavated, and the engineers there saw the 617 raid as a minor setback only. Minor or no, the fact remains that no V1 was ever launched from Siracourt.

St Leu d'Esserant, near Creil, north-east of Paris, Tuesday 4 July 1944, and Knilans was back from leave. 'Our target was a storage site for buzz bombs and rockets. They were hidden in a large cave that had been used to raise mushrooms, 25 feet underground. Wingco Cheshire was in the Mustang. He swooped down to 200 feet to place two red markers at the cave entrance. Taffy claimed a direct hit on the markers.'

This was a *blockhaus* nature made, with a 200-million-year-old roof of limestone too thick for Tallboys, so the plan was to bring down as much debris as they could by the entrances. After 617 with the Tallboys, other 5 Group squadrons would bomb conventionally including No. 9 Squadron, which had been selected as the second special-ops squadron and should have been training with Tallboys by now, but supplies of the bomb could not keep pace with demand. American production, at Smith Corporation in Milwaukee and other factories, was only just gearing up.

The nightfighters missed Joe McCarthy and 617 but were there in plenty for the mainforce and shot down 13 Lancasters over a strip of France 100 miles wide. Reconnaissance next morning showed that the Tallboys and the normal bombs of the other squadrons appeared to have wrecked the transport routes, which the Germans were frantically repairing, and a Tallboy, possibly Knilans's, had blocked one of the cave entrances. Much of the objective had been achieved, of sealing up the stored weapons and rendering a large proportion of the place useless, but another trip would be required by 9 Squadron and others of 5 Group to make sure.

That was Cheshire's century of ops and McCarthy's sixty-seventh. The boss, Air Vice-Marshal Cochrane, at a stroke removed the four heads of 617 Squadron and put them in the heroes' gallery: Cheshire and his three flight commanders, McCarthy, Shannon and Munro. All protested, all said they could carry on, but Cochrane knew it was time.

Sqn Ldr Joseph Charles McCarthy DSO, DFC and Bar, officer and gentleman, late of 136th Street and Alexander Avenue, New York, had flown something like five times the average number of ops for a Bomber Command pilot. If he had indeed been statistically average he would have been killed a long, long time ago but Joe, whatever else he might have been, certainly could never have been called average. What seemed like centuries before, 31 July 1942, Joe had flown his first op, in a Hampden to Düsseldorf. At that time, Andy Storey and Howard Burton were flying in Wellingtons on 9 Squadron, Dinghy Young was over in the USA getting married, Howard Lewis and Maurice Buechler were nearing the end of their training, Eric Roberts had a year to go in his, Ray Baroni and Jonah Reeves likewise, Ed Walters, Bob Cummings, John Hannon, Pappy Wilkes, James Stevenson, all in training in July 1942 and now all dead by July 1944, while Big Joe flew off to be a test pilot.

On the second trip to St Leu, the statisticians would collect more of the usual evidence. That same 100-mile strip of France this time soaked up the impact of 31 falling Lancasters, almost all successes for nightfighters, although 1 is believed to have been shot down by another Lanc.

Mimoyecques, Pas de Calais, home of the well-kept secret that was the London Gun, was only a few miles from the coast and less than 100 miles from the English capital. If the dome of Wizernes was an engineering marvel, Mimoyecques was a miracle on the grand scale. Again built on the Verbunkeren principle, the roof of this *blockhaus* was 18ft thick and the excavations beneath the roof were astonishing. There were tunnels and platforms and chambers enough and of a size to make several London Underground stations, all carved out of solid rock by hand, by slave labourers, thousands of whom died in the process.

The main accommodation and service departments were 100ft below the surface. There was a mass of complex and innovative machinery, living quarters for 1,000 soldiers, and everything else necessary for a subterranean village in wartime. At the heart of it were 25 launching tubes in groups of 5, 416ft long, with breech chambers 250ft down and firing loopholes in the roof protected by steel shutters 8in thick. Together, they were planned to fire ten missiles a minute, a rate that could only be achieved with highly automated handling and loading.

The technology was very advanced. As a missile shot upwards in its tube from its firing point, it received boost after boost as charges exploded in side inlets to the tube, until it reached a muzzle velocity well over 3,000mph (roughly 4,400ft per second; muzzle velocity of M16 rifle approx. 3,000ft per second). The shells were like darts, 9ft in length but only 6in wide at the base, narrowing to a sharp point. They carried quite a small charge; various designs had between 11lb and 22lb of HE, so the result would be more like an intense naval barrage than an air raid.

There had been many problems with the development of the gun, some so severe that the project probably should have been shut down but, as was so often the case, nobody dared tell the Führer that one of his pet schemes was a waste of money and time. Time for the secret-weapons programme was of the essence. With the Allies ashore it might only be a matter of time before the sites were overrun. Racing against that time were the secret-weapons personnel, 5,000 of them at Mimoyecques alone. Trying to stop the clock, or at least turn it back by weeks and months, was 617 Squadron.

Cheshire marked in his Mustang but the markers didn't show up too well in the daylight. Nevertheless, there was a direct hit and a large crater appeared. It looked as if the site was now out of commission and, unlike the other large sites, there would never be any follow-up raids. One of the engineers on the project reported to his superiors that the site was no longer of use; it had not been designed to withstand bombs like the Tallboy. Others saw that only one out of the five shafts was disabled and everything else was unserviceable merely because of the great quantities of collapsed earth and rubble, which could be cleared. No mention was made of the many hundreds of slaves from a dozen occupied countries whose bodies were mixed up with the earth and rubble.

While development work continued on the gun itself – two mobile versions would be used later in the year against the advancing Allies – Mimoyecques was indeed finished. When the V2 rocket panics began to grip later in the summer, American bombers would throw everything at the four large sites, in case they were anything to do with it, but they had no further operational role to play.

Wg Cdr Willie Tait DSO and Bar, DFC had taken over command of 617 Squadron and his first op with them was in a Mosquito, a daylight return to Wizernes, 17 July. Knilans was there with 15 other Lancasters. They did some damage, not knowing that the Germans had already given up Wizernes. Next day, Hitler signed orders to this effect. Without access to this information, 5 Group mounted a 100-bomber raid, 20 July, and sent 617 in again for good measure with Tait marking in the Mustang and continuing in the 617 Squadron tradition of commanding officers who, in any other context, would have been regarded as barking mad.

Knilans, watching his CO, wondered where the line was drawn between bravery and adventure:

Willie (Tait) dove into a hail of light flak and machine gun bullets. This time he used smoke markers. We could not see these plumes of smoke inside the ground haze 18,000ft below us, and told him so. He then had a good but foolhardy idea. He began to fly his Mustang in a tight turn around and around the blockhouse. Bullets and flak fragments flew about his airplane. 'Bomb on me,' I heard him say in my earphones. 'Taffy,' I said. 'Can you see the Wingco down there?' 'Just barely,' Taff replied. I didn't like this at all and told him not to bomb. 'R-Roger to Leader. We can't see you. Unable to bomb. Over.'

Maybe everyone was as appalled as I was at the thought of bombing Willie and his Mustang. No-one ever talked about it. We turned around and took our Tallboys home again.

It was Éperleques/Watten again, on the fine early morning of 25 July, so clear that Tait didn't need to mark the target. Several aircraft were hit by flak, one having the intercom disabled which was enough evidence for a gunner to be thereby persuaded to commit the airman's mortal sin of jumping out of a serviceable aircraft. Knilans's engineer, Ken Ryall, watched in wonder as a parachute opened over enemy territory while every Lancaster continued about its business.

The weather in Lincolnshire was grand around this time but, for 617 anyway, ops kept being cancelled. Crews were briefed, were stood down and went swimming, played tennis or, if they were the Knilans type, 'went cycling with young ladies'. There was a WAAF dance in aid of 'Salute the Soldier' week. There were 191 WAAFs at Woodhall Spa.

Perhaps the cycling young ladies weren't available on 31 July because Knilans was having a beer and a frame or two of snooker with Bill Reid VC in the Petwood when the call came to raid another V-bomb storage site, in a railway tunnel at Rilly-la-Montagne. Once again the plan was for 617 to destabilise the tunnel with Tallboys while the rest of 5 Group moonscaped the surrounding countryside. The planned bombing heights caused some objections at 617, as they were to fly with 90 or so other Lancs above them, dropping sticks of 1,000lb bombs. The danger of being hit, being 'bombed out', was probably no greater than in any of the dozens of night raids they'd been on in mainforce times, but this was worse because the danger would be visible. Objections were overruled.

There were northern and southern aiming points that in the bright daylight didn't need marking but that soon merged into one as clouds of smoke rose up. Knilans: 'I was airborne about 5.30pm. There were no clouds. The sun made it quite warm inside the cockpit as we climbed to 17,000ft. Several dozen aircraft from other squadrons in 5 Group flew above and behind us. The flak guns set up their usual box-shaped barrage as we began our bomb run.'

Nick Knilans was quite irritated when Ryall the engineer tapped him on the shoulder and told him to look up. The irritation disappeared instantly. Directly above them, not 100ft away, was another 617 Squadron Lancaster with its bomb doors open and its Tallboy hanging there on its chains, now a 21ft long, 5-ton air-to-air missile, shining and ready. Nobody in the upper aircraft would be able to see Knilans. He was in the blindspot.

He did what was required, skidding his aircraft to one side and immediately realigning on the aiming point. The run continued and a hit was claimed. The 617 Tallboys blocked the tunnel entrances and the bombs of the several dozen other aircraft, in fact 81 Lancasters, thoroughly cratered the immediate district. Nothing much else happened to Knilans that evening, apart from having to feather an overheating, flak-damaged engine, but since this would be his sixth three-engined landing he wasn't too bothered about that. Others were not so fortunate. In ME557 AJ/S, skippered by Flt Lt Bill Reid VC, nobody saw the bombs above them. Roy Learmonth, Knilans's rear gunner, was a witness, as Knilan explained: 'Roy shouted to me on the intercom. "Skipper, one of our planes has just had a bomb dropped on it." "Can you see any chutes?" I asked. "Not yet. Oh, she's breaking up. There, I see one, no two chutes. There she goes, into the ground."'

The pilot had heard and felt the impact of two bombs, one on the tail section and one shortly after on the port wing. The end was swift. The two chutes Learmonth saw belonged to Bill Reid himself, who fell out of the front as she broke up, and Dave Luker, the w/op. The others in the crew were unable to free themselves from a spinning and disintegrating aircraft. All five were killed.

Chapter 13

TIME FOR THE KRIEGSMARINE

An abortive, cloud-covered return to Siracourt was Nick Knilans's forty-fifth op. He and his crew originals hadn't had their due rest between tours, which made it somehow seem a good idea to volunteer for another 5 ops, to take them to 50 and an obligatory rest, possibly of sufficient length to see the war finished. After the first joint special op by 617 and 9 Squadrons together, a railway viaduct at Étaples, which they mostly missed, attention was turned to the German Navy.

One of the first things the Germans did after conquering France in 1940 was to build bombproof shelters for their U-boat fleet on the Atlantic coast. Sailing from their bases in Germany had meant a surface journey of 12 days or more, through northern waters patrolled by the RAF and the Royal Navy, before they could consider themselves operational in the open sea. By the end of 1941 there were bunkers at Lorient and St-Nazaire and soon afterwards also at Brest, La Pallice and Bordeaux. From these new bases, they sailed the Bay of Biscay and were in among it straight away, and the RAF had missed an opportunity. Had the Air Ministry so decided, Bomber Command could have attacked these bases while they were being built. Instead they waited until they were bombproof.

The U-boats' objective was to destroy the lifeline of Britain, the convoys of merchant ships bringing everything from America which could not be produced on the besieged islands – at all, which included every drop of petroleum, or sufficiently, including huge quantities of food and general supplies, weaponry, vehicles. Without this lifeline, there is not the slightest shadow of a doubt that Britain would have gone under. To sustain it, the Royal Navy and the RAF fought the Battle of the Atlantic against Adm Dönitz's *Unterseeboote* and very nearly lost.

Increased numbers of U-boats and Dönitz's wolf-pack tactic initially brought him great success. A pack of 12 sank 32 ships in 4 nights in October 1940. It was common for a U-boat to sail into home base with three, four or even six victory pennants flying from her rigging. U-boats sank around 1,100 ships in 1942. Such losses could not continue without bringing about the defeat of Britain.

British technology was one key issue. There was excellent and ever improving sub-finding kit in RAdio Detection And Ranging (radar) and Anti Submarine Detection Investigation Committee (Asdic, later known by its more apt US name, sonar, SOund Navigation And Ranging). Operational researchers came up with better convoy-management techniques, the forces provided more convoy escorts, better air cover and better sub-hunting tactics, and in May 1943 these combined to sink 42 U-boats. Now they no longer dared to cross the Bay of Biscay on the surface, which meant a cut in their operational time at sea of 50 per cent. Still the Germans were building U-boats faster than the Allies could destroy them and at the turn of the year, January 1944, they had almost 450.

Even so, the Battle of the Atlantic had swung irreversibly against the Kriegsmarine and U-boats were being sunk more frequently than they were sinking other ships. From the brilliance of the early years, the 'happy time', U-boat crews became one of the most endangered species of the war, almost as likely to die as Bomber Command aircrew. While sinking around 2,800 ships, out of the 40,000 sailors who went under the sea for Germany between 1939 and 1945, 28,000 were killed and 5,000 taken prisoner.

The first U-boat-pen raid with any chance of success was mounted by 617 Squadron on Brest, 5 August 1944, with Tallboys. These pens had always been beyond Bomber Command, simply because the German designers had 'bombproof' as their *sine qua non*. From the air, bomb aimers could see the latest addition, the *Fangrost* bomb trap, which looked something like large-scale, white corrugated iron but was a roof topping of U-shaped concrete beams laid across heavy concrete joists, 6ft high. The beams were to detonate the bombs and the void beneath would damp the explosion. Below that, what couldn't be seen was a massive thickness of reinforced concrete on top of a series of tilted rectangular concrete beams, laid like gable ends to produce more force-absorbing voids. Below that was yet more reinforced concrete and finally the steel-girder roof trusses, which themselves were entirely encased in concrete. The pattern varied from pen to pen and most of the roofs didn't have a complete *Fangrost* on top but they were all formidable obstacles, between 16ft and 22ft thick altogether.

Important since the Middle Ages, Brest harbour faced south into the estuary bay of the Rivers Penfeld and Aulne on the Cap Finistère (*finis terrae*, the end of the earth). In the summer of 1944, the news from the invasion front was becoming more disturbing for the U-boat captains and shipyard staff. They could be caught in an American trap, between the Devil and the deep blue sea.

The crews of 617 flew in and saw the *Port de Commerce* to the east and the *Port Militaire* in the centre, where the *Gneisenau*, *Scharnhorst* and *Prinz Eugen* had lain unhittable in the winter of 1941–2. Over to the west, near the naval school and where the seaplane station used to be, was the U-bunker. It was about 350yd by 200yd and contained 15 docks. The *Fangrost* was hardly begun but the strongest parts of the roof were getting on for 20ft thick anyway. Unseen, beneath the concrete, lay 13 U-boats. Some were ready to sail to the Channel. Others were being prepared to lift staff and equipment to the relative safety of La Pallice.

When the air-raid warning sounded, the men in the bunker were not concerned. The heaviest bombing so far had had no effect. Some U-boat crews were taking a swim from the quay outside. They strolled back into the shelter, drying themselves, followed by the dockers who had been sunbathing. What followed, nobody had witnessed before.

Two Mosquitos went to mark but the smoke bombs fell in the water. Then 15 Lancasters attacked through a mighty box barrage. Knilans: 'Some naval guns around the harbour were sending up very heavy shells that made a loud crack when exploding near my Lancaster. The markers were in the sea and useless, but Taffy aimed visually. He said he'd had a direct hit.'

Heiner Ruhe, a switchboard operator from U-963, gave this report:

I was in the lavatories in the middle of the bunker when the alarm went. I was calm and casual. The shelter was secure. No bomb had ever even cracked the concrete. As I heard the flak open up, there was an enormous noise and roar. The whole of the bunker seemed to shudder and dance. Debris was flying through the air. Somehow I made it to the central gangway. A cart swept past me, its horses bolting out of control. I was anxious to get back to my boat, through frightful noise and air which was filled with dust and smoke. When I reached the dock, I could not believe what I saw. There was a piece of the roof there, concrete and steel, hanging from a hole behind the stern of my U-boat. With my comrade Karl-Heinz Kröger I closed the gates of pen 3 because there was water flooding in and there was water flowing through the bomb damage too.

As we recovered from the shock, the damage was assessed, which was lighter than we had thought. Tremendous holes had been ripped in the roof but the mass of the explosion had gone upwards. Two motor boats [E-boats, *schnellboote*], S112 and S145 had been hit by flying debris but looked repairable.

In a superb display of bombing, five crews hit the roof with their Tallboys, three drilling 15ft-diameter holes right through before exploding, two producing huge craters with corresponding bulges beneath of tangled iron and concrete. In both cases, no serious damage was done to U-boats. Some lifting gear and electrics were destroyed, very little had happened to anything or anybody else but there was a lot of mess and the place did not appear so sound as it had been. Clearly, the Germans now knew their pens were not impenetrable.

The day was coming when they would have to remove back north. Knilans: 'I had a call from the tail gunner. "One of the Lancs behind us is going down. It looks like V-Victor. Six parachutes." V-Victor was Don Cheney's kite.'

Flg Off Don Cheney, a 21-year-old Canadian, was well into his second tour, as were several of his crew. They alone of the squadron were hit by flak above Brest, one shell exploding right in the bomb bay, badly wounding the navigator, Plt Off Welch, and the w/op, Flt Sgt Pool. With the aircraft on fire, Cheney held her steady as most of the men got out, but had to pull and push the barely conscious Pool to a hatch while making regular dashes back to the controls to keep V-Victor in some sort of trim. At last Cheney could jump himself and he and two of his men fell into Resistance hands and were later repatriated via the American Army. The bomb aimer, Flt Sgt Curtis, met German soldiers who took him prisoner. Plt Off Welch was not so lucky. His Germans shot him dead as he floated to earth. The Resistance found his body, and those of Pool and rear gunner Plt Off Wait, and the village bravely gave them a fine funeral with their skipper present.

In the U-boat pen, life returned to normal. Although not smashed as had been hoped, the roof was no longer secure and the rocky tunnels under the navy school were designated as the new air-raid shelters. At Kriegsmarine HQ there was much excitement and incredulity. The impregnable shelter, object so often of Hitler's proudest boasts, had proved vulnerable. What next? Would the sun fail to rise?

Lorient was the first and foremost U-boat base with its gigantic complex built on the Kéroman headland. Here they housed 28 boats at once and performed almost half of the French-base U-boat overhauls and regular services of the war. Activity was much curtailed by 6 August 1944 and the Americans were waiting to attack on land the next day, but Lorient had been awarded the dubious status of *festung*, fortress, and ordered to hold out at all costs.

The flak into which the Lancs flew in the early evening was as plentiful and accurate as anybody had seen. Tait in his Mosquito, as the Germans called him the *Zielmarkierer*, the goal-marksman, had been ordered to stay above 8,000ft because of the exceptionally fierce defences. He dropped two red TIs on the roof of one of the pens which, from bombing height, looked about the size of a postage stamp. Knilans:

The flak barrage was very thick as we began our bombing run through it. My Lanc bounced and bucked from the explosions near by and it was difficult to keep the straight-and-level needle on its spot. Taffy and Roy, one at each end of the aircraft, both claimed a hit on the AP and our photograph confirmed it next day.

The German report scores one Tallboy hit on Kéroman III and 14 Lancasters damaged. It was probably more; certainly, every Lancaster of 617 had holes from the flak. Wilhelm Abele, a naval engineer, was outside Kéroman III at the time:

200 crew men had just left for La Pallice when the siren went and shortly after that we could see the flying formation [12 Lancs and 2 Mosquitos of 617, 16 Lancs of 106 behind, escorted by 17 Spitfires and a camera Mosquito]. I had just got inside the door when the bombs began to fall. I was familiar with the way that explosions can cause tremendous pressures and powers of suction so I sought shelter between walls. Others were sucked off the docks into the water. Pieces of concrete were everywhere and the U-boats swung about. A hit on the land beside us pushed clouds of dust through every fissure

in the walls and we could not see anything. Even the light of a torch which I held up to my eyes I could not see. Parts of the workshops collapsed and the surrounding area was devastated.

The direct hit was on pen 21/22 which had a roof almost 25ft thick, and the result was that the corrugated iron on the undersurface of the roof sagged a little. This roof seemed to represent the limits of the Tallboy – and some sort of limit had been recognised in Nick Knilans and his crew.

We had been given a week's leave, having finished a second tour non-stop. My crew headed off to their homes or the homes of their English girlfriends. I went off to the fun and games of old London town for a farewell visit. The bartenders and bar girls of the Chez Cup or the Chez Moi seemed to be glad that I was still alive. I sent my parents in Delavan, Wisconsin a cable each month. The message always read 'Still kicking'.

The squadron without Knilans went to Lorient again, 7 August with 9 Squadron, and were called off moments before bombing because American troops were believed to be right there, on the attack. They were there but they weren't attacking. From now until the end of the war it was stalemate. American infantry regiments resting from the front were camped outside Lorient while the German garrison, its U-boats long gone, refused to surrender.

La Pallice, 9 August, again had 617 and 9 operating together, no Nick Knilans but with another American making his debut, Flt Sgt John Edward 'Jesse' Stowell, a groundcrew erk at the start of it all who was at last where he wanted to be, captaining a Lancaster on ops. He and the others of No. 9, still with no Tallboys available, attacked the diesel-oil tanks with 1,000lb bombs while 617 went for the concrete.

Originally the big-ship port for the ancient fishing and mercantile town of La Rochelle across the bay, La Pallice now had a ten-dock U-boat base with a roof between 21ft and 24ft thick, connected to the harbour by two canals, one with a concrete roof. There were 23 separate anti-aircraft emplacements with 73 guns altogether, plus 7 firing 24in rockets.

The results seemed good enough from above. Stowell thought his bombs fell slightly to port of the AP; others saw a mixture of good and bad. The Germans admitted to two direct hits with Tallboys but, as with the other raids, the real success was not so much the damage caused by the bombs as the destruction of the complete trust placed in the bunkers by Hitler and, therefore, by everybody else.

Ed Stowell was away with a raid on the oil installations at Bordeaux the next evening, and his third in three days was for the railway yards at Givors, described later as 'exceptionally accurate'.

At 09:30, 12 August, as the air-raid sirens went again at Brest, everyone ran for the rocky tunnels under the school except those on duty in the pens. The siren found officer of the watch Marinebaurat Otto Feuerhahn of U-963, wearing his steel helmet and 'waiting with fatalism for the bombs to fall. We felt in need of more protection. Then everything went quiet.'

A deckhand on U-963 saw what happened next:

The first bomb missed the bunker but still the whole bunker shook. An officer and two hands, Sekula and Laskowski, tried to run for it but at that moment a bomb hit and ripped a hole in the bunker roof. Laskowski was killed instantly. Sekula died next day. The officer stood in a corner completely covered in concrete dust but, amazingly, unhurt.

Another sailor, Karl-Heinz Patzer, described the same attack:

Our boat U-953 was in Brest for repairs. I was on guard duty. The others were in the navy school. I went to the open end of the dock to look at the sky and saw a formation of aircraft heading for the bunker. The flak started up. I drew back to try and avoid any pressure surges from the bombs but felt as secure under seven metres of concrete as on my mother's lap. La Pallice had already been hit without any damage worth mentioning, but now the world began to fall. A hit shook the bunker with a massive detonation. I thought the bunker would rise up into the air in one piece. There was darkness for a long time and the dust took my breath away, and then dead stillness. My first thought was for my boat. It was undamaged.

Like Herr Patzer's boat, almost everything was unscathed. Two of the three direct hits had made craters in the roof but the damage was light inside the pens. One bomb went in only 6ft from the back wall of the bunker but there was no earthquake effect. The bombs exploding in the water caused no tidal waves.

They went again the next day. Shortages meant only 4 of the 13 Lancs of 617 had Tallboys. The rest had 1,000lb bombs, as did the 14 Lancs of No. 9. The German Army was trapped on the Brest peninsula but still fighting hard to prevent the Allies from taking the harbour, which would then be able to accept shipping direct from the USA and greatly increase supplies to the invasion forces. Gen Patton had issued his famous order 'Take Brest', 1 August. Brest, like the other U-boat bases, had been classified as *Festung* and the Americans wouldn't get in until 18 September, by which time they had lost 10,000 men, the docks had been smashed to pieces by air raids and artillery so they were not much use anyway, and the front line was 500 miles away.

Still Brest, and the Germans were looking to block the harbour with shipwrecks. The whole of 617 was assigned to the *Gueydon*, an ancient French battle cruiser, 14 August, and 9 Squadron was given another old warship to destroy for the same reason, the *Clémenceau*. This was Stowell's fourth; he'd be doing six in eight days. At this rate he'd be tour complete in 40 days and 40 nights, except there was a big project on the horizon. Meanwhile, the squadron was switched to a nightfighter base in Holland, Gilze Rijen, part of a co-ordinated effort against military airfields and part of the preparations for a new bomber offensive against Germany. Stowell reported *Whole aerodrome was left in a cloud of smoke. Woods round aerodrome on fire.* The squadron all bombed within 1½ minutes and the base was obliterated.

It was the first op for another American, the quiet man from Michigan, Flg Off Clifford Sinclair Newton, son of Archibald Place Newton and Lucinda of Detroit, husband of Bethia Margaret of Rockwood, Michigan. He was a graduate of No. 9 Service Flying Training School (SFTS) at Centralia, near Exeter, Ontario, where he progressed as far as the Anson and the Harvard. Over in England he converted through the Wellington and the Stirling to the Lancaster, gathered up his crew with two Canadians in the gun turrets and another as bomb aimer, and on his first attack he too saw *the whole aerodrome covered in smoke* and thought it *very successful*.

La Pallice, 16 August, 25 Lancs of 9 and 617, only four carrying Tallboys, but this time Stowell and Newton found it rather unsuccessful. The clouds were thick, Tait marked the wrong AP, Newton bombed a corner of the submarine pens glimpsed briefly, one other 9 Squadron crew bombed and the rest were called off. The same target two days later provided a different story. Knilans was back from leave and he was one of the six with the big bomb. Newton, Stowell and the rest had 1,000lb conventionals or 2,000lb armour piercing. They set off between 11:15 and 11:30 in fine weather and, apart from a couple, all felt they'd hit the target.

Photoreconnaissance showed two good hits with Tallboys and the surrounding area like a First World War battlefield after an artillery barrage. A German report stated a remarkable coincidence. One of the Tallboys exploded almost exactly on a spot hit on the previous raid, over pen No. 10, where U-262 lay. It killed three men of the crew, injured another and damaged another boat, U-382. Men climbing onto the roof to inspect after the raid were astonished to find a steam locomotive up there.

There was a change of emphasis. Something big was going to happen. Nick Knilans:

> My flight engineer Ken Ryall, still only 20 years old, was made the squadron's engineer leader. He and I were detailed to make a series of fuel consumption tests, precautionary landings and heavyweight take-offs. Mr North, a civilian engineer from A.V. Roe [designers of the Lancaster] flew with us to give helpful hints on engine care and fuel. We were making ready for an undisclosed and distant target.

A few miles away based at Bardney, No. 9 Squadron was similarly engaged and practising with the new bomb, the Tallboy. No one had the slightest idea what the target could be. They would never guess either, because it was too far away for any Lancaster to reach.

Knilans and his engineer droned up and down the coast to see which propeller pitch and throttle settings would give the best miles per gallon. On the op, they would be carrying the full load of 2,154 gallons to try and make about 2,400 miles and 12 hours. The usual 1 mile to the gallon was not going to be enough – and the unbreakable Knilans was feeling the strain too. 'I began to have trouble flying. On one of these exercises the low, broken clouds were casting fast-moving shadows on the ground and that, with the constant in-and-out of sun and cloud was making me disoriented. Ken said 'Something wrong, skipper?' I said the clouds and shadows were making me dizzy.' Knilans had given his engineer some flying training so asked him to drive for a while. This magnificent flyer, who had been through so much, was at last falling victim to the one thing that got them all in the end: the sheer stress of repeated operations. 'I had never had a single dream or nightmare about flying combat missions, but I decided that, whatever it was, this next op, my 50th, would be my last.'

The next day they wanted an all-up weight test with 70,000lb of bombs and petrol which was 5,000lb over maximum:

> Someone was stalled on the main runway so I took the short one. The aircraft would not become airborne as we roared along. I pulled her off the tarmac. We sank down and bounced off the grass 100 yards beyond the end of the runway. We were just above stalling speed. We skimmed over a field towards a row of telegraph poles and wires. 'Ken, should we go over them or under them?' I said. 'I don't care, just bloody do something,' was his response. I put the nose down to get a little more speed and milked the flaps.

They rose over the wires. The Avro engineers watching from the control tower said later they couldn't believe it, taking off in such a short space with all that weight. 'I told my commanding officer that, with respect sir, I wouldn't recommend doing it again.'

Bomber Command aircrew very, very rarely gave up on the job for any reason other than being shot down, or tour expired or, in occasional cases like McCarthy's, being ordered to stop. Except for the early part of the war, aircrew were all volunteers. They chose to do it. Of course, once they were in it they were under military law; they couldn't choose to walk out, even though something they had elected to do had turned into Russian roulette.

The stresses of going on ops in that war are hardly imaginable by anyone who never went, nor is the mental strength that enabled them to get up and go again and again in the almost sure and certain knowledge that one day they would fail to return. No matter how much they told themselves that it was going to be the other guy who got the chop, it was demonstrably true that those who did get the chop had thought the same thing.

Nick Knilans had flown 18 ops with 619 Squadron. Apart from one trip to Milan and one to Modane in southern France, all were over Germany including four to Berlin. Hagen, No. 12, he flew back on three engines; Kassel, No. 13, rear gunner killed; Kassel, No. 14, hit by flak, returned on three engines. This was Knilans's schedule but the same kind of schedule was the burden of all aircrew, with the difference that Knilans got through his. The mystery mission coming up would be a thankful farewell.

It would be more of a hello for Stowell, promoted to pilot officer as Bomber Command at last implemented a long-discussed policy of having all pilots, *ipso facto* commanders of the ship, of officer rank. Since La Pallice back in mid-August he and most of the squadron had been on intensive practice, and the reason was about to be made clear.

The awe-inspiring battleship *Tirpitz*, sister ship to the film star *Bismarck*, was a weapon of mass destruction long before that phrase was coined. She had 8 15in guns, 12 6in, 16 4in, 8 quad torpedo tubes and a huge number of anti-aircraft guns. She could steam at over 30 knots, had a range of 9,000 miles at 19 knots and was manned by 2,400 crew. Presumably because there were no plans for her to have to go through the Panama Canal, her designers had made her much wider in beam than her length would normally require, thus making her a very stable and accurate gun platform. Clearly, she would alter the balance of power wherever she went.

Any direct attack on her in a conventional naval engagement would bring heavy losses to the attackers. The deadly calculation – would the losses be worthwhile if the *Tirpitz* was sunk? – could not be made with any certainty, partly because of her armour. From 6½ft below the waterline to the gun-battery deck above, she had armour plating over a foot thick. Above that it was 6in thick. And 3in and 4in armour protected her vitals from the enemy in the sky; she was designed to expect and to be able to resist all forms of aerial attack, by bomb or torpedo, known about at that time.

Tirpitz was launched at Wilhelmshaven, 1 April 1939, in the presence of Adolf Hitler by Frau von Hassel, a granddaughter of Alfred P. Freidrich von Tirpitz (1849–1930), father of the German Navy, architect of U-boat strategy and supreme naval commander 1914–16. Sea trials of the ship named for him were completed by February 1940 and she was commissioned early in 1941 under Kapitän Karl Topp, whereupon she became a constant cause of violent mental exercise in the Allied governments.

Bismarck broke out into the Atlantic in May 1941, sank HMS *Hood* on 24 May and caused unprecedented alarm in the Admiralty and everywhere else. More than 50 British warships were sent to find her – battleships, aircraft carriers, cruisers, destroyers and submarines – and she was sunk on 27 May. Perhaps rueing a missed opportunity – what havoc and destruction might have been caused had he sent the *Tirpitz* with the *Bismarck*? – Hitler ever after seemed reluctant to risk his pride and joy and the ship hardly went to sea, staying almost entirely in Norwegian fjords.

Still, she remained a constant threat. A considerable proportion of British naval resources was always deployed, watching and waiting, in case the *Tirpitz* should sail. There was continuous reconnaissance and espionage activity to establish whether she was at anchor. So jumpy were the authorities about her that, on an occasion in July 1942 when intelligence could not confirm the *Tirpitz*'s whereabouts, the order was given to Convoy PQ17 to scatter. Now unprotected, many merchant ships were sunk by the German Navy without a shot being fired by the mighty battleship, in her fjord all the time. Convoy PQ17, like so many, was bound for Murmansk with aid for the *Sovietski Soyuz*, the USSR. The convoy programme was always liable to be interrupted by the menace of the *Tirpitz* if not by the *Tirpitz* herself and pressure increased constantly on Churchill and the British, from Stalin and the Russians, and Roosevelt and the Americans, to do something about it.

Churchill ordered that *Tirpitz* must be destroyed and, over the months that turned into years, more than 30 attempts were made by over 700 British, Russian and American aircraft and midget submarines. An early try was by the Royal Navy aircraft carrier HMS *Victorious* which launched a dozen of its new Fairey Albacore torpedo bombers, their pilots doubtless thinking about that time back in May 1941 when, with their Fairey Swordfish, their flying stringbags, they'd punched the first hole in the *Bismarck*. This attack was quite different.

The Albacore was meant to replace the Swordfish in the Fleet Air Arm but never proved quite up to the job and was retired from the war while the Swordfish carried on. Here, *Tirpitz* simply sailed at full speed into a 30-knot wind and, into such a wind, the Albacores could not go fast enough to mount a decent attack. They launched their torpedos much more in hope than expectation. *Tirpitz* sailed on after shooting two of them down.

Halifax bombers went four times at night in 1942, when *Tirpitz* was in Fættenfjord, near Trondheim, but the only damage done was to the Halifaxes. By September 1943 the battleship was in Kaafjord, an offshoot of Altenfjord in the very north of Norway, and the Royal Navy did achieve something with midget submarines which planted four mines. Of these, two went off and *Tirpitz* was under repair for several months. In April 1944, the Fleet Air Arm went with their modern, single-winged Fairey Barracudas and dive-bombed her, claiming hits but causing nothing apart from a little inconvenience, and in the August several more attacks were made from Royal Navy carriers. Again, hits were claimed but the Corsair and Hellcat crews had little chance of achieving the big objective: to put *Tirpitz* right out of the war.

Thoroughly protected by her own armour and armoury, plus anti-submarine booms and nets, shore batteries of anti-aircraft guns, permanently installed smokescreen gear, and nearby squadrons of fighter aircraft, *Tirpitz* looked well set to survive. In Kaafjord she was also out of range of heavy bombers flying from the UK.

One last navy based attempt was planned. An RAF Mosquito squadron would be removed from active service to train for a special mission, taking off from aircraft carriers, attacking *Tirpitz* with their 2,000lb bombs and landing in Russia. It looked like a long shot but so desperate were the chiefs and the planners and the joint service staff that anything would be considered, and anything looked better than it really was in such a light. Eventually the Mosquito idea was dropped amid argument at the end of August 1944, but the urgent imperative remained. Arthur 'Butch' Harris later told the short story of how the job of sinking the *Tirpitz* was passed to him.

'Churchill rang me and said "I want you to sink the *Tirpitz*."' Harris's view was that such a mission could only be the result of a mating between a red herring and a wild goose. Admittedly, Allied resources were tied up and these would have helped shorten the war if deployed elsewhere, in the Far East for example, but the weapon of mass destruction was not an active combatant. So, Harris recalled, 'I said "Why bother, Prime Minister? She's not doing any harm where she is." Churchill replied "I want you to sink the *Tirpitz*". So I sent the boys out and they sank the *Tirpitz*.'

The boys in question were those of Nos 9 and 617 Squadrons, with Tallboy bombs, the only ones that could slice through *Tirpitz*'s armour plate. Sending the boys out was not quite as simple as Harris implied. The northern winter was coming and with it the darkness that would postpone the job into next year, making it more likely that the Germans would commit *Tirpitz* to battle as the Allies took charge of the war. If the boys were to be sent, it would have to be soon, and September was a poor month for bombing weather in those parts.

Kaafjord was too far, even for Lancasters modified well beyond specification. Overload tanks originally designed for the Wellington were installed in the fuselage, first removing the rear turret to get the tanks in, then replacing it. To save weight, the mid-upper turret was removed and was not replaced. Assuming they could get off the ground, a conventional approach by two squadrons of Lancs from across the North Sea would mean an early warning for the target. The smokescreen and the fighters would be up before any attackers could get there.

If these problems were solved, there remained the little local difficulty of actually hitting the bullseye. Both 9 and 617 Squadrons were practising hard, day and night, every day, for the mystery mission but *Tirpitz*, big as she was, wouldn't look so big from 3 or 4 miles high. She was hugely powerful and heavily armoured. A high-level attack would be necessary. This would give aircrew a better chance of survival against intensive shelling and the bomb enough time to build up armour-piercing speed. Of course, the higher you flew, the tinier the ship looked in the bombsight.

Kaafjord was only 600 miles or so from Archangel. The plot was therefore hatched to send the boys to Russia. The two squadrons would fly to Scotland and top up on fuel, fly beyond the Arctic Circle at night, bomb the *Tirpitz* soon after dawn, then carry on to an airfield near Archangel. They would recuperate in Russia, patch up their Lancs, and fly home. This plan was outlined to the two squadrons, 8 September.

Some of the Lancasters would be detailed to take the new, untried Johnny Walker mine, an ingenious, idiosyncratic and oh-so-British design which was actually classified as a bomb because it went off if it was dropped straight onto a solid object. It was a self-powered, roaming mine which was supposed to keep looking until it found its target. Lancaster crews didn't like it much because its self-power was something of a bomb in itself, a bottle of compressed hydrogen. Crews were under instruction to jettison their mines if they came under fighter or flak attack, which also made them wonder what might happen in a dodgy landing or other out-of-the-ordinary, mine-jolting circumstance.

The bomb/mine had a parachute and an arming pin, both deployed by a fixed line as the weapon left the aircraft. It was extremely difficult to drop accurately but, in theory, this didn't matter too much. When it hit the water and detached its chute, it sank to 50 or 60ft then, using its compressed hydrogen system, rose up again. If it didn't hit anything, for example the underside of *Tirpitz*, it sank again and 'walked' 30ft to the side. To which side was anybody's guess. Up it rose again. If it missed again, it did another sink, walk and rise, wandering around at random until its gas ran out whereupon it exploded, thus preventing German mine designers from finding it and having a good laugh.

It could only be deployed in deep water, such as in a fjord but not in normal harbours, canals and so on where the shipping tended to be. Johnny Walker had never been used operationally before the *Tirpitz* raid. This was the novelty mine's chance to prove itself. Hopes among the boys were not high. Plt Off Mick Maguire was 9 Squadron's armaments officer: 'If by some remote chance one of them had hit the *Tirpitz*, the armour plating would have shrugged it off. It had a very small charge. I thought they were a waste of time and it would have been far better to have all the Lancs carrying Tallboys.'

In the event, weather changed the main plan. There was no point flying all the way to Kaafjord then finding cloud obscuring the target. Cloud was forecast so the revised scheme was to go straight to Russia, missing out Scotland, and wait there for the clear day which must surely come along shortly. This decision was passed to 9 and 617 Squadrons around the middle of the day, 11 September 1944. Orders were to put together an overnight bag and take off at 15:00 DBST, land soon after dawn at an airfield on an island called Yagodnik in the River Dvina, near Archangel, and be prepared to attack the *Tirpitz* that afternoon if the weather was right.

The task force initially consisted of 12 Lancs from each squadron with Tallboys and 6 from each with 12 Johnny Walker mines, but 617 sent 2 extra Tallboy aircraft. The groundcrews and the officer in charge of the op, Grp Capt McMullen, and his staff for the operational HQ were carried in two unarmed Liberators of 511 Squadron, Transport Command. There was also a Lancaster of 463 Squadron armed with

201

cameras and a film crew, plus a Mosquito of 540 Squadron for reconnaissance and additional photographic duties. Altogether, there were almost 300 RAF personnel headed for Russia and the Arctic Circle. Mission: sink the *Tirpitz*.

The Liberators set off first from Bardney – they alone were going to Lossiemouth to top up with fuel before turning for Russia – then 18 operational Lancasters led by 9 Squadron CO, Wingco Jimmy Bazin, and including Ed Stowell in NF925 WS/T, probably disappointed after all that Tallboy training to be carrying JW mines, plus the camera Lanc. One Tallboy worked loose in its bomb bay and that crew had to jettison and come home.

Meanwhile, 20 Lancs of 617 Squadron took off from Woodhall Spa, led by Wingco Willie Tait, and including Nick Knilans in a brand-new aircraft, LM492 KC/W, with Tallboy and a scratch crew, a mixture of old and new. Flt Sgt Paddy Blanche, representing the Republic of Ireland, was now rear gunner. Flt Lt Larry Curtis, w/op, was the squadron's wireless leader and veteran of more than 100 trips. Plt Off Don Bell, a Canadian, was navigator.

The British forecast said cloud above 1,500ft and visibility 6 miles at Archangel. The Russian forecast said that for the last hour or 200 miles of their epic journey, the Lancs would be in ten-tenths cloud down to a few hundred feet, with heavy rain squalls. The latter forecast was correct but the two squadrons never heard it, which was why the Russians were astounded when their guests started arriving in such atrocious conditions. The guests were, many of them, equally astounded that any of them managed to arrive at all.

Don Bell, flying with Nick Knilans:

As we turned parallel to the Norwegian coast I remember the blazing sunset as it hung over the Orkney Islands only to sink slowly into the north Atlantic. Then the flight into utter darkness began, without any aids for me to navigate: no radar, no astro, no beacons, no wireless, no visual pinpoints, no bearings. We could see nothing but haze as we crossed the Norwegian coast with no position check and total overcast above us. Using the radar altimeter which had been installed that day and was the first one I had ever seen, I was able to plot the highest points we crossed over Norway and . . . I got an exact groundspeed check and position check as we crossed the Gulf of Bothnia. As we approached our ETA, Knilans let down to 50 feet on instruments. The tops of evergreen trees stuck out of the clouds around us.

We had been up 12 hours and had a 20 minute reserve. We had been given no alternative airfields so our options were running out with our fuel. We turned back to reach an area over the White Sea where we at last had some visibility. Our 20 minute reserve had gone; maybe ten minutes were left in the tanks reading empty.

Knilans: 'Don's maps were from the British Army, World War One, and nobody ever heard the radio signal we were supposed to home in on. I kept descending as the cloud base lowered. Finally I was at tree top level and the clouds were there too.'

Even if they had had decent maps, the countryside was against the aircrews when they could see it. Someone who had lived there all his life might have recognised the subtle differences between one small lake and a thousand others, one seemingly infinite stretch of pine forest and another, or this marshy wasteland and that marshy wasteland. The crews of the RAF in the worst-possible flying weather had no chance. It was a situation that threatened disaster, possibly complete disaster, before they came anywhere near the *Tirpitz*.

Knilans was right out of petrol:

There was a fishing village on the shore so I circled over it. In a large hayfield near-by, five barefoot boys about ten years old made vigorous motions with their heads and hands. I gathered that they were signalling that it would be OK to land there. The field was slightly downhill. A chimney's smoke showed that our approach was nearly downwind.

Knilans plopped his aircraft down the moment they were over the fence and the mud in the field brought them to a halt against a tree. Two of his engines cut out before he could shut them down. Minutes later, a 617 flight commander, Tony Iveson, came in to land, managing to stop just before the trees. It was still raining and both crews were cold, tired, hungry and increasingly damp. After a while, a Russian Army jeep came out on a suspicious inspection, followed by two more with a senior officer and an interpreter who did not have English among her languages.

Through another interpreter it gradually emerged that they were at Onega, on what had once been a fighter airstrip, last used in the Russo-

Finnish war. Language or no language, the needs of the exhausted traveller require no translation and a meal of salmon, potatoes and black bread was brought in, with large glasses of water.

Knilans: 'We had been warned about drinking the water but Paddy Blanche let his thirst overcome his good sense and he drained his glass in several quick gulps. Then he began to choke, gasp and change colour. We were alarmed. "It's bloody vodka," he sputtered.' Bell: 'Paddy Blanche turned white as a sheet and sagged to the floor as he passed out.'

Both crews were put up in relatively lavish log-cabin quarters which were part of a military hospital for veterans of the Battle of Stalingrad. Knilans:

> A soldier with a rifle and bayonet stood guard at our door. He accompanied each of us going to the latrine, which consisted of a log raised knee-high over a ditch. I told the sentry that they might have peeled the bark off for such eminent visitors, but he remained inscrutable. When we did get an English speaking interpreter, the Russians asked why I, an American First Louie, was in command over higher ranking British officers. I told them I was the pilot so I was the boss, but they didn't understand.

Bell:

> Our only complaint was about the sentries pacing around our buildings who wouldn't let us go out. The interpreter explained that Russia was a vast country and they didn't want us to get lost. We were warned not to attempt to get shaving kits from our aircraft as the guards had orders to shoot anyone approaching. At least we didn't need to worry about the safety of our Lancaster.

Knilans: 'They gave us dinner that evening, which was borsch, sour bread, cold bacon, potatoes, and vodka.'

Flt Lt Mac Hamilton, 617 Squadron, flying PD233 KC/G, was Knilans's best pal among the pilots. He had an experience nearer the plan:

> We set off well overweight, carrying a 12,000lb Tallboy and full fuel tanks. We flew at low level over the North Sea and made a sharp climb over Norway at dusk, then on past the northern border of Sweden.
>
> My crew were young and although we had completed two tours of ops, they had never seen lighted streets or towns from the air. Britain

and Europe had been blacked out since war began. To our starboard were the lakes of Sweden, the roads around them lit up like strings of pearls on black velvet, their bright reflections shimmering across the water. Then came the dazzling beauty of a large town with its myriad twinkling lights glowing with life.

Then on through deteriorating weather over the endless, featureless forests and lakes of the great Gulf of Finland. Many long hours later, dawn broke grey and dull with a steady drizzle. Easing down to below 500 feet we could still see nothing and fuel was getting dangerously low. 'We should be coming up to Archangel soon,' said Jackie [navigator Plt Off J.T. Jackson] and, right on cue, a boat appeared below. We were right over the harbour. At 400 feet we followed the river Dvina and found the rough grass airfield of Yagodnik. We circled and landed with fuel tanks almost empty and were the first to arrive.

Apart from a brass band to play the heroes in, the Russians had supplied very little. It was a grass field, marked out, with a windsock at the end. A few other Lancs followed Hamilton and were lined up by the Russians, facing the runway. Tait was among them and asked Mac if his wireless and loop aerial were working. They were, so Hamilton's Lanc was appointed as control tower and he as flight controller. Instead of going to what he imagined, a hot bath, food and drink after the longest operational flight in history, early bird Hamilton was rewarded with another 2 hours of duty.

Ed Stowell, now with his second promotion in a month to flying officer, a comparative novice with a navigator likewise experienced with six trips across the English Channel and one to the Dutch coast, was one of those who succeeded where Knilans and others could not, being called in to land by Hamilton at the designated aerodrome.

Hamilton:

When all hope of further arrivals had passed, I made my way to the houseboat, our allotted quarters. Above the gangplank was a banner: 'Welcome to the glorious flyers of the RAF'. I started up the stairway and was stopped by a Russian in a smart uniform who said 'Nyet!' and pointed to the lower deck. Kit Howard then appeared and called down 'Come on up, Mac, you're sharing a cabin with me.' I replied 'The admiral here has just directed me to the lower deck.' 'He's not the admiral,' laughed Kit. 'He's the orderly corporal.'

Orderly or not, the uniformed ambassador wasn't up to his job. Hamilton's cabin was infested with an exceptionally vicious strain of extremely large bed bug, as was everyone else's, and the medical officer's spray gun was only partly effective.

All the w/ops complained that the radio navigation aids had not been available but the Russians did have their beacons turned on. The briefing had been with the wrong call sign, the Cyrillic letter 'B' being the equivalent to the Roman 'V' but, like the maps, that hardly mattered since nobody had realised that they worked on an incompatible system anyway.

No navaids, the filthy weather and nothing left in the tank induced 13 out of the 38 Lancaster crews to go astray. Some picked the wrong aerodrome; some came down wherever they thought they could. They landed – and crashed – all over the place. By a marvel, 19 Lancasters had landed safely at Yagodnik. Including that of 463's photographer, Flt Lt Buckham, 11 had landed not far away at Kegostrov of which one was permanently u/s, or 'category E'. Of the two that went in at Vascova, one became category E and one got stuck in a bog. Knilans and Iveson at Onega still had serviceable aircraft. The rest were Es at Belomorsk, Chubalo-Novolsk, Molotovsk and Talagi, all outlying and outlandish places even by local standards.

Not a single one of the Lancasters was fit to operate as planned that afternoon. The crews were exhausted in any case but every aircraft needed work doing to it and, because of the late change of plan, groundcrews and spare parts were not already there as they should have been but were in the Liberators, one of which was at Kegostrov.

Two Lancs needed an engine change, one had extensive flak damage, one had a burned out exhaust valve. One had its nose in a potato patch, there were broken ailerons, cowlings, fuel tanks, and the best of them needed adjustments. As if that were not enough, the refuelling arrangements were quite inadequate for this number of hungry big birds and it would take 18 hours before they were all filled.

Bell:

Willie Tait was flown over to assess our situation in an ancient Russian biplane. He said it looked like a coffin, flew like a coffin and he was afraid it would be a coffin. Next came an ex USAAF Dakota with its white stars painted red, with enough fuel to get us to

Yagodnik, and we saw that our aircraft bearing the heavy bomb had been turned 180° ready for take off, with the brakes still on. We had seen no tractors so I asked how they'd done it. The interpreter said 'Many manskies.'

After hand-pumping the fuel from 50-gallon drums into the two Lancs, Iveson and Knilans were away, following Tait who was now in the Dakota. Knilans throttled back to keep pace and, with dirty spark plugs from the long flight before, all four engines stopped.

Knilans dived, expecting the increased airspeed to turn the props over and restart the engines. It did, but for no accountable reason the flight engineer decided it was time to pull up the flaps which were still at 30°. The Lanc, loaded with the Tallboy bomb, mushed down into the treetops and began trimming them off like a hedge-cutter. The natural instinct was to pull back on the stick but Knilans knew this would have put the tail right in among the trees and that, probably, would have been that.

One lonesome pine stood out above all the others and Knilans was going to hit it. The question was, with what? With a wing and a propeller? Not likely. He skidded W-Willie sideways so the nose would take the impact. As the tree smashed the Perspex of the cockpit and the bomb-aimer's compartment, the Lancaster chopped the tree. A 3ft section of log,* lopped off the top, fell into the cockpit and along the fuselage, missing everyone but leaving behind it an open wind tunnel. The blast of air took the navigator's maps and the wireless operator's new cap and threw them into Russian airspace. Knilans, his hand over his face so he could peer into the wind through gaps between his fingers, flew to Yagodnik one-handed. Knilans: 'The rest of the 60 mile flight was uneventful and we landed at the island on three. The starboard outer had had to be feathered, overheating because its radiator air-scoop had filled with pine needles and cones.'

A damage inspection showed that Knilans's kite needed a new bombsight, new pitot head, new nose, two engine cowlings and a radiator, plus repairs to an undercarriage door, the bomb doors, the starboard tailplane and the starboard wing. Even with all that, it was

---

* This trophy was displayed on the wall of the Petwood Hotel at Woodhall Spa for many years, with the caption 'Believe it or not'.

still easier to repair Knilans's aircraft than change an engine on the 9 Squadron Lanc belonging to Flg Off Adams, so most of the spares for KC/W were robbed off WS/W and poor Adams, who had flown half the way to Russia on three engines, would miss out on what looked like being the op of a lifetime.

The Russians had sent out search parties for the crashed crews and somehow over the next day all were assembled, present, correct and unharmed, at Yagodnik. For the next two days, frantic efforts were made to collect, repair and refit as many Lancasters as possible. RAF groundcrew, with Russian mechanics and sheet-metal workers, laboured continuously for almost 48 hours, until they were ordered to take a rest. They allowed themselves 4 hours sleep then went back to their aircraft, which were dispersed in a line a mile long, in the cold and the rain, with no transport to carry anyone anywhere.

Those aircrew not quartered in the houseboat were in an underground shelter where they soon found that the already legendary strain of bugs inhabiting the boat was also fully adapted to life on land. As officers, they were provided with Russian Army batwomen. One of these, a quite elderly lady in the uniform of the Russian Marines, pressed their RAF uniforms using her own ironing technique, taking a mouthful of water and spraying it on the cloth as she went. Knilans had his attention focussed on 'a large, pleasant-mannered female soldier on night duty. We became friends. We could not communicate in words but I gave her cigarettes and talcum powder and we walked about in the starlight.' As Knilans proved, there's nothing quite like cigarettes, talcum powder and starlight to cement an alliance between two great nations.

Not all aircrew proved so able to supply their own entertainment. Some had to be provided and the Russians took their responsibilities seriously. The Soviets of those days certainly knew how to make massively boring films which, without English subtitles, signally failed to impress the eager RAF audience used to frothier and more amusing productions. Other cultural events similarly did little for Anglo-Soviet relations and even the dance was something of a failure, the Russian girls seemingly being under instructions to socialise in general but not in particular and not for any length of time.

The mess dinner was, by contrast, a riot. Following a meal of raw fish, borsch and roast meat – possibly yak, possibly not – there were many toasts in vodka and red wine, to King George, General Secretary

Stalin, President Roosevelt, the RAF, 9 Squadron, 617 Squadron, the Red Army, Yagodnik aerodrome, the Union of Soviet Socialist Republics, and tomorrow or possibly the next day they would tarmac the runway.

Thursday 14 September, the proposed attack on the *Tirpitz* was scrubbed at 04:00. It was the weather again. Such holidays could not last and soon there was a war on for definite. Operation Paravane was about to commence. Friday 15 September, all available Lancasters were to attack the battleship, 10 of 9 Squadron and 17 of 617 Squadron, 20 altogether with Tallboys and the rest with Johnny Walker mines.

They began taking off at 09:30 local time, 617 Squadron first. All were up and on their way soon after 10:00. Most of the Tallboy aircraft came in more or less directly astern of the target which, to the bomb aimers, looked about the size of a Swan Vesta. Not only were they 3 miles or so above her. To hit from an aircraft flying at about 200 miles an hour they would have to release their bombs a mile and a half in advance. Over the target something like 25 seconds later, flying more slowly than the bomb was falling, on a clear day they would have been able to see if their own near-supersonic speck had hit the matchstick. As it was, they bombed from various heights and all within 13 minutes, sometimes aiming for a piece of the ship they could see, sometimes for her gun flashes in the midst of the smoke.

As they neared the *Tirpitz* they all climbed up to 15,000ft to avoid the shells. Knilans:

> The Germans ignited smoke pots on the mountain sides surrounding the fjord. The smoke from the pots rolled down the steep slopes and spread over the battleship. Those of us near the front of the formation were able to bomb before the smoke completely covered the ship. Taffy claimed to have hit the target, but then he never failed to claim a hit on the target, and we front ones were asked to circle among the exploding shells so the gunners below would have more to shoot at rather than just the few left to bomb. I had lost one engine already so was told to head back to our island aerodrome. That was my seventh and last time coming back from ops on three. Mosquito photographs later showed that someone had put a hole through the *Tirpitz* but she was still upright.

The someone was an experienced 9 Squadron crew led by Flt Lt Dougie Melrose in a famous old Lancaster, W4964 WS/J-Johnny, allegedly on her hundredth op but actually on her hundred and second. That anybody came anywhere near was a marvellous tribute to the determination and sheer flying abilities of these crews. Without enemy fighters it had not been as hazardous a trip as they might have expected. Even so, they had flown thousands of miles through freezing air, been unable to rest properly because of voracious, man-eating fleas, and had been subjected to huge quantities of Russian hospitality, and they still hit the *Tirpitz*.

Ed Stowell dropped his JW mines he believed in the correct area. Certainly some fell in the fjord, although some were seen to fall on land. None performed their tricks and the Johnny Walker synchronised swimming mine was never seen in action again.

The flight back to Yagodnik from the fjord was without incident. It was time to go home to Bardney and Woodhall Spa, as soon as the aircraft could be fixed. Meanwhile, a little celebration had been arranged. While *Russian baths and entertainments* were set up for the groundcrews on the Friday evening, something slightly more Bacchanalian was in store for the airmen. There is one common language understood by all service personnel, especially the comrades of the Royal and Red air forces, and that is the one spoken after much alcohol has been consumed. The premier event in this connection was clearly going to be the special stage show and luncheon to be given at the Intourist Hotel in Archangel on the Saturday.

Alas for those crews scheduled to fly home on Saturday night, getting sloshed beforehand was not permitted. That still left 23 crews available to embark on a river boat for the 15 miles or so to Archangel. Whatever they had expected, they could not have imagined the fact of Archangel. It was a frontier town in the middle of an infinite mudflat but still managed to have a certain charm. That the Intourist Hotel and auditorium had been adjudged suitable for entertaining, wining and dining the glorious flyers of the Royal Air Force must have been due entirely to the lack of suitability of the other options, if there were any.

Nick Knilans and his pal Hamilton were not keen on the stage show. It was Russian opera. They slipped out into the street with a supply of roubles acquired through the local sale of cigarettes. They met two Royal Navy men in a bar. They ran out of roubles. The sailors took them to a navy provisions store where they picked up a large quantity of jam, which fetched a very good price in roubles on the market square.

Meanwhile, after the show had been endured by the majority, the bottles were out and a sincere effort was made by the hosts, with the limited resources available to them in wartime Arctic Russia, to be as hospitable as they possibly could. They offered vodka, potato soup, vodka, fish, vodka, black bread, vodka, blinis, and vodka.

Back in the bar Knilans, Hamilton and the sailors were joined by a couple of Russians and a good time was had. By the time the sailors had fallen asleep and the Russians had slid off their chairs, Hamilton and Knilans didn't have a care in the world and were moderately surprised to see an RAF wing commander, not known to them, turn up in the bar.

Mac and I were feeling no pain when this guy came up to our table. 'Pardon me,' he said, 'but aren't you gentlemen part of the group from the auditorium?' 'Yes, sir,' we said. 'Well, the rest of your chaps are down on the dock. They've been there about an hour by now.' He led us from the bar to a waiting staff car, telling us he was the British Air Attaché at the consulate. Wingco Tait and the others didn't seem too amused at our holding them up. I decided to stay out of the way and went below. The Russian captain gestured me into a galley where the cook gave me a plate of fried fish and mashed potatoes. All in all, I felt quite pleased with the day.

Next morning, there was nothing left to do but go home. Everyone was looking forward mightily to seeing what effect there had been on their bank accounts of the 10 roubles per day special allowance added to their pay for the trip and were wondering how that might translate into pints of bitter in the Petwood, the Jolly Sailor, the Railway and other similar establishments.

Knilans, on the last leg of his last operation, might have thought it was downhill all the way. 'Our flight would take us across southern Finland and down the Baltic Sea to Denmark.' Bell: 'We began to ice up rather badly. Nick wanted a position as we were going to have to come down below the clouds to get under the icy weather. My dead reckoning had us over the Baltic, between Sweden and Germany.' Knilans: 'We wanted a landmark and we got one all right. We came out of thick cloud right over the centre of Stockholm.' Bell: 'It came as quite a shock to break out over a busy street in a big city with flashing neon signs and high buildings all around us. As Nick pulled us back up into the clouds, the Swedish flak was dense and very close. "Hey," he shouted, "I thought these guys were supposed to be neutral."' The last twist in the Wisconsin Farmer's Tale was a message that Woodhall Spa was fog-bound so they were diverted to Lossiemouth.

For days after the raid, reports from Norwegian intelligence and intercepted German coded messages gave differing versions of the damage caused during Operation Paravane but in summary it seemed that there had been one direct hit. A Tallboy had drilled through the foredeck at an angle and come out of the ship's hull near the waterline, before exploding some distance away. Had it exploded inside the ship it might well have sunk her.

Tirpitz was far more badly damaged than her attackers realised or the Germans would admit, except to themselves. A huge quantity of sea water, 1,500 tons, had flooded in through a hole big enough to sail a boat through. They hadn't sunk *Tirpitz* but now there was no need. *Tirpitz* had been reclassified by Germans as u/s for war. Adm Dönitz and a group of senior naval officers decided only a week after the raid that *Tirpitz* was no longer fit for duty. She would need to sail to the fatherland for repairs and could only manage slow speeds, less than 10 knots, which would be a highly dangerous journey for her. Even then, it would be the following June before she could be ready to fight again and it was thought that she could cause more short-term disruption to the Allied cause by doing the same as she had so far, hanging around in the fjords. So long as the Allies didn't find out what a mess she was in, they would continue to hop about in anxiety and tie up large resources in case their fears were realised.

Chapter 14

FLYING INTO THE SUNSET

Normal service at No. 9 Squadron was resumed 23 September. Full control of Bomber Command was back with C-in-C Harris after his summer of following Eisenhower's demands. Although army support work would still be on the roster and 9 Squadron would be closely involved where great precision was needed, the overall emphasis swung back to the industries of Germany. Some other things had changed, too. The Luftwaffe was no longer the power it was and, with the resources of Fighter Command much more at his disposal, Harris could order daylight raids with strong escorts. France and Belgium were German-free zones but Arnhem had proved a bridge too far, showing how German resistance would increase in ferocity as the fatherland came more and more under threat. For the bombers, all the other risks remained, of course, and the flak was still there. You could never forget the flak.

First up was an evening raid, take-off at seven, back around one, to aqueducts near Münster on the Dortmund–Ems canal, a target of the highest importance to the Germans. Since 617's dreadful night in 1943, Bomber Command had drained it several times. It would be breached again tonight, by a force including 12 of No. 9, 6 with Tallboys. Another 90 or so of other 5 Group squadrons went with 1,000lb bombs. A warm welcome was guaranteed; the Germans expected the bombers all the time and were ready.

WS/W, Adams's *Tirpitz* aircraft, was back, mended and skippered by Ed Stowell carrying a Tallboy. Doug Melrose, also with the big bomb, was leading the attack, the other Tallboy carriers being Laws, Begg, Taylor and Tweddle. They had had to hop over to Woodhall Spa to get their bombs, production and logistics not yet being up to demand. As they took off it was pouring with rain and the weather just got worse. Spirits were further depressed by the sight of two Lancs going down together at the rendezvous, after a collision, but flak on the way into and over the target was light. Melrose found ten-tenths cloud over the aqueduct and it was still thick down as far as 7,000ft. He flew around for 10 minutes but it was hopeless for the Tallboy men so he set off for home with his still in the bomb bay, as did Stowell and the others. They were expensive things, Tallboy bombs. They were not allowed to waste them, even if landing with one was a hazard.

Flak and fighters were much greater hazards and 15 Lancasters out of 136, 11 per cent, were lost on this operation including 2 from 9 Squadron. Old hands returning to Bardney thought it one of the worst jobs they'd been on. Still, there was more to come.

Stowell's tenth op was not so bad. Kaiserslauten, only a medium-sized city but one of the most important industrial centres of Bavaria, had never been the subject of a major raid and it never would be again, as the force of over 200 Lancs destroyed a good third of it. With little flak expected, 9 Squadron went in low. Stowell, bombing from 4,400ft, saw *one fire near church and large glow reflected on cloud later*. Others saw bombing well concentrated near the autobahn. One Lanc was lost, from 463 Squadron, and one Mosquito of 627, piloted by Flt Lt Harold Earl Brown RCAF, aged 29, husband of Jessie, of Rolla, North Dakota.

Stowell and crew went on leave but Cliff Newton carried the 9 Squadron American flag to Wilhelmshaven, 5 October, a morning raid but cloud covered. They bombed on instructions from the controller who was working off H2S and the results were scattered. Newton went to Bremen the next night, the last and most successful of more than 30 attacks on this city. In clear moonlight, 250 Lancasters destroyed 5,000 houses and 50 factories, including some of Focke-Wulf and Siemens, for the loss of 5 aircraft. If only they were all like that.

Newton's third in a row was to Vlissingen (Flushing) and the sea walls, part of the plan to bomb the Germans out of their fortress at Walcheren Island. They were on the run everywhere else but here, at the mouth of the Scheldt, the route into Antwerp. The city was already in Allied hands but could not be used for urgently needed supplies because the Germans controlled the Scheldt Estuary from Walcheren, most of which 'island' was below sea level. Newton and the rest took 4,000lb cookies and 1,000lb standard issue, everyone saw the dyke hit and water flooding in and, from a force of 121 Lancs, no losses.

Where McCarthy had failed in May 1943, perhaps 9 Squadron could succeed with a different bomb and so, 15 October 1944, 18 Lancasters went to the Sorpe dam, escorted by almost 60 Mustangs. The Sorpe was the one in the great 617 Squadron dam-busters' raid left to the last, hit by McCarthy but not usefully damaged, and which kept the Ruhr supplied with water while the breached Möhne dam was rebuilt. At the time of the dam-busters' raid, the Germans had speculated on what might have happened had the second dam on the list been the Sorpe rather than the Eder, the breach of which didn't affect the Ruhr. In view of the construction of the Sorpe, the answer was almost certainly 'much the same'.

All the skippers on that famous moonlit night had been very experienced; most were so on 9 Squadron's morning effort – it was Ed Stowell's eleventh – but not all. *Two aircraft were jostled by others over the target and as a result were unable to make an attack. No definite breach of the dam was seen to have occurred although several hits were registered.*

Stowell had a complete view of proceedings before his own drop: *First two bombs went to starboard of compensating lake, third and fourth overshot, next four in SW corner of dam face, next two in centre of dam face, and the next on top of the dam.* There were nine hits and near misses, with one direct hit on the very crest of the dam, smack in the middle. If Stowell's timings are right, that was the eleventh bomb to fall; Ed's was thirteenth.

Accurate though the bombing was, the dam was proof against the Tallboy, being 2,000ft thick at its base with its concrete centre reinforced and protected by many, many tons of earth and rubble. Perhaps, had the Germans kept the water level as high as it had been pre-dam busters, the extra pressure would have made a breach. More likely, the Sorpe would have stood however many bombs hit it, bouncing, spinning or otherwise.

On the same day *Tirpitz*, her every move watched by Norwegian spies for the Allies, steamed very slowly down the coast to Tromsø where she anchored off Haaköy Island, to be a floating gun battery against the expected Allied invasion of Norway. The spies reported extensive damage to her forward hull. Her low speed, plus a huge escort of more than 50 warships, might have convinced an independent mind that she was *hors de combat*, no longer an independent fighting force. A more enticing thought was that she had sailed herself into range. No need for Russian adventures now. Lancasters with a few further modifications could reach her from Scotland, but before that there was a trip to Nürnberg.

It was fairly routine. The squadron sent 19 Lancs, 1 came back with the Gee box u/s, 1 didn't come back at all, and Jesse tried something new. He conceived a pressing desire to relieve himself and, though the flight engineer offered to keep the ship straight and level while the skip went back to the Elsan, the good captain didn't fancy leaving the flight deck while over Germany. The navigator suggested that the matter could be resolved by opening the side window but the bomb aimer cautioned against this, citing frostbite on the procreative member as a potential hazard.

In need and nothing loth, Ed Stowell undid his straps, stood up, opened the window and bestowed his bodily fluids upon the German nation. Settling back into position, he heard the mid-upper gunner complaining that he'd gone blind. Stowell asked the navigator to check the poor man's oxygen but that wasn't the reason. The gunner wanted to know why they were suddenly flying through fog, yellow fog, at this height. Thankfully there were no fighters about because it wasn't until they were making their descent over the sea that the yellow ice melted on the mid-upper turret. Jesse resolved that henceforth he would carry an old paint pot under his seat.

The Lancasters were having more powerful engines installed and their gun turrets were again being removed so that two additional fuel tanks could be fitted in the fuselage. With all that extra weight they would be lethargic and vulnerable if they were attacked by fighters on a long outward journey, so the aircraft were lightened. Non-gunning crew members were relieved to see that at least the rear turret was put back; as before, the mid-upper turret was left off but now the front guns were dropped as well.

After four days of bombing practice and air tests with the new engines, the truth was revealed, as if they hadn't guessed. They, including Ed Stowell with a Tallboy this time, and 617 were going to fly to Scotland and then it was to be the *Tirpitz* again, 29 October, Operation Obviate, a 2,400 miles, 12-hour round trip flying over the spectacularly beautiful Norwegian landscape in glorious weather. As they reached the fjord, they saw broken cloud starting to appear in an otherwise cloudless sky, against the forecast and right over the target.

Egil Lindberg was a Norwegian Resistance radio operator, a meteorologist at Tromsø put out of work by the Germans who had their own weathermen. He regularly sent covert signals to London and naturally was a close observer of the battleship. 'The situation in Tromsø was hectic, to say the least. Russian troops had crossed the Norwegian border and the German army, retreating from Finland, adopted a scorched-earth policy. The result was 15,000 German soldiers in Tromsø and many thousands of new refugees every day. Then, when the *Tirpitz* arrived, everybody knew something extraordinary was going to happen.'

On board ship, a senior gunnery officer, Lt Willibald Völsing:

In Tromsøfjord we discovered quite different geographical conditions [from Kaafjord]. Here there were no mountains close at hand. Rather, for a distance of some 30 kilometres around, everything was open, so it was no longer any use to have land-based observers. On 29 October a sailor on watch at the ship's foremost observation post sighted the enemy approaching at a range of 70km. The Captain awarded him the Iron Cross on the spot. We had enough time to make ready and go to action stations on that day.

Egil Lindberg, as the air-raid siren sounded:

The Lancaster bomber squadrons came sailing in above the town from the east, above Tromsdalstind, the highest peak in the vicinity [just over 4,000ft]. The Germans immediately struck up with their anti-aircraft guns and there was a deafening noise. Shell fragments rained down upon the town. You could see the planes dive into the clouds and out, while the anti-aircraft shells exploded around them.

Wg Cdr Bazin led 9 Squadron in and bombed at 08:54. He thought the ship seemed to be beached at one end. Sqn Ldr Williams at 08:55 had the centre of the ship in the bombsight. Light and heavy flak were moderate to intense from shore batteries, flak ships and the *Tirpitz* herself, also firing her heavy guns from aft. Lt Völsing: 'Our salvoes gave us cover and the British had to scatter.'

Stowell had taken off at 01:26 and bombed at 07:57 from 13,000ft. He saw 3 explosions, 2 in the bows and 1 in the stern. A rear gunner in another crew saw a direct hit on the bows followed by a big explosion and a column of brown smoke. Several others saw the brown smoke and a hit on the bows.

Lt Völsing: 'A near miss caused an influx of 8,000 cubic metres of water but we did not list because of compensating currents in the fjord. Several

Lancasters were shot down or lost on their way home. Even an attack by four-engined aircraft can be fought off if there is enough warning.' The Lancasters had had one bomb each and all the bombs were dropped, and only Carey of 617 didn't return, crash-landing in Sweden, which hardly counts as scattering, being driven off and several shot down.

Most of the 617 Squadron crews had also seen hits and smoke but, when it all cleared and reconnaissance pictures could be studied, *Tirpitz* was still there, apparently unharmed. Sure that another, third attack would come, the Germans got on with the job of saving the *Tirpitz* by the only method open. Lt Völsing: 'We now set about encasing the ship in sand so as to make her unsinkable.' They built up the sea bed beneath her. They had believed their berth would meet this specification anyway, with a clear fathom of water only, but it proved to be much deeper than that. So, they got busy with their dredgers in the mud.

Bomber Command's orders, from the very top of the top, said to sink the *Tirpitz*. Not render her u/s, not turn her into scrap, but sink her. It was becoming as much psychological warfare as anything. The negative effect on German morale of sinking the mighty *Tirpitz* could hardly be underestimated. The value of her staying there, defiant and indestructible, was opposingly great. If she was to be sunk, increasingly shallow water was not the only problem. The days in the fjords were already very short and in three weeks the sun would dip below the horizon, not to reappear again until the spring. So far, two squadrons had been twice in the daylight and hit the target with a single bomb between them. How many night trips would it take?

They flew up to Scotland, 4 November. There was a gale warning so they flew home. Every day they practised. With the few daylight hours and the possibility of cloud, if they got one more shot at it they would have to make sure. Somebody, some pilot and bomb-aimer combination, in 9 Squadron or 617, absolutely had to stick a Tallboy right on the money. Off they went again up to Scotland, 11 November.

At around 03:00 the following morning, it was exceptionally wintry and those responsible for de-icing the aircraft did not get up soon enough. In any case, some Lancasters were refreezing as fast as they were defrosted and it was snowing. To his great frustration, Doug Melrose, commanding B Flight, was among those who couldn't take off, likewise Wg Cdr Bazin, commanding the squadron. With two of the top men grounded, Sqn Ldr Williams moved up from commanding

A Flight to take charge of all of 9 Squadron. Ed Stowell and Cliff Newton were among those able to get away.

They were to rendezvous over a lake, 20 minutes south of Tromsøfjord, after a long flight in the dark on dead reckoning. As dawn broke they saw a seemingly endless vista of mountain tops covered in snow, separated by valleys filled with mist. It was like Finland on the way to Archangel; no distinguishing features but with better weather. They found the lake.

Tait shot off some Very lights as a signal to form up. Lt Völsing was in position on *Tirpitz* as range finder for the heavy guns: 'The alarm was given and in 40 seconds the guns were cleared for action. The Commandant spoke words of encouragement and optimism and held out the prospect of support from squadrons of fighter aircraft. Since we had so far survived without outside help, this time the optimism was all the greater.' The fighters were FW190s of 9 *Staffel, Jagdgeschwader* 5 (coincidentally, No. 9 Squadron, 5 Group) but the support never got beyond the prospect stage.

As the leading Lancasters cleared the last peak, crews were astounded and delighted to find that the fjord they wanted seemed to be the only one in Norway with no white mist and there, in front of them, tiny but perfectly visible, was the *Tirpitz*.

Egil Lindberg: 'It was an unusual day for the time of year. The sky was bright and there was not a breath of wind.'

Lt Völsing: 'Electronic range calculation was in its infancy and never were the calculations so far out as on that day. The First Gunnery Officer [in the armoured command post] repeatedly ordered the heavy guns to open fire, but there was no data and so the automatic firing devices could not be used. We fired too late and overshot.'

Wingco Tait led the attack and his bomb, the first to fall, was almost certainly a direct hit on the ship. Egil Lindberg:

> I and some other Norwegians were watching from the Weather Office, on top of the island of Tromsø, while the huge bombs were dropped in a circle around the ship. As the bombs burst, our own windows were blown from their fastenings and panes were shattered, and from the sea columns of water rose several hundred feet into the air.

Lt Völsing: 'There was no longer any distinguishing between our firing and the enemy's bombs.'

219

Stowell saw his own bomb fall approximately at the centre of the port side, before he was hit in the tail by flak. Newton didn't hit the *Tirpitz* but he did have a shoot-out with two E-boats 10 minutes after he bombed and his rear gunner, Sgt Stevens, put one of them out of action.

Flt Lt Bruce Buckham DSO, DFC was captain of the 463 Squadron camera Lancaster:

> We descended to about 2,000 feet and the bombers were right overhead doing perfect bombing runs, bomb doors gaped open and the glistening Tallboys suspended. Now they were released and to us they appeared to travel in a graceful curve like a high diver. [I thought] the first two were near misses and then Pow!, a hit which was followed by two more in as many seconds. There was a tremendous explosion on board and the *Tirpitz* appeared to try to heave herself out of the water.

Egil Lindberg:

> The anti-aircraft fire of the *Tirpitz* soon became more tame. Only the aftermost guns were still firing angrily. Some minutes later the guns fell silent and a tremendous mass of smoke rose from the ship and we assumed there had been an explosion of the boilers or magazines. When the smoke lifted and lay like a dark cloud in the sky, we could see the battleship stripped of masts and towers, as if she was part-finished in the shipyard.

Johann Tröger was a signaller, aged 22, who had been blown into the fjord by a direct hit on the bridge:

> The ship seemed to leap out of the water when the magazine went up, making a huge hole through the side. There were men everywhere in the water. It was bitterly cold and there was black smoke billowing over everything, then another bomb hit the water-line alongside. The suction pulled the ship sideways and she stayed there for what seemed a very long time but water was pouring in through the hole and suddenly she keeled over and slid bow first into the harbour sand.

Bruce Buckham in the camera Lanc: 'We decided to call it a day, when our rear gunner Eric Gierch called out "I think she's turning over".

We flew in at 50 feet and watched with bated breath as *Tirpitz* heeled over to port, ever so slowly. We could see German sailors swimming, diving, jumping and there must have been 60 men clinging to her side.'

Tröger was among those picked up by a motor torpedo boat. 'We were crowded on deck when a single aircraft came back and circled overhead at very low level. I said to the man next to me "There you are. They've come back to make sure we're really finished and take a picture of us."'

Where had the fighters been all this time? For once, the Germans were inefficient. At the nearby fighter base at Bardufoss, the FW190s were scrambled to attack enemy aircraft in the east but were ordered to wait on the ground for the commander. There didn't seem to be a commander so one of the more experienced pilots among a fairly raw lot, Heinz Orlowski, took off and the rest followed:

We saw anti-aircraft fire in the Tromsø area and set course for it, not knowing why anyone would want to raid the fjord because the fighter base had not been informed about *Tirpitz* being there. On the way, we met two Bf109s flying in the opposite direction. I assumed that one of them must contain the commander, so I wheeled around and the rest did the same and we flew back with the Messerschmitts to land at Bardufoss. By this time, flights of four-engined aircraft had been reported as coming and going high over Tromsø but it was too late for us to catch them.

Egil Lindberg: 'Only a few hundred men were saved. About a hundred dead bodies drifted ashore; the rest remained inside the ship. There was a great enthusiasm in Tromsø over the successful attack and the joy manifested itself loudly, which resulted in quite a number of arrests among the civilians by the Gestapo.'

There was a great enthusiasm in Britain too, with congratulatory messages to both squadrons from the King, the Prime Minister, the War Cabinet, the Admiralty, the Russians, President Roosevelt and all the biggest brass hats in the RAF. The very top man, Air Chief Marshal Sir Charles Portal, Chief of Air Staff, wrote privately to Harris:

I have just heard of the splendid achievement of 9 and 617 Squadrons in sinking the *Tirpitz*. Please pass to them my warmest congratulations and an expression of unbounded admiration which I feel for their skill, courage and perseverance now so happily crowned with full success. Apart from the effect on the war at sea of the permanent removal of the most powerful unit of the German Navy this exploit will fill the German Nation with dismay at a critical time and will enhance the fame of Bomber Command and the Royal Air Force throughout the world.

The two squadrons were pleased with the praise and the fame but were more immediately concerned not to be filled with dismay at a critical time, and so went to manifest their joy at full speed in the mess. The parties at Bardney and Woodhall Spa were most memorable, except hardly anyone could remember.

There were many post-mortems, bomb plottings and analyses of the final *Tirpitz* raid, all of which disagreed with the men who were there, but the consensus was that the leader of the op made the first hit. Errors of 200yd were accepted in such plottings since they relied on data given by the pilots – time of bomb release, aircraft speed and height – but, as with the plot for the first attack in September, there seemed no reason to doubt the central premise. Just as Melrose and his crew dealt the blow that time, so did Tait and his men on this fine November morning. Other 617 pilots claimed hits and very near misses.

Whatever the claims and witness accounts, there were only two direct hits on the battleship, almost certainly Tait's and one other from 617 Squadron. It was enough. *Tirpitz* was a kill. She was finished, at last, after all those attempts, but she hadn't sunk immediately after the direct hits. The tradition grew that 617 Squadron had put the holes in the ship and 9 Squadron had blasted all that extra sand and gravel away from the sea bottom so that she could turn over. It was certainly the case that 9 Squadron bombed after 617 with the smoke from previous hits obscuring their bombing. They also had an error built in to their bombsights; the wind at the target was different from the wind they were working on.

In any case, the inglorious fighting career of the *Tirpitz* was concluded when she keeled over on her side and lay there, a useless steel island and giant coffin. Among the dead – figures varied from 971 to 1,204 – were the captain and most of the senior officers, trapped in their heavily armour-plated command post with massively thick doors which, twisted by the explosions, could not be opened.

The squadron scribe at Bardney summed up in near biblical style: *As is now known, this operation was completely successful, and was no doubt the outstanding operation of the month, and when it became known at the station great jubilation was evident amongst the ground crews, the extra work called for being thought well worth while.*

Cliff Newton's next trip was to Munich, a long way. He was away just before midnight, 26 November, dropped the 12,000lb triple cookie around 05:00 from 20,000ft, home around 09:00 with the following wind. Out of 270, 3 Lancs crashed but none due to enemy action. Bomber Command's renewed assault on Germany had had particular emphasis on oil installations; success had largely grounded the Luftwaffe. As the nightfighter menace decreased from an enemy in retreat and reversal, so the strength in numbers, power and accuracy of the Allied bombers went up and up. German industry more or less disappeared under the unparalleled weight of bombing by day and by night. In the last nine months of the war, RAF Bomber Command dropped very nearly half of their entire war's worth of explosives. Harris could send 170 bombers to Cologne and lose 1, and over 300 to Essen and lose none. Tell that to the boys of 1943. They'd never have believed it. Nevertheless, as Newton would find out, perils remained.

By 8 December American troops of the First and Ninth Armies had fought their way to within sight of the River Roer/Rur, which rises in Belgium but flows mainly through Germany before joining the Maas in Holland. Crossing this river would be a key operation in the invasion of the fatherland. Bomber Command and the USAAF had already mounted the biggest attack of the war in support of ground troops, featuring almost 2,500 heavy bombers and smashing completely the 3 main cities on the Roer, Düren, Jülich and Heinsburg, for the loss of 4 aircraft.

The river crossing itself, opening up the way to the Rhine, could not be attempted with any confidence while the Germans controlled large dams across the river's upper reaches. They could literally open the floodgates, swamping any troops in the valley, and plans had been laid to do this. A precision strike with Tallboys might pre-empt the flooding and leave the American soldiers in control, so 617 and 9 Squadrons went to the Urft dam, 8 December. This dam, like the Sorpe, was possibly beyond breaching by aerial bombardment but the spillway down the side was wreckable. On the morning, the bombers could do nothing in the cloud so came home and went back three days later.

There were 20 Tallboy Lancs of No. 9, including Ed Stowell's, 17 of 617, plus almost 200 fighters giving cover and 230 more Lancs of the mainforce which were to go in first carrying standard bombloads. Despite the smoke caused by mainforce bombs and intermittent cloud cover, most of 617 and all of 9 managed, sometimes with repeated runs in, to let go their Tallboys. Stowell thought his own bomb had overshot a little, but saw others hit. There had been several direct hits but, partly due to the newly lowered water level, no bust on this dam. Further raids on it were cancelled for bad weather and it was eventually given up as a viable target. When the Americans came to attempt the Roer crossing in early February 1945, the dams were opened the night before and the crossing could not be made for another three weeks.

A month and more after they had been together on the last *Tirpitz* raid, Newton and Stowell were again on the list, for Munich, 17 December. They both thought it had been an accurate attack; reconnaissance the next day showed 'severe and widespread damage'. It wasn't only the lack of opposition that made life different for 9 Squadron in late 1944. Daylights on dams made a change from nights over Germany, and another change was attacking ships in a harbour. Back from Germany by 02:30 they were off again before 17:00 and the ship in question was sister to the *Graf Spee* and *Admiral Scheer*, the pocket battleship formerly known as *Deutschland*, renamed by Hitler *Lützow* after a famous 18th-century Prussian general. She was lying at Gdynia, a far-Baltic port in the Gulf of Gdansk (Danzig), in German-occupied Poland soon to become Russian-occupied Poland. Cliff Newton had to return early with his bombsight u/s but there were over 200 other Lancs at Gdynia, attacking various targets, and damage was done but not to the *Lützow*.

Now came a spell of very poor flying weather, mostly thick, freezing fog with few breaks, the first result of which was only four getting down at Bardney from Gdynia, while the rest mainly diverted to Langar in the Vale of Belvoir, between Newark and Melton Mowbray. This would prove highly inconvenient. The crews could come back by road but bad weather prevented the aircraft and it would be 1945 before they were all available for selection.

At Pölitz, near Szczecin in what used to be called Pomerania, on the Polish side of the border with Germany, was one of the Germans' most important synthetic oil refineries. They were making aviation spirit out of coal and very good at it they were, but this had always been meant to supplement their natural oil from Romania, the government of which had decided to swap sides seeing as they were completely overrun by Russians and Americans. Now synthetic oil was all there was in Germany. USAAF raids had put the plant out of action for two months but it was back in full production again, 21 December. Lancasters of 617 Squadron took Tallboys, the wrong weapon for the job. Pölitz was pipes, pipes, storage tanks and more pipes; No. 9 Squadron could only send six aircraft but they took the 8,000lb double cookie, the blockbuster, much better for blasting pipework. Cliff Newton saw his bomb exploding in the target area and the raid was a good one, with a power station chimney knocked down and various parts of the synthetic-oil plant smashed.

There was more fog at home but the first one back tried to land and crashed into a tree. The irregularity this caused at the debrief was noted thus: *FLG/OFF J.A. Read. Presumed target attacked. Crew not interrogated owing to the fact that the aircraft crashed on return to Base, the Flight Engineer and Air Bomber being killed and remainder of crew admitted to hospital.* The other five landed elsewhere.

Christmas Day was relatively warm; only 6 degrees of frost compared with 9 the day before and 12 on Boxing Day. It was still -12 °F when Stowell and four more went in a force of 67 to attack a mixed fleet in Oslofjord, 28 December, anchored off Moss, about 35 miles south of Oslo. Each aircraft was to make two low-level runs with 1,000lb bombs; those of No. 9 were detailed to attack the flagship, lying off the village of Kambo. Stowell: *Two runs were made, 2336 at 7,000 feet and 2344 at 7,700. One large and one small ship seen. Four hits seen on large ship, also an explosion.* After the squadron's first run, only one gun on the flagship was still firing, and that soon stopped. Another year of war was over. Maybe when they got their Lancasters back from Langar they could help finish the damned thing.

For off-duty aircrew, every night was party night. Eat, drink and be merry, for tomorrow we die. Even so, there was a special atmosphere about New Year's Eve, 1944. Most people hoped and many expected that this year coming would be the last of the war in Europe. Bomber Command was now an extremely effective and powerful force. Butch Harris was by no means alone in thinking that, if the invasion faltered or was repelled, the RAF on its own could render Germany incapable of further resistance.

Von Rundstedt's counter-attack in the Ardennes had been greatly aided by the bad flying weather in the second half of December but eventually bomber attacks on roads and railways had severely disrupted his troop movements. Bombing had also reduced tank production to a trickle and fuel was desperately short after the raids on synthetic-oil plants. What new tanks there were, often couldn't be delivered to the battlefield and, if they did arrive, they couldn't do what was wanted without petrol.

The news on New Year's Day was that Ed Stowell was promoted to flying officer and, possibly less cheering, that the boys had to be up for a briefing at 03:00. They were off to the Dortmund–Ems canal again, to Ladbergen. This waterway was of such essence to the German system that every time the bombers hit it, everything was thrown into the effort of repairing it at whatever cost, especially to the forced labour.

New Year's Eve had been a very cold day with sleet showers and the temperature dropped well below freezing at night. It was perishing, frosty and black dark as the crews were taken to their dispersals at around 06:45 and inside the aircraft it was little better. There was a cabin heating system based on pipes filled with glycol, heated by the engines, and it was as big a contributor to passenger comfort as everything else in a Lancaster.

Flg Off Harry Denton, a New Zealander, captain of U-Uncle, was first up. Next, at 07:47, Cliff Newton surged down the runway in R-Robert and took off. Immediately filling his place in the queue was Flg Off Buckley in A-Able. He and his flight engineer began their usual last-minute checks. At the moment they were expecting a green from the caravan, there was a huge Wooomph! and a great flash of fire, some distance away. Everyone thought some poor souls at Woodhall had gone in. Woodhall Spa, base for 617 Squadron, was 6 or 7 miles away. The explosion was much nearer home.

Once in the air, Newton's engines had cut and the Lancaster, powerless when it needed power the most, had crashed into a field. The pilot and five of his crew, four originals including the gunners who had done for the E-boat on the *Tirpitz* raid, were killed in the fire. Another founder member, the bomb aimer, P/O Paddy Flynn, was thrown clear and escaped with injuries.

Unaware, Buckley tried to take off and almost suffered the same fate, his engines cutting out when hardly off the ground. After a truly hair-raising ride across the aerodrome in an out-of-control Lanc, they crashed and suffered one broken leg between them.

Clifford Sinclair Newton was 22 years old when he died, a long way from Detroit. His body was buried at Harrogate Stonefall Cemetery in Yorkshire, where most of the war graves belong to Canadian airmen, as were those of his two RCAF gunners. The cause of his and Buckley's crashes was never confirmed but the general opinion was in favour of frozen droplets of water in the petrol.

The day was not over. Denton was hit by flak over the target and fell in Holland, all the crew surviving, although two later died of their wounds including wireless operator George Thompson, who was awarded the Victoria Cross posthumously for his efforts in saving the lives of his colleagues. Another 9 Squadron Lanc went down with four killed. And after all that, Stowell and seven others were sent to Gravenhorst in the afternoon to breach the Mittelland canal. They took off 2 hours after the remnants of the Ladbergen force had landed back so they knew the squadron had already lost four aircraft in a morning, but they dropped their bombs from 9,000ft and all were back in the mess by midnight.

The draining of these canals was to have a significant effect on 9 Squadron's targets in the next month or two, but first Stowell and crew were due some leave, and there was a squadron stand-down, so Jesse's next op, his twentieth, was 3 February to the E-boat pens at Ijmuiden, said to be in use by suicide squads of midget submarines. The suicide aspect was not intended; it was simply that the *Biber* (Beaver) class of one-man sub was liable to poison its operator with carbon monoxide, and the *Molch* (Salamander) class of electric one-man sub was no use. Making 102 sorties in early 1945, 70 of these subs were lost. Crews of such boats may have been grateful that damage to their bases by 9 and 617 Squadrons with Tallboys prevented their going to sea for the whole of February.

Empty canals meant even greater importance for railways. Priority was assigned and Nos 9 and 617 were ordered to knock down some key viaducts, weak points in a huge system which, if rendered u/s, could cause severe paralysis. Weak points they may have been, but very hard to hit. The squadrons were to keep at the job until it was done.

The Altenbeken viaduct, by the town of Paderborn in Westphalia, had been on the list of desirable precision targets since such lists had been compiled. It carried one of the two railway routes from Dortmund and the Ruhr/Rheinland beyond, to Hannover and thence to Berlin. It was an ancient structure, part of the golden age of railway building, about 500yd long by 40yd high but, from the bombers' point of view, only the width needed to carry two railway tracks. Attacks by the USAAF in late November 1944 had put it out of commission but the Germans had it up and running again by February with a steel construction filling in the gaps the Americans had made. Stowell went in an attack of 18 Lancs of 9 Squadron on a solo raid with Tallboys, 6 February. There was ten-tenths cloud so Bazin ordered them home.

If there was no raid that night for a particular crew, there were no official duties. They could do more or less what they liked – go into town, have a game of snooker in the mess, go for a walk, read a book, whatever. Some crews had rather strict captains who didn't like time wasted, so they might find themselves doing extra dinghy drill while the rest went off to the pub, which might be the Jolly Sailor, the Black Horse or the Railway in Bardney, or maybe the Snakepit as they called the Saracen's Head in Lincoln, a notorious haunt of waifs, strays, vagabonds, ladies of the night, and airmen. They might travel as far as Nottingham where there were fewer aircrew competing for the girls.

If there was an op and it was a daylight, similar procedures applied for the evening. When Altenbeken called again, Ed Stowell took off at 07:43, found ten-tenths cloud so couldn't bomb and was back by 13:53 with plenty of time still left for relaxation. The squadron would have been in need of same, having flown through flak from the German lines to the target and back again and having watched one of their number going down. On night raids, of course, you never knew who was in the falling ball of flame. On a raid like this, with only your own squadron there and all in sight as you flew along in loose formation, with your CO calling on the VHF if anyone strayed too far, everybody saw everything. The aircraft going down was WS/E, they could all see it, so that was Flt Lt Johnny Dunne DFC, only 3 or 4 trips short of his 30, and the strange thing was, nobody baled out. The aircraft had been hit by one flak shell and an engine was on fire. It fell, slowly, from 12,000ft, with Stowell, crew and every other man on that op shouting jump, jump. They didn't jump. They died, and that was the topic of conversation that night in the Jolly Sailor. Jesse and the boys always preferred the Jolly Sailor.

Stowell was not required next time No. 9 went to Altenbeken, on this occasion in good visibility, and knocked one end of it down. Ed's next was back to Ladbergen, to the aqueduct, 9 Squadron with Tallboys plus 200 or so other Lancs with conventional bombs. It was a nerve-racking few hours, with take-off time constantly being postponed because of the weather forecast at the target, until day turned into night and they were up around half-six, bombed on the dot of ten and were home around midnight. They had attacked through gaps in the cloud with delayed action bombs so they had no idea if they'd done the job or not. Photographs next day showed the canal dry, empty, breached in two places. That, and the earlier attack on the Mittelland, meant disaster for the Germans. It also meant that Bomber Command would not need to go there again.

Sassnitz, a Baltic holiday resort and fishing town on Rügen Island, had attracted quite a collection of fugitive shipping, far more than its little harbour could cope with. There were destroyers and other ships in port and outside, the target for 9 Squadron with Tallboys and 170 other Lancs with thousand-pounders. Stowell aimed for one of the bigger ships at anchor a mile and a half outside the harbour. In the dark and partial cloud it was impossible to be sure about whose results were which, but certainly three ships were sunk and the town took a hammering from the mainforce.

They were back from Sassnitz around 04:00 and would be off again, to the oil refinery at Harburg, at around 18:15. The Germans had retreated from the Ardennes but the Allies hadn't yet crossed the Rhine. The war was not going quite according to plan and the bombers had a great deal of work to do, trying to make an early conclusion more likely. In March 1945, more bombs were dropped than in any other month of that war, a quantity almost equal to the amount dropped in the first three years of it. Harburg was like old times, with Lancaster losses at 5 per cent and the oil installations and a rubber factory demolished, but that was the last German city at night for Ed Stowell. From now on it was precision targets only.

Arnsberg viaduct was a fairly short and curving thread, only 7 spans, and 17 of 9 Squadron, all with Tallboys, went to try and cut it in misty weather, 13 March, and again next day when Ed Stowell saw a direct hit, and again the next. Apart from a crater at the mouth of the tunnel leading to the viaduct, the structure stood firm, and so did a railway bridge at Bremen when they attacked that, 22 March, and another at Vlotho. It had to be said that targets like these, looking from above like a short piece of string, were largely beyond the technology of the day, or so it seemed.

Near misses with the new super-super bomb, Barnes Wallis's Grand Slam, 22,000lb and pushing the Lancaster to the very edge of its capability in carrying it, were powerful enough to knock these bridges down. Only 617 ever got around to taking the Grand Slam, in modified Lancs with the bomb hanging outside and the aircraft's wings flapping in alarming fashion. Meanwhile, 9 Squadron went to Bad Oeynhausen, a well-defended railway bridge with a new dimension, encounters with the Me262 jet fighter. Stowell was on his thirtieth op and he thought part of the bridge collapsed and he was right. They did fell it with their Tallboy Mediums that only a few months before had been thought by everyone except Wallis to be the ultimate bomb.

There was a huge oil store at Farge near Bremen, next to the new 'bombproof' U-boat factory, and both were attacked by 115 Lancasters, 27 March, including 15 of 9 Squadron with Tallboys and 20 of 617 with Tallboys and Grand Slams. Here prefabricated components for the latest Type 21 U-boat, shipped from the Ruhr on the Dortmund–Ems canal if it was open, would be assembled when the project was commissioned in a couple of months. The Type 21 was a much-improved weapon that could have made a big difference if it had got to sea.

Fuel, hundreds of thousands of gallons, was stored underground and camouflaged by a pine wood. Hits would cover the area with smoke and so they used delayed action bombs. It was a 4-hour round trip to this small port on the Weser, up around 10:45, back about 14:45, and Stowell thought the Tallboys were falling in the target area. The raid was a complete success because 617 also smashed the U-boat pens, Grand Slam bombs penetrating roofs 15ft thick, just then in the process of being reinforced to 23ft, and bringing down many hundreds of tons of concrete. Farge would never recover and never be functional.

Friday 13 April 1945, and Ed Stowell's last operation was a washout. They set out shortly before midday to find the battleships *Prinz Eugen* and *Lützow* anchored at Swinemünde, but ten-tenths cloud meant they couldn't see a thing. So, that was that. For Jesse, the war was over. Flg Off John Edward Stowell of Royal Oak, Michigan had survived, unlike the dead sons of American mothers, Flg Off Charles Douglas Fox and Sqn Ldr Henry Melvin Young DFC and Bar, and unlike Sgt Raymond John Baroni, Glendale, California; Flt Sgt Maurice Emanuel Buechler, Newark, New Jersey; Plt Off Howard Houston Burton, West Virginia; WO2 Robert Cummings, Pennsylvania; Tech Sgt James John Hannon, Bronx, New York City; Flt Sgt Howard Clark Lewis, Ann Arbor, Michigan; WO2 Frank Goheen Nelson, Wilkinsburg, Pennsylvania; Flg Off Clifford Sinclair Newton, Detroit, Michigan; Flt Sgt William Harvey Penn, Tulsa, Oklahoma; Sgt Warren Thompson Ramey, Whitefish Bay, Wisconsin; Flg Off Jonah Bruce Reeves, Oneida, New York State; 1-Lt Eric George Roberts PH, Merchantville, New Jersey; Plt Off James Morton Stevenson, Parkchester, New York City; Plt Off Anderson Storey, Jamaica Plain, Massachusetts; WO Edward Joseph Walters, Oakmont, Pennsylvania; and Flt Off John Enoch Wilkes, Barrington, Rhode Island.

There were many more, of course. In Bomber Command, 55,000 aircrew died in the Second World War but these volunteers from America were different. Either it wasn't their war when they joined, or they were so determined to join it that they enlisted in Canada when their own air force refused them. They, above all else, had no need to die.

Epilogue

THE *BOULDER DAILY CAMERA*, 8 NOVEMBER 1954

Word was received this morning by telephone of the death of Robert O. Van Note, younger son of the late Charles O. and Grace Van Note, of Boulder. Death occurred at his home, Rolling Hills, near Los Angeles, after an extended illness.

He was the first American officer to receive the British Distinguished Flying Cross from King George VI at an investiture at Buckingham Palace, London.

While in England he married Miss Marjorie Sullivan and to them three boys were born. The first died at birth. The others are Stephen, now 6, and Keith, 4, residing with their mother at Rolling Hills.

After the war, Robert Van Note was an intelligence officer with the A2 detachment of USAFE, policing the American Zone of Germany from the air. Later he became a precision engineer with an oil company and lived in Stanton, California. He remained with the US Air Corps Reserve.

William W.W. Turnbull moved to Honduras after the war, and he received his DFC medal there in 1947. He died sometime before 1978.

The *Litchfield Enquirer*, Thursday 13 March 1980:

Private funeral services were held Monday for Sedgwick Whiteley Webster, 75, of Old Mount Tom Road, Bantam, who died March 6 after a long illness.

Mr Webster was born in Cape Town, South Africa, on October 28 1904, a son of the late Edgar Fletcher and Lillian Whiteley Webster. He was a member of the Royal Air Force, serving as a flight lieutenant in the Second World War. He was a representative in this country for the Dorland Advertising Agency of London and later was a freelance advertising executive.

Joseph Charles McCarthy stayed with the RAF, at first as a test pilot and later as a squadron commanding officer. His last posting was in Norfolk, Virginia, 1969, when he retired to nearby Virginia Beach. He died in 1998 at the age of 79.

John Edward Stowell moved to New Jersey where he met and married Jane in 1950. He worked as a mechanic with Flying Tiger Airlines in Arleta, California, until his retirement in 1986, raising four children, and died in 1999 after suffering from Alzheimer's disease for five years.

Hubert Clarence Knilans got his promotion at last, but Major Knilans suffered two years of depression through combat fatigue after the war, before going to the University of Wisconsin followed by post-graduate studies at the University of Minnesota. He began teaching history in 1953 at Corona, California. After working with the Peace Corps in Nigeria and with his old friend Cheshire in India and other places, he retired in 1978.

BIBLIOGRAPHY

Beck, Pip. *A WAAF in Bomber Command*, Goodall, 1989

Becker, Cajus. *The Luftwaffe War Diaries*, Gerhard Stalling Verlag, 1964

Brickhill, Paul. *The Dam Busters*, Evans, 1951

Chorley, W.R. *Bomber Command Losses of the Second World War* (various volumes), Midland Publishing, 1992

Darlow, Steve. *Sledgehammers for Tintacks*, Grub Street, 2002

Florentin, Eddy. *Quand les Alliés bombardaient la France*, Perrin, 1997

Flower, Stephen. *A Hell of a Bomb*, Tempus, 2002

Fydenchuk, W. Peter. *Immigrants of War*, WPF Publications, 2005

Goss, Chris. *It's Suicide But It's Fun*, Crecy Books, 1995

Holmes, Harry. *Avro Lancaster: The Definitive Record*, Airlife, 1997

Mason, T. *9 Squadron*, Beaumont, 1965

Middlebrook, Martin and Chris Everitt. *The Bomber Command War Diaries*, Viking, 1985

Neitzel, Sönke. *Die Präzisionsluftangriffe auf die Ubootbunker in Frankeich im August 1944*, Bernard & Graefe Verlag, n.d.

Postlethwaite, Mark and Jim Shortland. *Dambusters in Focus*, Red Kite, 2007

Thorning, Arthur G. *The Dambuster Who Cracked the Dam*, Pen & Sword, 2008

Turner, John Frayn. *VCs of the Air*, Airlife, 1960

For further details of Americans who flew with all Commands of the RAF in the Second World War, see: www.immigrantsofwar.com.

INDEX